LE MANS
24 HOURS

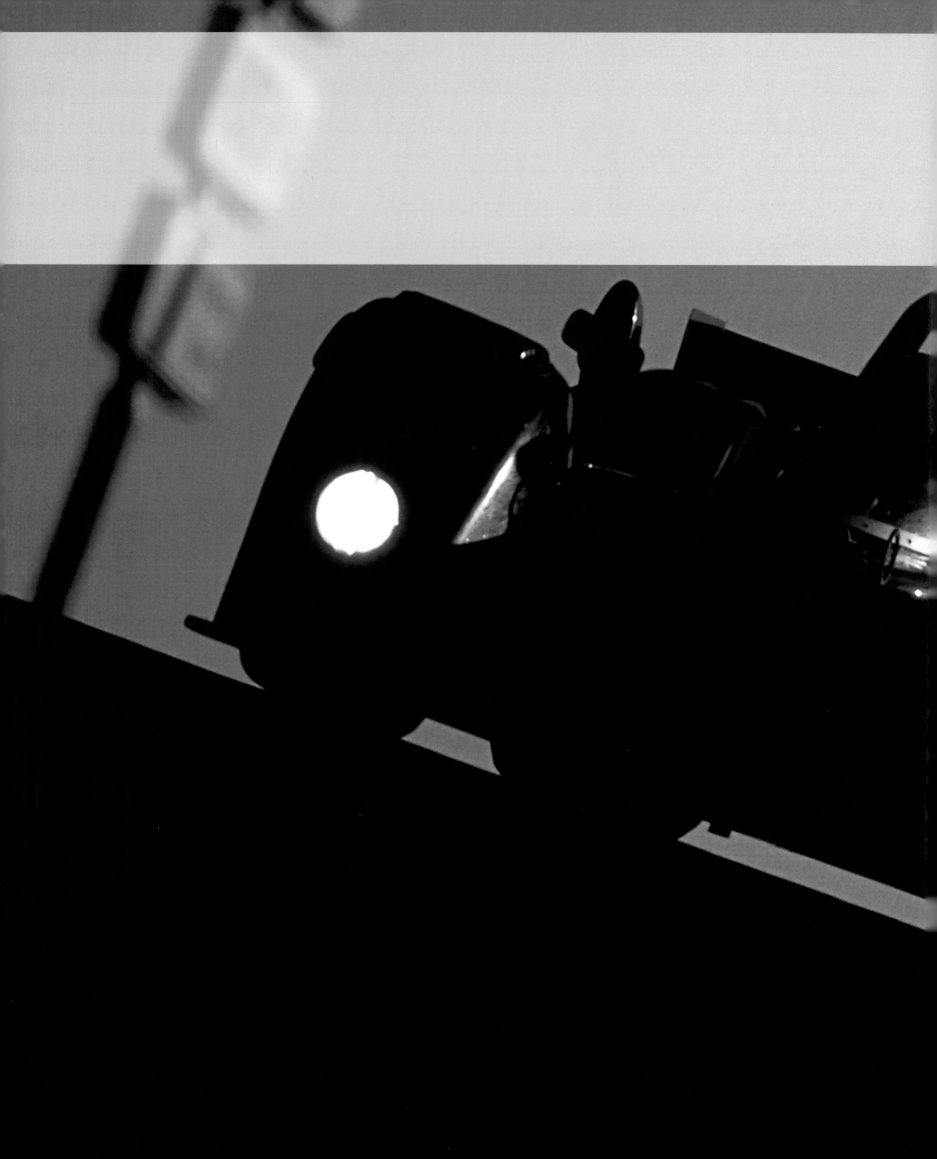

LE MANS
24 HOURS
BRIAN LABAN

MBI Publishing Company

LE MANS
24 HOURS

For Mary, for 24-hour support

This edition first published in the United States in 2001 by
MBI Publishing Company
Galtier Plaza, Suite 200
380 Jackson Street
St Paul, MN 55101-3885
USA

First published in the United Kingdom in 2001 by
Virgin Books
Thames Wharf Studios
Rainville Road
London W6 9HA
UK

ISBN 0 7603 1256 7

This book is not sponsored or authorised by, or connected in any way with the Automobile Club De l'Ouest.

Every effort has been made to trace the ownership or source of all photographs and illustrations used in this book. We regret any inadvertent error concerning the attribution given to any such material. Those claiming copyright in any unattributed photograph or illustration should contact the Publishers.

Publishing Consultant: Philip Dodd
Editorial Consultant: Simon Taylor
Project Editor: James Bennett
Le Mans motor racing results supplied by Mike Cotton
Art Direction, Design and Picture Research by Derek Slatter, Emma Murray and Daffydd Bynon at Slatter-Anderson

Printed and bound in Italy.
Repro by P2 Digital.

CONTENTS

FOREWORD
BY DEREK BELL

It's fair to say that, one way or another, Le Mans has played a very important part in my life. My first memories of of the race take me back to the 1950s, while I was still at school. In those far-off days, when the BBC used to broadcast from Le Mans every year, I would lie in bed in the dorm in the middle of the night on that traditional June weekend, with my portable radio switched on, listening to the news from the circuit. And although I suppose it was natural enough that as an impressionable schoolboy I would dream of racing there myself, I don't suppose that I ever believed that one day I actually would.

But having done so, I know that Le Mans is just as special as I always dreamed it would be. For any racing driver, along with the Monaco Grand Prix or the Indy 500, a win at Le Mans has to be one of the most sought-after victories of them all. And like the drivers, the teams, manufacturers and sponsors can dine out on victory at Le Mans, not just for the following year but for many years to come.

Having driven in 26 Le Mans races I can look back with many memories – some glorious, some painful. As with any great race, the start at Le Mans is very special. Everyone wants to talk to the drivers, everyone is clamouring to take photographs. By mid-afternoon the noise and atmosphere are almost overpowering. Ticking along to 4pm on Saturday, standing in the heat waiting for the start, there are times when our bodies already feel drained. For any Le Mans driver, the next 24 hours are going to seem a very long time.

Every driver has his or her own approach to the race. I shared three Le Mans victories with Jacky Ickx, and Jacky liked to do the start of the race – but he preferred me to do the finish. He seemed to think I could bring a sick car home, and in 1983 I had to do just that, in a Porsche with non-existent brakes. That was one 24 hours that we didn't win, but we did finish second – just 26 seconds behind our team-mates after a truly exhausting drive. I believe I drove the last hour on adrenaline alone. In fact at the end I was so drained that I had to be lifted from the car and drip-fed mineral replacements intravenously. Sometimes not winning is the hardest thing of all ...

In contrast, in 1995 I shared one of the McLaren F1 GTRs with Andy Wallace and my son Justin. We led the race for fourteen hours or so, in appalling conditions – only to suffer clutch problems with just a couple of hours to go. We did hang on to finish third, however, and to stand on the Le Mans podium with my son beside me was the proudest moment of my life.

I have to admit that in the early stages of my career I never had any great desire to race at Le Mans – it was F1 that I wanted to pursue. But I became involved in sports cars through my contacts with Ferrari, and one thing led to another. In fact my first sports car race was at Spa, in 1971, in a Ferrari 512. After that race Enzo Ferrari hired Ronnie Peterson and me to drive together at Le Mans, and it was a disappointing encounter. Engine problems eliminated us early on. The following year I was to drive the infamous 917 Porsche Longtail as a member of the Gulf Team under the expert eye of the famous team manager John Wyer. He left us in no doubt as to how important the race was, and he guided us all the way. Unfortunately, our rather too special 917 succumbed to an oil leak – but before it did we had been running at up to 246mph on the Mulsanne Straight!

I had to wait until 1975 before we won, with Gulf again but this time in the Ford-powered Gulf Mirage. And winning at Le Mans really is special. Having won once, a driver realises just how prestigious it is to be victorious in one of the toughest races in the world, and then the event takes on a different meaning in one's life. As much as any sporting event in the world, Le Mans requires a massive effort in terms of financial resources, technical expertise and immense dedication from the whole team. The drivers are really the icing on the cake. On the day the only extra item you need is luck. And I have been very lucky to be a part of the Le Mans story.

INTRODUCTION
BY BRIAN LABAN

Like Derek Bell, the first I knew of Le Mans was listening to it on the old BBC steam radio in the 1950s, when there would be regular updates right through the race – the night-time hours included. That alone made it unique, and it's maybe not insignificant that I (and I'm sure thousands of other people of a certain age) can remember those old Le Mans broadcasts but don't remember hearing a thing about 1950s Grand Prix racing.

This was unique reporting of a unique event, and from that day on Le Mans had a mystique for me. For a while it was worship from afar, but in the early 1970s, as a fledgling motor sports writer, I finally made the pilgrimage, and I've been going back there, watching and working, virtually every year since.

For many of those years I was also covering a large number of Grands Prix, but the one event of the year I really looked forward to was the 24 Hours – both for the race itself and everything that surrounds it. Over the years I've written tens of thousands of words about Le Mans, been burned alive by the sun, almost drowned by the rain, bitten to hell by insects, and slowed down by too much celebrating and too much soaking up of the atmosphere. But through it all I've always thought that if there was only one race a year, this should be it.

This book isn't a lap-by-lap, car-by-car account and makes no attempt to be – that would be a different kind of book altogether, and it would need to be a hugely bigger one. My aim in *Le Mans 24 Hours* is to convey some of the unmatched atmosphere that makes this the greatest race in the world. If you've been to Le Mans and this brings it back to you, that's great; if you haven't been to Le Mans and this book makes you want to go, that's even better. There really is nothing like it.

THE EARLY DAYS
SETTING THE SCENE

To a casual observer, Le Mans is a medium-sized provincial town with plenty of history, just like many others in central France. About 110 miles south-west of Paris, Le Mans stands on the river Sarthe, a winding northern tributary of the Loire, which it joins at Angers. Western Loire (or, to the locals, Pays de la Loire) is the district, La Sarthe is the département, and Le Mans is its capital. To the south of the city is a motor racing circuit, used annually for Les Vingt-quatre Heures du Mans, the Grand Prix d'Endurance. It is this event which, since its inauguration in 1923, has made the name of Le Mans famous around the world.

Today, away from race-time, the Circuit Permanent de la Sarthe (or more correctly nowadays the Circuit International du Mans) is mainly evident in the towering pits complex. It was built in the early 1990s to replace the old pits, and is topped by the huge sweep of the glass-fronted hospitality units and press gallery, which look down over the broad pit lane where so much of what is important at Le Mans takes place, and the start-finish straight. Across the track there are older buildings, big in their time but now dwarfed by the new complex. Right by the start-finish line is the older multi-storey grandstand, which used to house the press desks on an open terrace, facing the pits and, for most of the race, the blazing sun. To either side are covered stands, some new, some very old, bearing the names of drivers who were once famous here, or who perished here. In front of the covered seats are the dusty, open terraces where the atmosphere of Le Mans reaches its peak at the start and finish of each year's event.

Previous Spread: Ferenc Szisz in a Renault on his way to winning the first Grand Prix of the Automobile Club de France, held in June 1906 on a 65-mile road circuit to the east of Le Mans. **Above:** the town square in the 1920s. **Right:** the scene of the White House crash, 1927.

The track itself runs up from the Ford Chicane to the Dunlop Curves, under the famous Dunlop Bridge, over the brow where the plunge to the Esses begins, past the noisy funfair and the campsites. That part of the circuit is no longer public road, but further into the countryside, for 51 weeks a year at least, the everyday traffic comes and goes with little except the stretches of raised, painted kerb and triple-layered steel barriers to show the road's alter ego. The rippled kerbs and steel barriers aren't there for normal, law-abiding French motorists, they are for the benefit of the two-seater racing cars that thunder down these roads for a few days each summer at speeds of well over 200mph, through the night and the morning mists as well as in the heat of the day.

Le Mans isn't a modern, antiseptic, artificial, closed circuit like the ones which are now the norm for Grand Prix racing – it developed naturally and organically over a number of years. In the beginning it was made up entirely of public roads. For the most part it still is, and in spite of many changes over the years its layout remains very similar to that of the original. Only the northernmost tip is significantly different, since the original longer layout (with its hairpin at the Le Mans suburb of Pontlieu) was replaced in the early 1930s by a purpose-built road running from the end of the pits straight through to Tertre Rouge.

From the point where the cars turn onto it at Tertre Rouge, the famous Mulsanne Straight is more usually the RN158 towards Tours. Where the circuit leaves the 158 at Mulsanne Corner, turning sharply right towards the Indianapolis and Arnage corners, is normally a pleasant run through wooded countryside, past the golf club in the pines on the inside of the track at Mulsanne.

From Arnage (named for the nearby village) the circuit turns sharp right again, onto the old 'White House' section. This was the old route CD139, and in the early years of Le Mans it was the scene of some of the most famous incidents in the race's history. Eventually, as speeds rose, it became too dangerous to be used, and now the old White House is bypassed by the still fearsomely fast but considerably more open Porsche Curves, where the racetrack splits again from the public road (which heads on to Le Mans town) and spears back towards the pits.

The circuit used today is officially the eleventh variation. Its lap distance is 13.605km, or 8.503 miles. The fastest cars, in qualifying trim, cover the lap in less than three and a half minutes – an average of around 235kph, or 147mph. In places they are travelling at over 220mph for relatively long periods. Even this, though, is not the fastest that Le Mans has ever been. In the late 1980s, before the Mulsanne Straight was punctuated by chicanes, maximum speeds topped 400kph, or 253mph. Before these and other chicanes intruded, the all-time lap record during a race was set by Jackie Oliver during the 1971 race, in one of the mighty Porsche 917s, at 244.387kph, or 152.740mph.

But all this is getting ahead of the story of Le Mans. Even before the 24-hour race, the local government had granted permission for racing on the town's roads as and when required. That was clear evidence of how, in its early days, France supported the motor car (and motor sport) just as unequivocally as the Luddite English establishment frowned upon it. In fact Le Mans played a leading role in the early days

Even before the 24-hour race, the local government had granted permission for racing on the town's roads as and when required.

Above: for much of its life, the Circuit Permanent de la Sarthe was entirely made up of public roads, and even now a large part of the circuit is still public road. For a couple of days a year, this junction is better known as Tertre Rouge. **Right:** towering over Vieux Mans, the imposing gothic cathedral of St Julien.

of European motor sport, and few organisations have been more enthusiastic in promoting the causes of motoring than the Le Mans organising club, L'Automobile Club de l'Ouest.

It is also worth remembering that the city of Le Mans has a history of its own, which began some two thousand years before the motor car was invented.

It is an old place, once occupied by the Romans, whose visible legacy is the towering walls surrounding the oldest parts of what has been described as the largest and best preserved medieval city centre in France. Within the third- and fourth-century walls, high above the broad river to the north and reached on foot by flights of stone steps through the old Roman gates, is a jumble of narrow streets, steep alleyways, small shops and old half-timbered buildings: Vieux Mans. Above it all is the imposing gothic cathedral of St Julien, with its beautiful stained glass windows, ancient tapestries and the longest nave in France.

Long before the annual British pilgrimage which has been arriving here since the mid-1920s, and which is such an intrinsic part of the modern Le Mans story, Le Mans had notable English connections. It was reportedly here that William of Normandy met with his nobles to plan the invasion of England in 1066. Here in 1128 Geoffrey Plantagenet, Count of Maine et Anjou and at the time just fifteen years old, married the Empress Matilda, ten years his senior, already once widowed, and daughter of King Henry of England. In 1133 Le Mans was the birthplace of their son, also Henry, who, in 1154, nineteen years after his father's death, became Henry II, first of the Plantagenet kings of England.

Two years before he became king, Henry II had married Eleanor of Aquitaine, recently divorced from Louis VII of France and with Aquitaine returned to her control. Henry and Eleanor never lived in Le Mans (their estate was a hundred or so miles to the south, in Poitiers) but Le Mans was capital of the province of Maine and through the Plantagenet connection it remained under English rule into the early thirteenth century.

The newer parts of Le Mans grew up mainly to the south-east of the old walled town, and were spreading even by the eighteenth century. Le Mans has been growing ever since, to include what is now a busy modern commercial district – around the Place de la République – alongside the Roman and Belle Epoque buildings of earlier generations.

The wooded area near the Indianapolis and Arnage corners is as far from the bustle of the pits and main grandstand area as you can go, and during the small hours spectators in the dusty trackside enclosures watch cars racing through the night illuminated by nothing more than their own headlights, just as the first Le Mans spectators did almost eighty years before.

The modern racers travel at rather greater speeds: this is another 200mph-plus section of

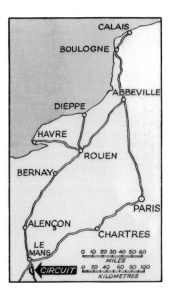

track, and these two ultra-fast corners are among the most challenging of all.

Before Le Mans was famous for its motor race it was known for its pioneering motoring family, the Bollées. The Bollées were long established in Le Mans as bell-founders and engineers, before Amedée Bollée built his steam coach, *L'Obeissante* (right), in 1873. It was one of France's first practical road vehicles and the first of a series of vehicles, steam and petrol, from the Bollée family. It still survives, in the Musée des Arts et Metiers, Paris.

In the nineteenth century, Le Mans formed its first connections with what would become the motoring world through a family of local industrialists, the Bollées. The Bollées were principally bell founders, and had been since the sixteenth century, but they also had interests in other technologies of the day, from hydraulic engineering to windmills, locomotives and sundials. Amedée Bollée was born in Le Mans in 1842, and in 1873 he built one of France's best known pioneering vehicles, *L'Obeissante* – the obedient one. It was a twelve-seater steam carriage, steered using the elliptical cam steering gear Bollée had invented in 1872. In 1875 Amedée Bollée drove *L'Obeissante* to Paris and back. He arrived in Paris on 9 October, the journey having taken around eighteen hours – not because *L'Obeissante* was particularly slow, but because Amedée had to stop so many times on the way to explain his journey (and probably his machine) to the authorities. It doesn't seem to have helped that he had a document of authorisation from M Caillaux, Minister of Transport, Deputé for La Sarthe, and presumably one of those Sarthois with an early affection for automobilism. Bollée arrived in Paris with more than seventy summonses!

After *L'Obeissante*, Amedée built several other steam carriages and coaches. These included the *Marie-Anne* in 1879, a four-wheel-drive carriage with twin-cylinder steam engines driving each wheel, and then, in 1878, a much lighter steam carriage, *La Mancelle*, which was notable for its layout. Many years before the 'Système Panhard' established the 'conventional' format for petrol automobiles, *La Mancelle* had its multi-cylinder engine at the front with the crankshaft in line with the chassis; it had a propellor shaft to a rear axle which turned the drive through ninety degrees to the rear wheels; and in some versions it had a sliding pinion gearchange. The Bollées were automobile pioneers, and by 1880 they were selling so many of their Le Mans-built vehicles that the manufacturing operation, already employing around seventeen people, was separated from the bell foundry.

Steam, however, was the technology of the past; the petrol-engined automobile was the future. By the late 1880s, Amedée's son, also called Amedée and distinguished as Amedée fils, had started to experiment with the new technology, and in 1887 he built a prototype petrol engine. By 1896, with his brother Camille, he was building petrol-engined cars, while another brother, Léon, had already started building petrol cars just a couple of doors away in Le Mans. In the first Michelin Red Guide, published in 1900, Amedée was listed as *constructeur* and *mechanicien*, at 104 Avenue de Paris, and Léon similarly, at number 99.

Léon played an important part in another episode of Le Mans history: the town's association with the aviation pioneers Orville and Wilbur Wright. Léon was an early aviation enthusiast, and was instrumental in attracting the Wright brothers to Le Mans when they were planning their first experiments in Europe. In December 1903 they had made the world's first controlled powered flight, at Kitty Hawk, North Carolina. In 1907, Wilbur came to France, and with the encouragement of Léon Bollée to Le Mans, where the Automobile Club de la Sarthe already had a companion organisation in the Aero Club de la Sarthe. The Club arranged for Wright to be able to use the Hunaudières racecourse, home of the Le Mans Horse Racing Club, for his work. In August 1908, having assembled his biplane in Léon Bollée's workshops, he made his first flight in Europe from the Le Mans 'hippodrome', and made several more before moving to more spacious (and safer) locations nearby. The racecourse is still there, hidden in the centre of the circuit almost alongside the well-known Restaurant des Hunaudières, part-way down the Mulsanne Straight. In the middle of the racecourse there is a stone

Below: Wilbur Wright in the Wright Flyer II coming in to land at Auvours on 8 November 1908. He made the first flights in Europe in what is now the centre of the modern circuit, on the horse race course, near Hunaudières. He moved to Auvours, on the old Grand Prix circuit, when he needed space for longer flights.

Le Mans had the distinction of hosting the first ever race to bear the title which would come to symbolise the pinnacle of racing: the Grand Prix.

monument to Wilbur Wright and his pioneering flights here, and there is another monument to the American aviator in the town, where he went on to work on a number of experimental aero engines with his new friend Léon Bollée.

Back on the motoring scene, although the Amedées (père et fils) were selling as many as a hundred cars a year by the late 1890s, and although Léon's designs were built under licence in even larger numbers, the Bollées failed to put Le Mans on the motor manufacturing map. Their contribution to the town's future fame lay more in giving it an awareness of motoring as a sport. Léon's very quick, lightweight 'voiturettes' were outlawed by the rule

makers, but in 1898 Amedée fils designed a pioneering streamlined racer, shaped like a truncated boat and called 'Torpilleur' – Torpedo. It performed well in the 1898 Paris-Amsterdam-Paris race, where Etienne Gerard finished a creditable third behind the two Panhards of Fernand Charon and Louis Girardot. It had seemingly underlined the Bollées' reputation for producing successful sporting cars, but

a year later the Torpilleurs failed badly in the Tour de France (which passed through Le Mans on its penultimate stage), and Amedée fils turned his back on motor racing forever. In addition, production was already drying up, and would peter out completely by the outbreak of World War I.

Even before Wilbur Wright had arrived, Le Mans had its motor racing baptism, and it could hardly have been with a more important race. Again, the initiative was a local one, from the Automobile Club de la Sarthe – forerunner of the present-day Automobile Club de l'Ouest. The Sarthe Club was founded in October 1905 and officially recognised by the Automobile Club de France, the pioneer and governing body of world motor sport, then and for many decades to come.

In 1906 the Automobile Club de la Sarthe proposed its circuit – in competition with

a number of others – to the Automobile Club de France for the running of a major race to re-establish the French Club's pre-eminence. This was a time of transition for motor racing, which was moving from the early inter-city races towards shorter, closed circuits. Inter-city races had been outlawed after the disastrous Paris-Madrid race of 1903, which was halted by the authorities at Bordeaux after the deaths of Marcel Renault and a number of others, both competitors and spectators. By this time, racing had already begun to take place on long, closed circuits without the need for the 'controlled' low speed sections that the inter-city races endured through towns en-route, and with hugely better protection for spectators and competitors alike. The first, in 1902, was the Circuit des Ardennes, held over six laps of a circuit of approximately 53.5 miles and won by Charles Jarrott in a Panhard at an average of some 54mph. The Circuit des Ardennes became a regular fixture over the next five years, and alongside it other prestigious, circuit-based road races grew up, including the Gordon Bennett Cup races, the Vanderbilt Cup and the Targa Florio. The Automobile Club de France needed a showpiece event to recapture its own status.

And so, in 1906, Le Mans had the distinction of hosting the first ever race to bear the title which would come to symbolise the pinnacle of racing: the Grand Prix.

Above: Szisz's 90hp Renault during the 1906 Grand Prix. His race average on the triangular road circuit was over 63mph and here, on the long straight between Conneré and la Ferté Bernard, he reached more than 90mph.
Far Left: Amedée Bollée in the 1898 Paris to Amsterdam race.
Overleaf: Alessandro Cagno's 120hp Itala retires from the 1906 Grand Prix, in Conneré – victim of the heat, dust, and car-breaking pace.

The club organised safety features for the racers and viewing for the spectators.

Above: cars lined up outside the offices of the Automobile Club de la Sarthe before the troubled Grand Prix de France in 1911, won by local star Victor Hémery for Fiat. The Sarthe Club, founded in 1905, was the forerunner of today's Automobile Club de l'Ouest. **Below:** Selwyn Francis Edge (fourth from right) with his Napier at Brooklands. Before Britain's famous banked circuit opened for racing in 1907, Edge and the Napier set a world 24-hour distance record. Brooklands never ran a real 24-hour race as the circuit didn't allow racing at night, and Europe was a long way behind America in adopting the 24-hour format.

The race, sanctioned by the Automobile Club de France, was known retrospectively as the Grand Prix de l'Automobile Club de France. The circuit devised by the Automobile Club de la Sarthe (whose committee included Amedée Bollée père and an important figure in our later story, general secretary Georges Durand) was to the east of Le Mans, and north-east of today's 24-hour circuit. It was approximately triangular in shape, some 65 miles in length, with its three main corners at La Ferté-Bernard in the north, St Calais in the south, and *virage de la fourche d'Auvours*, just west of Yvre and Le Mans itself. The smaller towns on the triangle – Conneré, Vibraye and Bouloire – were considered part of the circuit (not 'neutralised' by a speed restriction as in earlier road races) and between the legs there were specially laid wooden link-roads. The Automobile Club de la Sarthe made great efforts to put the roads into good condition, which included tarring some sandy stretches. They also organised safety features for the racers and viewing for spectators, from roadside barriers to grandstands, pedestrian bridges and underpasses.

The race was run over two days, 26 and 27 June 1906, which oddly enough were a Tuesday and Wednesday, not a weekend. The cars had to cover six laps on each of the two days – a total of some 780 miles – starting at intervals from six o'clock in the morning. Both days were swelteringly hot, and the shape of the circuit – essentially three long straights and three major corners – put an emphasis on very high speeds. Much like other major races of the time, each team was restricted to three entries, and the international field included three cars each from Mercedes, Fiat and Itala. The strong French entry comprised 23 cars, whose makers included Renault, Panhard, Gobron-Brillié, Gregoire, Darracq, de Dietrich, Brasier and Hotchkiss. Fiat, Itala, Brasier and Renault pioneered a new idea, detachable wheel rims for quick tyre changing, and these proved to be the key to success in an age when tyres were the Achilles' heel of many a racing car on the rough public roads.

At the end of the first day, Ferenc Szisz's four-cylinder 13-litre 90hp Renault (aided by its fast tyre changes) led Albert Clément's Clément-Bayard (hampered by non-detachable rims) and Felice Nazzaro's Fiat. Szisz held on over the second day to win quite comfortably, in spite of the road surface now breaking up and both cars and drivers becoming tired and battered. He won from Nazzaro, who had demoted Clément to third. Szisz's winning average was 63mph, while Baras's Brasier set a remarkable fastest lap of 73.3mph.

The organisers had lost a substantial sum of money on the event, and so for a few years the Automobile Club de la Sarthe turned its attention to other interests, promoting better local road conditions for the ordinary motorist and supporting the efforts of Wilbur Wright. Le Mans had clearly gained a taste for motor sport, however, and would soon return to it.

Between 1911 and 1913 a new circuit to the south of Le Mans was the venue for the Grands Prix de France and the Coupe de la Sarthe. For the first time the layout of the circuit incorporated roads which would later form part of the Circuit Permanent. The 1911 circuit was triangular again, and ran between Pontlieu in the south-eastern suburbs, along what is now the Mulsanne Straight, to Ecommoy where it turned left (away from the modern circuit) towards St Mars d'Outille and for the third side of the triangle left again, via Parigné-l'Eveque, back to Pontlieu – a lap of 54km, or 33.75 miles.

Reflecting internal upheavals in the Automobile Club de France in 1910, these races didn't have the prestige of the original Grand Prix, and the 1911 event gave the Automobile Club de la Sarthe huge headaches. At first the entry was excellent, and included three Nationals and a Buick from America as well as many fine Europeans. But several changes of date, added to uncertainty over the rules, meant that only fourteen cars lined up on 23 July – and a mixed bag of monsters and midgets they were. The race was run in fierce summer heat, the roads suffered badly, and there were many retirements. Worse, the race cost the life of Maurice Fournier and his riding mechanic when they crashed their Corre-La-Licorne. But Ernest Friederich's second place to Victor Hémery's Fiat was one of

Below: construction work on an underpass on the circuit for the 1906 Grand Prix – proposed, planned and financed by the ambitious Automobile Club de la Sarthe.

Above: Le Fèvre rounding the Pontlieu hairpin (soon to be part of the original 24-hour circuit) during the 1921 Grand Prix des Voiturettes – one rung below Grand Prix racing in the early days. **Top Right:** Thomas's Talbot Darracq takes the flag in the same race. **Overleaf:** Jimmy Murphy's Duesenberg wins in 1921. **Below Right:** in the main event at Le Mans that year, the French Grand Prix, Henry Segrave changes wheels on his Sunbeam. Detachable wheels were what made Le Mans' first sponsor, Rudge-Whitworth, famous. Before they were available, drivers had to remove the tyres from non-detachable wheels.

the first successes for the new Bugatti marque, and Hémery's win was especially popular locally because this hugely successful international star was a native of Le Mans. Hémery lived in the town, and assisted the Automobile Club in the early years of the 24-hours.

The 1912 and 1913 events were pretty low-rent affairs, held on the same circuit as 1911 but again with mediocre entries. In 1912 the Automobile Club de France had combined its Grand Prix with the Coupe de l'Auto (for voiturettes) and taken it away to Dieppe. Le Mans was left with the crumbs, in what became the Coupe de la Sarthe, run over 403 miles and won by Jules Goux's Peugeot. The programme also included a race rather over-billed as the Grand Prix de France and won by Paul Zuccarelli's Peugeot, and Le Mans even hosted its first motorcycle race as part of the 1912 mixture – as well as various other minor meetings during the rest of the year, for two wheels and four.

1913 saw more of the same, and this year the major race, again with a poor entry, was run in August as the Grand Prix de France. There was one major story, the reappearance of a team of three Mercedes. It wasn't the last time the three-pointed star would choose Le Mans for its re-emergence. In the event, Bablot's Delage won after a hard-fought race, and certainly the best of the series. It was a swansong, after which motor racing at Le Mans, as elsewhere in Europe, went off the agenda for the duration of World War I.

When the sport was revived after the war, it was revived at Le Mans, on another new circuit, backed by the authorities and known as the Circuit Permanent de la Sarthe. Again, the Automobile Club de la Sarthe (or the Automobile Club de l'Ouest as it had now become) was the driving force, and it has to be said that it was quite a remarkable organisation. During the war it had organised a Red Cross parcel service for prisoners of war, had helped families of missing troops find information, and at the end of the war had helped set up the first airmail service between Paris and Le Mans. For its war

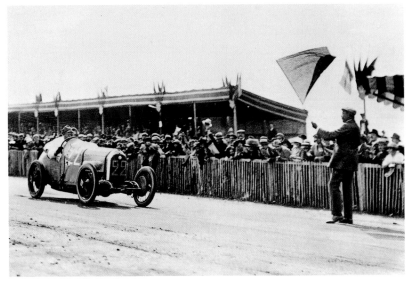

efforts the Club was awarded the prestigious Médaille de la Reconnaissance Française.

It would be a while before it was possible to go racing once more, but the Automobile Club began planning almost immediately – and this time for a long-term future. By 1919 they had proposed a new, shorter 'permanent' circuit to the south of the city – the direct forerunner of today's 24-hour circuit. It was the venue for some of the first races of the postwar era, and a reborn optimism. It ran from Pontlieu, down the Mulsanne Straight, turned right to Indianapolis and Arnage, and returned by the White House corners and the start and finish section to Pontlieu. The lap distance was 17.3km, or 10.8 miles – exactly as it would be for the first 24-hour race some two and a half years later.

The first day's races in August 1920 were for motorcycles and cyclecars; on the second day the main event, the Coupe Internationale des Voiturettes, was won in patriotic style by Friederich's Bugatti. In 1921 the Grand Prix de l'Automobile Club de France returned to Le Mans, and was the town's biggest event so far. This was the first post-war Grand Prix, and like many Le Mans races to come was a truly international event, with strong representation from America as well as from Europe. After a thrilling struggle, it brought an all-American winner, Jimmy Murphy in a Duesenberg, with the French Ballots of another American, Ralph de Palma, and Jules Goux second and third.

Succesful as the race had been, Le Mans lost the Grand Prix to Strasbourg in 1922. Its main event that year (supported by motorcycle and cyclecar races) was for voiturettes, and was won by British star Kenelm Lee-Guiness (the KLG of KLG spark plugs) in a Talbot-Darracq – a make which owed its origins to Léon Bollée of Le Mans, whose first four-wheelers Alexandre Darracq had built under licence.

The Le Mans club, meanwhile, clearly had even bigger ideas already forming. Towards the end of 1922, the French press began to carry news of a great event being planned for the following summer. As *L'Auto*'s headline read on 18 November that year, 'Une course de 24 heures pour les Voitures'. The brief story announced that M Coquille of the Société Rudge-Whitworth was planning a great race over 24 consecutive hours. Three beautiful 'triennial' trophies were to be contested consecutively, thus

Towards the end of 1922, the French press began to carry news of a great event being planned for the following summer.

covering the first five years of the competition. *L'Auto* announced that one of France's finest makers of fast touring cars had already promised to take part, and said that the event would be the reponsibility of one of the country's great regional motor clubs. For the moment it didn't say which club that would be, or where the race was to be held.

The results of the first 24 Hour race would count, with the results of the following two races in 1924 and 1925, towards the major prize, the Rudge–Whitworth Cup.

By 15 February 1923, *Le Temps* was writing about the great race being organised by L'Automobile Club de l'Ouest, and giving a few more details of the format. The results of this first race would count, with the results of the following two races in 1924 and 1925, towards the major prize, the Rudge-Whitworth Cup. M Coquille's company was also to donate 100,000 francs towards the organisation and prize fund.

Competing cars were to be strictly touring cars, and had to be manufactured in series – not one-off competition models. In the first instance the manufacturers would have to declare that they had built a specific number of identical models – originally thirty cars – and the competing cars had to be standard versions of the catalogued models. The original demand that the manufacturers bring a number of identical cars to the circuit for verification was dropped before the event. The cars would be classified mainly according to capacity, and depending on capacity would have to cover a minimum distance to qualify as a successful finisher. The sliding scale ran from a requirement of 920km (570 miles) for cars of up to 1100cc to 1600km (990 miles) for cars of over 6500cc, with a graph between those two points defining what was required of other competitors. The smallest cars were allowed two seats only, anything larger had to have four. Any car which was more than twenty per cent behind its target distance after six hours would be subject to instant elimination. Similarly any car fifteen per cent behind schedule at twelve hours or ten per cent adrift at eighteen hours would be out of the running.

Any car which achieved or exceeded its required distance, however, would become eligible for the second part of the triennial Rudge-Whitworth Cup. And so that the field did not fade away to nothing with each race's eliminations, each year a new rotation would start for the next Rudge-Whitworth Cup – allowing in new competitors, while still being open to existing ones. The technical checking of the cars would be done the day before the race started, and the start would be a simultaneous one for all competitors, lined up in decreasing order of cylinder capacity. The colours of the cars were to be as dictated by international racing rules: blue for France, red for Italy, yellow for Belgium, green for England and white and blue for America. The rules made no mention of Germany, or any other possible entrant country.

Two drivers had to be nominated for each car but only one could be in the car at any one time. Driver changes, and the length of driving spells, were at the team's discretion. Ballast was to be carried for each passenger the car was nominally capable of carrying: bags of lead weighing 60kg for each notional passenger. Running repairs could only be carried out by the driver, except in the refuelling pits, and the engine had to be switched off during all refuelling and repair operations. Refuelling could only be carried out in the designated pits, observed by an official who would record the amounts of fuel taken on board. Time taken for refuelling would not be added to the running time. 24 hours was 24 hours, and no more. Other makes who weren't actually racing but who wished to 'observe' (presumably as putative future entrants) could occupy a pit of their own for a fee of 500 francs so long as they applied before the end of February, 1000 francs if they applied between then and the end of March. Each car had to carry accident insurance for a minimum of 200,000 francs, each driver had to be insured, and each team had to have fire insurance for their refuelling pits! Anyone not complying would not be allowed to start.

Entries opened at 9am on 22 January, and could be received either at the

GEORGES DURAND

CHARLES FAROUX

Top Left: the Rudge-Whitworth triennial Cup. **Below Left:** Georges Durand and Charles Faroux, fathers of Le Mans. **Above:** the three 3-litre Chenard et Walker team cars of 1923, in remarkably clean condition after their dominant performance in the first 24-hours of Le Mans. Winners Lagache and Leonard are in number 9. Raoul Bachmann and Christian Dauvergne were second in number 10, and Fernand Bachmann and Raymond Glazmann seventh in the number 11 15hp 'Tourer' – seen here between the two 'Sports' models.

offices of the Automobile Club de l'Ouest or of *L'Auto* magazine. Entries would close at 6pm on 28 February, although as with the rent-a-pit scheme an entrant could still join up to 31 March by paying twice the normal fee. Those fees were on a sliding scale depending on capacity: 1000 francs for each car up to 1500cc, 1500 francs up to two litres, 2000 francs for anything over two litres. The ultimate sanctioning authority was the Automobile Club de France; the director general of the race would be Charles Faroux; and the sporting commission responsible for administering the rules would comprise Messieurs Paul Rousseau, Pol Ravigneaux, and Geo Lefevre et Charleau, engineer and professor of racing matters for the Automobile Club de l'Ouest.

The idea for the great race had come from three men: Faroux, Emile Coquille and Georges Durand, with practical as well as purely sporting intentions. Emile Coquille was the donor of the Rudge-Whitworth Cup; Georges Durand was general secretary of the Automobile Club de l'Ouest; Charles Faroux was a highly respected motoring journalist, and his complex character is well summed up by the obituary which appeared in *The Motor* after his death in 1957.

'The great French motoring journalist, Charles Faroux, died in Paris on February 9 at the age of 84, and the world of motoring has lost one of its greatest figures. He will be remembered as a motoring writer of true erudition, for he was an engineer and a brilliant mathematician, as the clerk of the course at all the major French motor races and rallies, as the man who founded the Le Mans 24 Hours Race, and as a Frenchman whose cultivated taste ranged from automobile design to the arts, to literature and to the sciences. Courteous, urbane, rarely ruffled, he placed the wealth of his experience and the guidance of his sage advice at the disposal of all who sought them.

'Many British drivers will miss his stocky figure, chequered flag in hand, at the finishing line of French races. Charles Faroux was a great man in an epoch when such are few and far between.'

By 1922 Durand and Faroux were already old friends, and while visiting the Paris Motor Show in October Durand found time to go and see Faroux, who by this time was editor of *La Vie Automobile*.

Above: today, away from race-time, the Circuit is mainly evident in the vast ultra-modern pits complex. That was built in the early 1990s to replace the old pits, and is topped by the huge sweep of hospitality units and the impressive press offices. Right: the starting point, the pits and main scoreboard in 1923.

He went with his ideas for a new kind of motor race at Le Mans: an endurance race with the aim of demonstrating the improving reliability of modern touring cars. Such a race would also, to some extent, promote the kind of improvements in public roads for which the Automobile Club de l'Ouest had long campaigned, often in conflict with government ideas. Durand had played a prominent part in this campaign, mainly in opposing what the authorities called their 'Golden Roads' programme. They proposed to concentrate on a limited number of major roads, which would be rebuilt in concrete, while leaving the majority of country roads in the dreadful state to which they had degenerated. Durand, and the ACO, were among the strongest opponents of this plan, arguing that the government couldn't simply abandon the countryside and country dwellers. In the end the efforts of Durand, the Club, and many others like them around France, prevailed, and in time the whole road network, not just the Golden Roads, was improved.

By the time Durand appeared in his office with his basic ideas for an endurance event, Faroux, coincidentally, had already had informal conversations with Emile Coquille about a race which would include a night section – as Coquille said, 'for the sole purpose of making manufacturers perfect their electrical equipment'. Faroux's initial ideas were for an event restricted to production cars (that, after all, was the point) to be run over, say, eight hours, of which half would be at night. Very soon Faroux and Durand had come up with a much bolder idea: a race run for a full 24 hours, not in two stints but straight through. Coquille was approached, responded enthusiastically and undertook to provide a trophy and the initial 100,000 franc prize fund. Faroux set about drafting the regulations, and Durand went back to Le Mans to start the mammoth task of organisation. And so the foundations were laid for the first Vingt-quatre Heures du Mans.

THE BENTLEY YEARS
THE 1920s

LE MANS 24 HOURS

Despite the excitement surrounding the inaugural 24-hour race at Le Mans, it certainly wasn't the first 24-hour motor race – even in France. The very first were track races held in America early in the century. There was a series of 24-hour races on the Point Breeze oval in Michigan, and races at other dirt and board tracks, including a track at Indianapolis some years before Indy became famous for its Motor Speedway. They were a very different proposition from Le Mans, which from the start would be a genuine road race. Lighting the whole of a small oval track was one thing; lighting the ten-plus miles of Le Mans would have taken more searchlights than even the French Army could muster. In fact the army did supply lights, but they were used only on key areas, such as Mulsanne corner, Indianapolis and Arnage, to show cars where they had to brake and turn even if their own lights were faulty.

Le Mans wasn't even the first 24-hour race in Europe. In 1922 a race for light cars, cyclecars and motorcycle/sidecar combinations, the Bol d'Or, was held on a circuit at St Germain, near Paris. Like Le Mans, the first Bol d'Or was run on a road circuit that was mostly unlit. Also like Le Mans it had a minimum average speed requirement. Unlike Le Mans, only one driver was allowed, although they had to carry a non-driving 'riding mechanic' and take a four-hour rest period during the 24. It seems probable from the timing that the first Bol d'Or was the inspiration for the first Le Mans, and the Bol d'Or also continued for a good few years (to 1955, in fact), although with changing formats.

Following his meeting with Faroux, and with Emile Coquille's agreement to back the race, Georges Durand returned to Le Mans with the task of turning an exciting idea into reality. That meant

Previous Spread: refuelling the winning Bentley in 1928. In the early days, drivers (in this case Barnato and Rubin) were responsible for virtually everything the car needed during the race, from fuel and tyres to running repairs. Fuelling was a potentially hazardous affair, and at every stop the fuel added was checked and the tank sealed by an official. Away from the pits repairs could only be attempted with what tools and spare parts were carried on the car. **Above:** the start of it all, with Excelsiors 1 and 2 and Lorraine-Dietrich number 5 leading away in 1923 – the first race.

obtaining permission for closing the public roads of the Circuit Permanent for two days of racing. To their huge credit the authorities readily agreed, and within a month Durand at least had somewhere to run the great race. Now he had to arrange for marshalling, providing pits, grandstands and other spectator facilities, and for the night-time illumination of those pits, certain areas of the racetrack, and even (at Faroux's suggestion) the racing numbers carried by the competing cars.

Durand was already in his late fifties, but his energy was clearly indefatigable. When the time came, everything was ready. There were overhead lights on the start and finish straight, and the Army searchlights further afield. There was a line of fairly basic pits under canvas tents by the start-finish line (on the stretch of road from the White House curves up towards Pontlieu, virtually where it is today). There were barriers to keep spectators from the trackside, and a two-tiered wooden grandstand opposite the pits. This area is now at the heart of the circuit's permanent buildings, but in the early years its location on private land would prove briefly contentious. There was a large scoreboard near the pits, and where the track ran through the village of Pontlieu, right between the houses on the narrow village streets, the pavements were lined with wooden barricades to keep cars and spectators apart.

Faroux's efforts had also been successful; his draft regulations had been speedily approved by the Automobile Club de France and had proved attractive to potential competitors. By the appointed date, eighteen manufacturers had placed entries for 35 cars – although only 33 of them actually made it to the start as Gabriel Voisin withdrew his two entries at a very late stage without giving any reason.

Even without the Voisins, the entry for the first race, perhaps not surprisingly, remained predominantly French. The only 'foreign' marques were Bentley from Britain and Excelsior from Belgium. The Bentley representation was, for the moment, strictly private. The marque's founder, W.O. Bentley, had apparently been unimpressed by the idea of such a race, but could nevertheless still be found on the sidelines in 1923, managing the pit work for the only Bentley in the competition.

This was one of the new 3-litre sports cars, entered by Bentley's London agent, Captain John Duff, of Duff and Adlington in Upper St Martin's Lane. His entry had been the first to be received by the race organisers. Canadian-born, British-resident Duff had been a purveyor of Bentleys since 1922, and as well as selling them he raced them. His credentials notably included a haul of almost 40 international records at Brooklands in 1922. Those records extended to 24 hours, but they were set in two twelve-hour stints, because Brooklands had banned night-time running very early in its history. So Le Mans in 1923 was Duff's first 24-hour race, and the first for his co-driver, Frank Clement. Clement, too, had already raced Bentleys both at Brooklands and in the Tourist Trophy, and he also worked in the company's experimental department.

Right: the Bol d'Or of 1922 beat Le Mans to the distinction of being Europe's first 24-hour race. The picture shows the Salmson team; two Salmsons also contested the first Le Mans, one winning the 1100cc class.

The entry for the first race, perhaps not surprisingly, was predominantly French.

'The weather, which had been threatening all the afternoon, showed its worst mood as the starter's flag dropped ...'

The Autocar

Although W.O. Bentley didn't want anything to do with entering Le Mans directly, he was happy to let Clement team up with Duff for the great race.

Despite all the preliminary work, the one thing the organisers couldn't control was the weather, which was awful. As the cars lined up in two rows in front of the grandstand, the heavens opened. As the starter's flag fell, at 4pm on Saturday 26 May, there was a brief hailstorm, which turned into heavy rain and continued for the next four hours. But the race proved to be a great success. Contrary to the original intention to start the cars in order of capacity, they lined up with the earliest entries at the front and later ones further back, promoting some early overtaking battles. Durand, with his interest in building better roads for all, had done what could be done to seal the Le Mans surfaces, but in the dreadful weather the road became a mudbath anyway. All but three of the cars were open-topped, and few of the remainder ran with hoods up, or even windscreens up, while mudguards were mainly pared down to almost nothing in the interests of minimising weight and wind resistance. Amazingly, according to contemporary race reports, not a single car had a mechanical windscreen wiper. The drivers simply had to make the most of it, and most (Duff and Clement included) couldn't even wear their goggles because of the mud.

The race to complete the greatest distance (there was no such thing as an outright 'winner' in the early years) developed into a battle between the 3-litre Chenard et Walckers, the 2-litre Bignan and the lone 3-litre Bentley. After 24 hours a French car had travelled furthest, followed by three more French entries, with the solo Bentley sharing fourth place. The order was André Lagache and René Leonard in a Chenard et Walcker, Bachmann and Dauvergne in another, then two of the Bignans – the second one, with the Bentley, 174 miles behind the winners. Lagache and Leonard (two coachbuilders who had built the bodywork for the Chenard et Walckers) had covered 1372.5 miles at an average of 57.2mph, and finished 45 miles ahead of their team-mates.

It was a considerable achievement considering how bad the weather had been for much of the race, the road conditions that this had created, and the newness of the challenge. It was certainly quicker than *The Autocar*'s preview had imagined, even assuming that the weather would be fair.

'While a few will be satisfied to qualify [for the Triennial Cup] by maintaining a slightly higher speed than the minimum average,' they had predicted, 'it is practically certain that the majority will attempt to set up records. There are reports that certain drivers will attempt to average more than sixty miles an hour for the full period, which, on a triangular road course with three right-angle turns per lap of about twelve miles, must be considered a bold enterprise.' To average more than 57mph in the wet was bolder still ...

Quite aside from the appalling weather conditions that afflicted the whole

Above: a 1923 pit stop for Courcelles and Rossignol's six-cylinder 3.4-litre Lorraine-Dietrich B3-6, number 7 (eighth on distance and 5-litre class winner) and the Molon brothers' 1.8-litre four-cylinder Vinot Deguingand, number 27 (26th on distance). **Left:** the 1923 winner, the Lagache and Leonard Chenard et Walcker, showing the mixture of loose dirt and brick paving at Pontlieu hairpin.

field, that first Bentley Le Mans entry had a torrid time of its own. It ran most of the dark hours with only one headlight after the other had been broken by a stone. Another stone punctured the petrol tank and cost more than two hours for repairs. That included the time it took for Clement to jog back to the pits from where the car had expired near Arnage, and to return on a bicycle carrying petrol in tins. He had 'borrowed' the bicycle from the trackside, and the French soldier in charge of it was reportedly very pleased to see it return in the back of the car. The Bentley's two-wheel brakes were bordering on inadequate, too, for a punishing circuit such as this with its long straights and several tight corners, but Frank Clement did make one mark by recording the 24-hour race's first fastest lap, at an average of 66.69mph.

Nowadays at Le Mans, drivers are whisked away between driving stints for physiotherapy, debriefing, some carefully regulated food and fluid replacement and maybe a few minutes' sleep. In 1923 *The Autocar* noted a less scientific regime. 'One of the most curious scenes at the covered pits was the "Hartford Hotel". The makers of the well-known shock absorber, having no motor supplies to give out, had fitted up their replenishment station as a restaurant and hotel. As the tired, wet and muddy drivers came off their cars they were hauled into the hotel, regaled with hot onion soup, found plates of roast chicken in front of them, and were called upon to assist in emptying innumerable bottles of champagne.' After the race they reported that 'fifty chickens, 150 gallons of hot soup, 450 bottles of champagne [surely not all consumed by the drivers!] and unknown quantities of red and white wine were given away ...'

As good as Duff and Clement's shared fourth place with the Bentley was in its own right, more important in the long term was that it qualified them for the second leg of the first Rudge-Whitworth Triennial Cup. That meant that they would surely be back the following year – and this time the

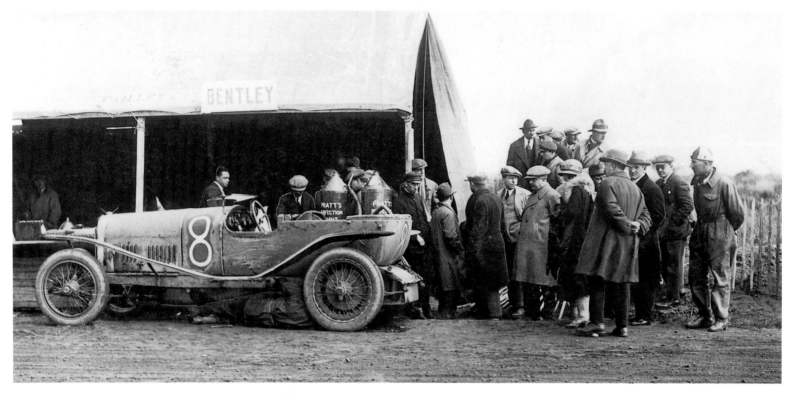

The pits have always been a focal point of Le Mans action, and frequently a place where the race has been won and lost. They have changed somewhat over the years. Above: Duff and Clement's 3-litre Bentley in 1923, the pits just wooden counters under canvas, the onlookers no more than that, as only the drivers could work on the car. Right: modern pit stops involve far more people working on the cars, a greater sense of urgency, and far less time spent at a standstill.

privateer Bentley effort would have an even greater impact on the race's future.

In 1923, the crowd, like the entry, had been predominantly French, and had that situation continued Le Mans would never have become the multinational circus that it is today. But the seeds of a very different atmosphere for Le Mans had been sown. The catalyst was that Bentley effort, and the following that the marque brought with it from across the Channel. It started a British love affair with Le Mans which far outlasted Bentley's original glory years, and which survives today.

Bentley's achievement on their second appearance was even more remarkable for the fact that in 1924 they were the one and only non-French entry, in a field which had grown to forty cars. There should have been a new 3-litre Sunbeam for Dario Resta and Kenelm Lee Guinness, but Sunbeam were too busy preparing for the Grand Prix at Lyon; Delage and Bugatti were also sidelined by Grand Prix preparations. This time, although W.O. Bentley still wasn't ready to enter cars officially, he gave more direct support to Duff, and the solo 1924 Bentley (now with four-wheel brakes) led all the others home. It had been a hard race. In the first year, in spite of appalling weather, 30 of the 33 starters had finished the 24 hours. In 1924 only 18 of 41 starters made it to the end. With the weather in mind, the 1924 race was put back to 14 and 15 June, when the daylight hours were longer and the weather was likely to be kinder. It has stayed on approximately that weekend (with very few exceptions) ever since.

In 1924 every car had to stop after five laps, erect its hood, and leave it up for at least two laps. Cars could only be started by their electric starter. Each was allowed a maximum of six wheels (four on the car, two spares – although the driver was allowed to change tyres or tubes on the spare rims so long as the replacements were carried in the car). Cars had to cover a minimum of twenty laps before being allowed to take on fuel, oil or water. Times for erecting the hoods were reported as Grand Prix pit-stop times are now. Duff was pretty quick in around forty seconds, but one of the tiny French SARAs set the record at 27 seconds.

As night fell, the unique atmosphere of Le Mans developed. 'As darkness settled down', *The*

Autocar reported, 'the scene at the grandstands underwent a complete transformation. The long, orderly row of replenishment stations burst into light, and with their luminous signs, the tidy array of tools laid out on the counter, the active attendants behind the wire netting, they looked like so many shops completely equipped for the requirements of customers. Electric arc lamps threw a brilliant glare over the entire grandstand stretch, acetylene flares were placed at frequent intervals around the ten miles of the circuit, and the cars added to this artificial illuminant with either one, two, three or even four headlights.'

More than once during the 1924 race – which suffered fierce heat during the daylight hours – the winning Bentley came close to joining the non-finishers. Towards the end it was docked many miles because the organisers said time lost while the rear wheels were replaced in the pits had reduced the average for one five-lap stint below the statutory minimum. In the end the previous year's headlines were reversed. Bentley won (by just ten miles) while 1923 winner Lagache, after leading for quite a time in the Chenard et Walcker, broke Clement's inaugural lap record – raising it to 69.5mph. The French pair's run ended as night fell when the Chenard caught fire on the Mulsanne stretch. Most of all, Bentley's win – the first for a non-French marque, and against all odds – helped put Le Mans on the wider European map. In fact it drew attention to the race even beyond that, as America also started to take notice of the new French phenomenon.

Le Mans is more than a motor race; it's a funfair, a vast weekend picnic, a giant all-night party, all rolled into one. It always has been. Previewing the first race, in May 1923, *The Autocar* didn't overlook the social side. 'For the first twenty-four hours race to be held in France, on the permanent circuit just outside Le Mans, on Saturday and Sunday May 26th and 27th, a series of side shows has been organised on a scale hitherto unknown in connection with racing.

'The Automobile Club of the West of France appears to be of the opinion that even with thirty-two cars there are apt to be dull moments in a race which lasts two rounds of the clock. In consequence, the evening hours will be enlivened by a display of fireworks depicting sporting scenes, moving pictures will be shown, wireless concerts will be heard from the Eiffel Tower, there will be a dance hall, an American bar from the Champs-Elysées, a jazz band and an orchestra, and the grandstands and pits will be brilliantly illuminated. At mid-day on the Sunday a lunch will be served to five hundred members of the Club'.

Reporting on the 1924 race, *The Motor* echoed the atmosphere. 'The stands emptied; the open-air restaurant, erected near-by, became crowded to overflowing. A jazz-band tinkled and a quartet of red-coated huntsmen played prettily on French horns.' The music may have changed, and the scale is now vastly bigger, but the all-night party feel is still a vital part of the Le Mans experience.

> 'The Automobile Club of the West of France appears to be of the opinion that even with thirty-two cars there are apt to be dull moments in a race which lasts two rounds of the clock.'
>
> *The Autocar*, 1923

'The only car entered from this side of the Channel, with J.F. Duff and F.C. Clement as drivers, takes the laurels.'

The Motor, 1924

In 1925, as leading contenders for the first Triennial Cup (and the first Biennial Cup, which had started in 1924), Duff and Clement were naturally back on the entry list, and finally supported by an official works Bentley, driven by Dr Benjafield and Kensington Moir. This time they weren't the only British entry, as Sunbeam joined in, and so did Austin. There should have been an AC too, but it was withdrawn minutes before the start with a broken frame. There were two 3-litre Sunbeams, for Sir Henry Segrave and George Duller, and Jean Chassagne with SCH 'Sammy' Davis – the latter a fine racing driver as well as a journalist for *The Autocar*. There were 49 starters, ranging in size from the 749cc Austin to the 4.5-litre four-cylinder Sizaire-Berwick. Chenard entered both its big cars and its smaller, streamlined 1100cc four-cylinder 'tanks', contributing to the variety that has always made Le Mans unique.

Le Mans was developing into a major event for spectators as well as manufacturers. *The Motor* suggested that the 1925 race attracted at least three times as many spectators as previous races. As dawn broke at 4am 'fully half of them still thronged paddock and stands,' and the day went on, 'every hour bringing more and more'.

This new interest underlined one problem that even the entrants were beginning to note. The race was widely known as the Grand Prix d'Endurance, but officially it was the Rudge-Whitworth Cup Race. In January, six months before the race, *The Autocar* observed, 'It is not an easy matter to follow the rules of this event, and in most cases the public simplifies the result, somewhat unscientifically, by looking upon the one having gone the greatest distance as the winner. It is necessary, however, to find a winner of the trophy, and according to the rules which have now been published, this will be done in the following manner for all those having qualified in the first two races. By taking the results obtained in 1923 and 1924, curves will be plotted, the points of which will show identical performances in the different piston displacement classes. The winner of the triennial cup and the holder of the two biennial cups will be the ones whose curve reaches the highest point, as based on effective distance covered.'

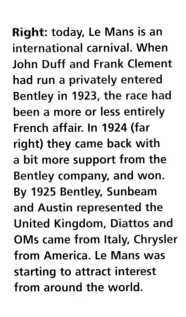

Right: today, Le Mans is an international carnival. When John Duff and Frank Clement had run a privately entered Bentley in 1923, the race had been a more or less entirely French affair. In 1924 (far right) they came back with a bit more support from the Bentley company, and won. By 1925 Bentley, Sunbeam and Austin represented the United Kingdom, Diattos and OMs came from Italy, Chrysler from America. Le Mans was starting to attract interest from around the world.

'The drivers raced for their cars, erected the hoods with all possible speed, leaped in, depressed the starter button and roared off . . .'

The Motor, 1925

This first, complicated completion of the Triennial Cup turned out to be the last, although the Biennial Cup would survive into the early 1970s.

In 1925, the start was held for the first and only time on the Mulsanne Straight near Hunaudières – directly opposite its traditional (and modern) location. The pits and start-line grandstands moved with it, because the owner of the land normally used had asked for too much money as the crowds continued to grow. This meant that it was Hunaudières, not Les Raineries, that witnessed the birth of another tradition: the running 'Le Mans' start.

As *The Motor* colourfully described it, 'As the loud-speaker gave out the final warnings the competitors' cars were parked diagonally down the right-hand side of the road with hoods folded and strapped down and with doors shut. The drivers stood tense and expectant on the other side of the course. Slowly the minutes ticked by until, with the dropping of a great flag and a stentorian "Partez!" from gargantuan loud-speakers the drivers raced for their cars, erected their hoods with all possible speed, leaped in, depressed the starter button, and roared off.' A similar starting procedure (save for putting up the hoods) would be a feature of Le Mans for another 44 years. In 1970, with a very different kind of car, and full harness seat belts an absolute necessity, the drivers sat belted in, with engines started on the drop of the flag. From 1971 it changed again, to a conventional grid, and nowadays the thunderous rolling start with the pace car peeling off into the pit lane at precisely four

Below: Bloch and Saint Paul's Lorraine-Dietrich and Pisard and Elgy's Chenard et Walcker pass the grandstand wheel-to-wheel in 1925. Neither of them finished the race.

o'clock on Saturday afternoon is as much a Le Mans tradition as the dash across the track once was.

In 1925 Duff was away first, and Segrave's Sunbeam led at the end of the first lap. But it was the Lorraine-Dietrich of De Courcelles and Rossignol which was ahead at the end of the race. The Bentleys had a tough time. Kensington Moir battled with the Sunbeam and led the race, but having already stopped to fix a loose oil-filler cap he was a victim of the rule which said a driver couldn't stop for fuel before twenty laps had elapsed. He ran out near the Pontlieu hairpin on his nineteenth tour. At much the same time the other Bentley had fuel pump problems near the old start line area. Duff ran across country to his pits, picked up a spare pump, made his way back, and fitted it to the car. It was an hour and a half before he re-started, but the Bentley was back in the race – until a carburettor cracked and the car briefly caught fire just before midnight, while Clement was at the wheel.

There were problems with the road surface again: the tarred Mulsanne Straight section stood up reasonably well to another hot weekend, but the sandy sections from Mulsanne to Arnage and from Arnage to Pontlieu broke up badly and gave the drivers horrible problems with the unpredictable surface and flying stones. Tragically, Le Mans also saw its first fatalities in 1925, and not the last on the already fast and dangerous Mulsanne. André Guilbert was killed while practising on Saturday morning, and Marius Mestivier's Amilcar went into the trackside trees during the race, killing him instantly.

As the Bentleys failed, Segrave and Duller's Sunbeam fell out with clutch problems. The English challenge was left to Chassagne and Davis in the other Sunbeam, but they could only finish second between two of the Lorraine-Dietrichs. The winners were De Courcelles and Rossignol, by 45 miles. Fourth and fifth were the Italian OMs, and sixth the lone American Chrysler – although that had failed to cover its allocated distance, and didn't qualify for the next round of the Biennial Cup. Sénéchal and Locqueneux's small Chenard et Walcker took the first and only Triennial Cup, Glaszmann and Manzo's similar car picked up the first Biennial trophy.

Second-placed Davis later wrote about the experience, and included some detail of a typical lap.

Right: 1925 was a rare bad year for Bentley. 'Bertie' Kensington Moir and Dr J.D. Benjafield ran out of fuel on the nineteenth lap – short of the minimum distance to be covered before refuelling was permitted. It was the first year of the 'Le Mans' start, and after running across the track to their cars, drivers had to erect their hoods before starting.

'At Le Mans there were at least fourteen gearchanges to be effected in each circuit; Mulsanne was taken at about 30mph, which is, incredibly, deceptively slow after 90mph, and seems like 5 or 6mph; Arnage's second bend at 25mph, and Pontlieu at 25mph or thereabouts. Then there were six gauges to watch, an air pump and a lap counter to operate, while one's own pit had to be distinguished among the others, the signals recognised and acknowledged ...'

Left and Above: 1968, nearing the end for the traditional sprint, which was revised in 1970, with drivers belted into their cars, and abandoned in 1971 for a rolling start behind a pace car.

Come 1926, Le Mans was developing a look of permanence. Having bought the disputed land, the Automobile Club de l'Ouest moved the start back to where it was first (and has been ever since) and surrounded it with more permanent pits, grandstands and a proper press stand. The Club continued its experiments with improved road surfaces, so the circuit was now far smoother and more durable all round, with the inside of Mulsanne corner newly concreted to stop it breaking up.

The magazines reported that record crowds stayed for the full 24 hours, and the Club catered for them with large new car parks, a new main scoreboard and several new bars and cafés. Le Mans was becoming a social magnet. As *The Motor* wrote in its race report, 'the Hartford hotel competed with the Rudge-Whitworth Bar and the Weymann Cabaret in

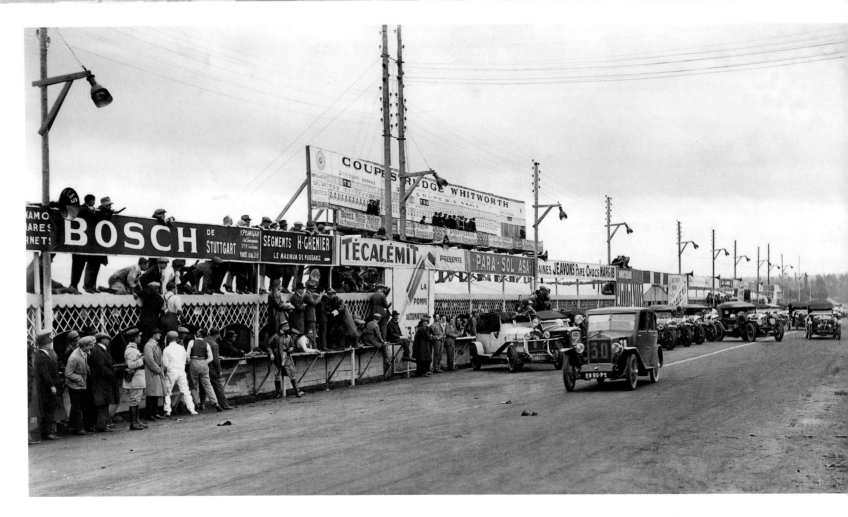

Above: in 1926 the echelon start with the cars lined up in front of the pits and drivers running across the track was still a fairly leisurely affair. The little four-cylinder 1.5-litre Jousset of Leon and Lucien Molon led away but failed to qualify as a finisher because it was five laps behind the minimum distance specified for it in the rules. **Overleaf:** Theo Schneiders in 1926, hoods up in the early laps.

distributing champagne from inexhaustible cellars, chicken and paté de foie gras from spacious ice-boxes, and in slicing Prague hams and Bologna sausages on American machines. Tastefully decorated, brilliantly illuminated with electric table lamps served by white-jacketed barmen, these temporary cafés were comparable with the best in Paris. They differed, however, in having no charges and no tips. Outside, the interest among the spectators was no less. Between 11 and 12 o'clock the immense open-air garage was packed with cars, and more were making their way towards the circuit than were proceeding in the direction of Le Mans, thus proving the deep-rooted interest of the French public in motoring competitions.' Today's hospitality may be even more lavish, but otherwise – *plus ça change.*

The Autocar captured the mood of the build-up, which still has a familiar ring. 'Near the place where the old grand-stands used to be is the single-storey Café de L'Hippodrome, with that air of extreme age which the rural French café invariably presents ... It is but a few paces from the border of the actual course ... In ordinary times one supposes that this Café exists precariously in supplying coffee and extraordinary drinks to the local farm labourers. During the practice week, however, it reaps a golden harvest, for to it come, from all parts of France and other countries, anybody who can possibly get there on any excuse. It becomes the rallying place – almost the club house – for everybody connected with the race, together with their friends and acquaintances. It is the accepted rendezvous for all ...' They described Le Mans town, meanwhile, as 'a place in which only the deaf can sleep'.

The 1926 race saw another win for Lorraine-Dietrich, and more disappointment for what had grown to a three-car Bentley team, officially entered by the company. This year's American challenge was from the big Willys and the smaller Overlands of the Willys-Overland company, but they were never a serious threat to the fastest cars: the French Lorraine-Dietrichs again, the Le Mans debutant Peugeots, and the British Bentleys. Perversely, better road surfaces made for a harder race, because of higher average speeds. In the end the winning car would average some 66mph, while Mongin's Lorraine would lift the lap record to 71.1mph. The sleeve-valve Peugeots were fast, but proved fragile. Wagner's went out with electrical problems and Boillot's was disqualified after losing its windscreen, both before daybreak.

The Bentleys had a nightmare. Duller, having driven his heart out to take the lead, stuck his into an earth bank at Arnage and took an age to dig it out, after which he was flagged into the pits for not wearing the crash helmet which had now become compulsory. Trying to catch up again, he suffered engine failure. The second Bentley, Gallop and Thistlethwaite's, followed suit early on Sunday morning. Having driven some all-out laps to pull the remaining Bentley into the lead with half an hour remaining, 'Sammy' Davis finally ran out of brakes and into the sandbanks at Mulsanne, where the car stayed. As he wrote, 'No badger has ever worked harder or removed more sand than I did in the next twenty minutes, but despite tearing down the barricade and mounting the rear wheels on the wood, and despite digging away sand in vast quantities, I could not move my poor old car.'

The Lorraines ran out 1-2-3 winners, for Bloch and Rossignol, De Courcelles with the record-breaking Mongin, and Stalter and Brisson. That gave De Courcelles and Mongin the second Biennial Cup, and Le Mans its first two-time winner. But Bentley was about to beat that.

The next four years were all Bentley. Four wins in a row from 1927 to 1930 and five in total including 1924. To many, the 1927 race was arguably the greatest of all. It was certainly the one which finally established Le Mans as an annual pilgrimage for the British.

The detailed regulations had changed again, as they did almost every year. Now 1100cc cars could have two seats, 1500cc ones had to have three and the rest had to have four. Foreshadowing modern homologation rules, cars had to be produced in minimum numbers to be eligible; in this case at least thirty production examples had to be built. Minimum distances were increased slightly, and there were minor changes to the rules about spares and repairs, lighting systems, acceptable fuels and pit stops. All cars had to run in national colours. Thus, on 18 June the British Racing Green Bentleys lined up against the gaggle of French blue Aries, Gregoires, EHPs, SARAs, Th Schneiders, Fastos and Salmsons. There would be just 22 cars on the grid, way down on previous years and reflecting the worldwide depression of the late 1920s. The number of starters would soon be forgotten in the amazing race that followed, however.

In the absence of the big French names, the three Bentleys, two 3-litre cars and one 4.5-litre, were strong favourites. From the moment Emile Coquille dropped the starting flag they confirmed their speed. Clement and Callingham's 4.5 took the lead, with Duller and Baron D'Erlanger second and Davis and Dr Benjafield third, ahead of the fastest Aries and a gaggle of Salmsons. Clement had soon lapped half the field and began breaking the lap record, eventually leaving it at 73.4mph. Then, around 9.30pm, with night falling, everything changed.

The sequence of events which *The Autocar* described as 'one of the most sensational accidents ever recorded in connection with the history of road racing' took place on the narrow, fast, blind and dangerous White House corners between Arnage and the start-finish line. As another car overtook him, Tabourin's Th Schneider slid broadside into the barriers and rebounded into the middle of the track. Callingham's leading Bentley was next to arrive, at perhaps 85 or 90mph, and rather than hit the Th Schneider he aimed for the ditch to his right.

'Night brought a complete change of aspect, and the grandstands, which had been well filled during the daylight hours, became even more crowded and animated.'

The Autocar, 1926

'As the twilight deepened to dusk, old Number 7 came fast round the White House turn and there in front, uncertain in the headlight's beam, was the tangled mass that was our other team cars.'

S.C.H. Davis

The impact threw him out of the car, into the middle of the road, but essentially uninjured he was able to run back to warn oncoming drivers. Thelusson's Fasto squeezed past the first accident but spun to a halt just beyond it, facing backwards.

Callingham was too late to warn George Duller in the second Bentley, who saw the Th Schneider across the track but didn't see his team-mate's car in the ditch, which was where he too was now heading. As *The Motor* described it, 'At the last moment, expert hurdle-race jockey that he is, he saw the obstacle and jumped clear over the steering wheel. His car crashed into the 4.5-litre model with such force that it threw it bodily into the road again ...' So the big Bentley was now on the track with the Th Schneider, the first of the smaller Bentleys was half in the ditch, half reared up on top of its sister car, and the Fasto was just beyond them. Duller, bleeding from the mouth but more or less uninjured, also set off to warn the next drivers, but having been thrown into the adjoining field he was on the wrong side of the hedge and too disorientated to realise it. Davis, in the third Bentley, was thundering towards all this mayhem at full speed.

If he had carried on like that the story may have been tragically different, but approaching the White House he sensed something wrong – dirt on the road, a few scattered stones – just enough to make him brake heavily. He still arrived on the scene at high speed, maybe 80mph, but picking out the biggest obstacles now piled in the road he braked as hard as he could, throwing the big car into a broadside slide to scrub off more speed and to ensure he was travelling backwards at the moment of the apparently inevitable impact. His right front wheel caught the pile comprised of the other two Bentleys, peeling back the off-side mudguard and running board, smashing the headlamp, and causing extensive damage to the front of the car. But amazingly, having satisfied himself that his team-mates and everyone else involved had survived, he decided that his battered car was still drivable, and that he was still in the race.

Right: the start in 1927, with Clement and Callingham in the number 1 Bentley and Davis and Benjafield in the number 3 leading their teammates Duller and d'Erlanger and the rest of the field. **Left:** the battered 1927 winner, wheels removed for transport by road to the victory celebrations in the Savoy Hotel, London.

Davis bent the front mudguard away from the wheel and set off for the pits, driving by his one remaining headlamp. It had started to rain. Even in the pits, of course, only the driver was allowed to work on the car, so Davis changed the battered front wheel and did what he could with the badly bent mudguard and headlamp mounting. He couldn't do much about the twisted chassis and bent front axle, and didn't want to think about the steering arms or the brakes. He particularly didn't want to draw W.O. Bentley's attention to the real condition of the car, which was now steering rather like a crab and braking with one wheel after another in a fairly random fashion. But Davis, and co-driver Dr Benjafield (the 'bacteriologist-cum-racing-driver') gritted their teeth, tried to forget the dangers, and set out to win the race. Ettore Bugatti once derided the Bentleys as 'the fastest lorries in the world', but their heavy engineering did have some advantages.

Immediately following the accident they were in the lead, but when Davis handed over to Benjy around midnight they had lost six laps on repairs (when the sidelight fell off Benjy replaced it with a torch taped to the windscreen frame). Now they were chasing the Aries, driven by Chassagne and Laly, through the foul weather of the night.

By daybreak the weather was bright and the Bentley was still running. It was now four laps adrift and apparently resigned to second place, but then the Aries started to falter, losing much time in the pits with a jammed starter. With two hours to go the Aries was back in the race but its lead was less than half a lap, until Chassagne put on the pressure to draw away again, to almost a full lap. Again the Bentley boys somehow found a bit extra to put maximum pressure on the French leader. It worked. In the 23rd hour the Aries stopped on the circuit and the Bentley took the lead. With only minutes to go Benjy pulled in and handed the car to Davis to take the flag in one of the most remarkable Le Mans races of all. They had covered 1472.6 miles at an average of 61.4mph. With the demise of the Aries they were 218 miles ahead of De Victor and Hasley's second-placed Salmson. Only seven cars finished, and although the winning Bentley carried the number 3, it was affectionately known ever after as 'Old Number 7' for the race number it had been carrying when it crashed out of the 1926 race. It went home, still battle-scarred, to be guest of honour at *The Autocar*'s celebration at the Savoy in London.

After this, the final two years of Le Mans' first decade could have been an anticlimax, but the dramas of 1927 had put the race even more firmly on the map, and the Bentley's success had brought the English flocking across the Channel. Bentley didn't let them down.

In 1928 there was more British interest, as Lagonda, Alvis and Aston Martin joined a field which had grown to 33 cars. French cars were now in a minority, and aside from the Aries were mainly smaller capacity cars with little chance of an outright win. For the first time there was officially such a thing, with a new award for the greatest distance covered. And there was the strongest American entry so far: four Chryslers and a straight-eight Stutz, the latter the biggest car in the race at 4.9 litres.

'The 24-hour race has always aroused considerable interest on this side of the Channel owing to the fact that ever since its inception Bentley cars have taken part.'

The Motor, 1927

The Bentley operation of the 1920s and early 1930s was the stuff that legends are made of: the quintessentially English team going to Le Mans to fight for national pride, and to do it with a certain style.

In 1927, as ever the team stayed in the Hotel Moderne in Le Mans, and final preparation of the team cars was carried out in the Hotel's yard (above).

In the late 1920s, the Bentley team was one of the most professionally organised in the sport, even though it was essentially made up of gentleman amateurs. Almost beyond its racing achievements the team would be known for its bringing together a group of personalities universally known as the Bentley Boys.

The 1927 team photograph (right) shows most of them. From left to right are Frank Clement, Leslie Callingham, André d'Erlanger, George Duller, and the winning driver pairing, 'Sammy' Davis (in the beret), and Dr John Benjafield. Behind d'Erlanger is Woolf Barnato, and between Duller and Davis is the boss, Walter Owen Bentley. The most famous missing face is Sir Henry 'Tim' Birkin, who didn't drive in 1927.

Clement was a talented driver who had known W.O. Bentley for many years before driving for him. Davis was a journalist who wrote wonderful accounts of his Le Mans exploits in *The Autocar*. 'Benjy' Benjafield was a bacteriologist. Millionaire 'Babe' Barnato's fortune was rooted in the South African diamond market. He raced at Le Mans three times, and won three times – in 1928, 1929 and 1930. By the time he won his third Le Mans he was also propping Bentley up financially, but by 1931 the team was no more and W.O. was headed for Lagonda.

The big Stutz, driven by Brisson and Bloch, led from the start, swapping both lead and lap record with the three 4.5-litre Bentleys, with one of the Chryslers never far behind. The Bentley shared by Chassagne and Sir Henry 'Tim' Birkin lost a lot of time with a puncture and collapsed wheel, largely because there was no jack in the car when the wheel failed. The Bentley shared by Benjy and Clement was put out by a broken chassis, leaving Woolf Barnato and Bernard Rubin to lead the chase, with Chassagne and Birkin fighting to recover almost three lost hours. One of the Lagondas ploughed into the sandbank at Mulsanne and d'Erlanger's sister car rammed it, but was able to continue and eventually to finish tenth. The Stutz v Bentley contest continued unabated while others fell by the roadside, and in the end it became a head-to-head contest between two almost crippled cars.

First the Stutz slowed with gearbox problems, allowing Barnato and Rubin into the lead, then the Bentley broke its chassis. But it was near enough the end of the race, and the Bentley had just enough of a lead, for Barnato to nurse it home before the leaking radiator killed it completely. So it was another dramatic Bentley victory, ahead of the Stutz and two of the Chryslers, with the Birkin/Chassagne Bentley surviving for fifth – and the front-drive Alvises a creditable sixth and ninth. The winners had covered 1658.7 miles at 69.1mph, winning by 64 miles. Birkin took the lap record to 79.1mph on his very last lap.

For 1929, the circuit had undergone the first of its periodic modifications. The hairpin at Pontlieu – a tight and dangerous turn hedged by houses (and people) behind the rudimentary barriers – was replaced by a short link between the two main straights, just before Pontlieu. The link was dubbed the 'Rue du Circuit' and reduced the lap length slightly, to 16.34km, 10.15 miles. That made the circuit safer but didn't significantly alter its character – or the status quo.

In 1929 Bentley had five cars, four 4.5 litres and a new six-cylinder 6.5-litre short-chassis Speed Six for Barnato and Birkin. The French challenge was limited to the smaller cars, led by the SARA team, which could hardly challenge for outright distance but could still contest the efficiency-based categories and the Biennial Cup, which reached its fifth finale. Of the absence of any big French cars, Clerk of the Course Charles Faroux exclaimed, 'It's a disgrace! I am ashamed for my own country! Perhaps next year.' This year, the real threat to the Bentleys again came from America, from Stutz, Chrysler and Du Pont.

It wasn't a great race, as *The Motor*'s man wrote, literally in mid-air, returning to England by light aeroplane. 'Touring pleasantly over an amazingly green countryside, with our Moth flying

Above: evening pit stop for Benjafield and d'Erlanger's four-cylinder Bentley in 1929. They finished third, behind Barnato and Birkin's Speed Six and the four-cylinder of Jack Dunfee and Glen Kidston, and ahead of the fourth-placed four-cylinder of Clement and Jean Chassagne. **Below:** Barnato and Rubin after their 1928 victory – both in their first drives at Le Mans. **Right:** the Stutz pit crew call in one of their cars for a spark plug change in 1929.

'By the end of the 1920s, Bentley and their British fans had fallen in love with Le Mans.'

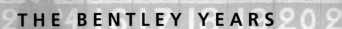

Left: another stop for the third-placed Bentley. While only the drivers were allowed to work on the cars, there was nothing to stop the crew examining them from a distance.

very low to keep out of the wet, misty clouds that drift barely 400 feet up, we seem to be creating something of a sensation. A mare and her foal have just galloped madly away from our threatening shadow. A yokel has gazed at us spellbound. He is probably more thrilled at the sight of an aeroplane over the Mairie gables than we have been at any moment during the Le Mans race this weekend. For it was not a thrilling race.'

Except for Bentley. They finished first, second, third and fourth, completing their hat-trick, and fourth win in six years, in dominant style. Their only retirement was the 4.5 shared by Rubin and Earl Howe, while their nearest challengers were the big straight-eight Stutz Black Hawks and the quick and consistent white Chryslers. All but one of the Stutzes failed, however, and the Bentleys underlined their superiority by taking the finish in line-astern formation. Barnato and Birkin in the big Speed Six led, covering 1765 miles at an average of 73.5mph, with 73 miles in hand over second placed Glen Kidston and Clive Dunfee.

Benjafield and d'Erlanger were third, Clement and Chassagne fourth, followed by Bouriat and Phillipe's Stutz and just five other finishers, including a privately-entered, British-built Lea Francis in eighth. Birkin raised the lap record to 83.5mph, and with Barnato won the fifth Biennial Cup, and the Index of Performance, which was normally dominated by the smaller fry. For Bentley it crowned a spectacular decade, but there was more to come.

GROWING IN STATURE
THE 1930s

0 KIL 000 DÉPART   13 KIL 626 ARRIVÉE   0 KIL 000 DÉPART   13 KIL 626 ARRIVÉE   0 KIL 000 DÉPART   13 KIL 626 ARRIVÉE   0 KIL 000 DÉPART   13 KIL 626 ARRIVÉE   0 KIL 000 DÉPART   13 KIL 626 ARRIVÉ

LE MANS 24 HOURS

The 1930s dawned at Le Mans with what looked like the recipe for a very second rate affair. Surprisingly, the 1930 race actually turned into a classic, with elements to rival the dramas of 1927 – albeit with a very different script. A week after their race report (written for the third successive year 'on the wing' as their man was flown back to Britain), *The Motor* reflected, 'Le Mans this year provided more thrills than it has ever done in the past. Indeed I am not sure that it was not the most exciting race of any kind to be held for at least five years ...'

This was a race with the smallest entry ever seen at Le Mans, bringing a meagre eighteen cars to the start-line (and one of those failed to go any further). However, this was more a sign of the economic climate in Europe (and indeed America) at the turn of the decade than of any problems with the race. It couldn't have been entirely true, either, as some of the press suggested, that other major teams were staying away simply because they thought the big Bentleys were unbeatable on the Circuit de la Sarthe. Motor racing has never worked that way. 1930 was also the year which saw the first female competitors at Le Mans, the all-French team of Madame Mareuse and Madame Siko, who went on to finish seventh in their Bugatti. That, remarkably, was one of only three French cars in this event, the others being a pair of the interesting 1-litre front-drive Tractas.

While the French stayed away, the Americans returned, joined by the strongest challenger so far from Italy, and the first appearance of a motor-sporting giant from Germany, Mercedes-Benz. The sole

Previous Spread: in 1935 R.P. Gardner's Aston Martin was one of seven Ulsters as Britain dominated the 58-car entry with 37 cars, including the winning Lagonda, plus Aston, Austin, Frazer-Nash, MG, Riley and Singer. Gardner and Beloe were fifteenth. Charles Martin and Charles Brackenbury's Ulster was third, winning the Biennial Cup and the Index of Performance. **Above:** in 1931 Birkin switched from Bentley to Alfa Romeo, and won. **Right:** final fling for the Bentley Boys: Kidston and Barnato after their 1930 win.

American entries were from Stutz (America was feeling the depression more than most), but they were known to be fast and durable. The single Alfa Romeo and Mercedes were unknown quantities, although both from very fine marques. The pale blue Alfa was really a British effort, driven by Earl Howe and Leslie Callingham – the former Bentley driver and survivor of the 1927 White House crash. The white Mercedes was entered for a young but already highly respected Rudi Caracciola with co-driver Werner, and looked after by legendary team manager Alfred Neubauer.

It was a year for superchargers, but while Mercedes loved supercharging and Caracciola's mighty SS used one of the biggest in the business, W.O. Bentley was not a fan. Yet this was the first year of the 'Blower' Bentleys. Over time, they became perhaps the best known Bentleys of all, but the blown four-cylinder 4.5-litre cars weren't built by the works – they were built by Birkin's team, supported by its rich patron the Hon. Dorothy Paget. Three were entered for 1930, but preparation problems saw Harcourt Wood and Jack Dunfee's car scratched, so only two made it to Le Mans to run alongside W.O.'s unsupercharged Speed Sixes. W.O. thought the way to more power was more capacity, and believed that supercharging made the cars unreliable, hence his 6.5-litre Sixes. There were three of those, for Barnato and Kidston, Clement and Dick Watney, and Davis and Clive Dunfee. The 'Blowers' were driven by Birkin and Chassagne, and Benjafield and Ramponi, with the Birkin-Paget pits managed by former driver Kensington Moir.

At the start, on 21 June, the longest day of the year, it was hot and sunny. Caracciola in the screaming 7-litre six-cylinder Mercedes took the lead, with the three big Bentleys behind him and Birkin's Blower next up. On the fourth lap Birkin, having clawed his way onto Caracciola's tail, and pulling over 125mph on the long straight, put in a mighty passing manouevre at Mulsanne corner. It was too much for his offside rear tyre, which threw its treads. Replacing the wheel, he resumed the chase a lap down and had just caught the Mercedes again when another tyre shredded, this time taking much of the rear mudguard with it. Over the next few hours that was how it continued, the

Bentley, with either Birkin or Chassagne driving, alternately catching the Mercedes and throwing tyre treads in the hot weather.

That allowed Davis's Speed Six to chase the Mercedes, until co-driver Dunfee stuck the car into the Mulsanne sand, where it stayed despite frantic shovelling by both drivers. The sandbanks on the faster corners were a long-standing feature of Le Mans, and along with the earth banks and woven wood fences on other parts of the circuit provided fairly advanced safety features for their time, but they did ensnare a good few cars over the years. Still the surviving Bentleys hounded the Mercedes, now led by Barnato's Speed Six, and just before 8.30 on Saturday evening he took the lead, if only for a lap. The cars now raced neck-and-neck for lap after lap. Around midnight Barnato's Bentley was leading, until it had its own tyre problems –

'The bonnet was never lifted, throughout the race, on No 4, the winning Bentley – a wonderful testimony to the engine's reliability.'

The Motor, 1930

but then the incredible battle was over, as the Mercedes retired, officially with electrical problems. The scene was set for Bentley's fifth victory.

The Stutz effort ended in the sandbank for one and in flames for the other. The Alfa ran steadily but not quickly enough to fifth place, and as W.O. had predicted, the Blower Bentleys failed, both with engine problems, albeit after Birkin had raised the lap record to 89.7mph. Barnato and Kidston triumphed, ahead of Clement and Watney, with the British Talbot of Lewis and Eaton a distant third – but winning the Index of Performance, related to capacity.

This was Barnato's third Le Mans, his third win, and his final appearance at the race. It was Bentley's finest hour, but it was also the end of an era. The works cars didn't come back for 1931, and although private Bentleys ran in the 1930s, 1940s and 1950s, it would be 2001 before a works Bentley effort returned in force. The irony was that Bentley in its original form was in deep financial trouble, and all its Le Mans glory (plus a good deal of Barnato's money) couldn't save it from becoming a part of Rolls-Royce, without W.O. at the helm and with some very different cars.

It was Alfa Romeo who took up Bentley's mantle at La Sarthe, winning the next four races in a row. Mercedes, like Bentley, didn't return as a works team in 1931, although there was a private entry for Iwanowski and Henri Stoffel, which would do rather well in a field which had also lost all its American challengers bar one private Stutz and two Chryslers, none of which saw dawn on Sunday. France, however, finally had a serious front-running chance in the shape of Bugatti.

Alongside a number of smaller private Bugatti entries, Ettore Bugatti entered three works cars, Type 50s, with 4.9-litre twin overhead camshaft eight-cylinder unsupercharged engines. His main opposition would be the Alfa Romeos, also works cars this year, and in engineering terms just as elegant as Bugatti's masterpieces. The three 1931 Alfas were the latest 8C 2300 model, designed by the brilliant Vittorio Jano and based on the company's Grand Prix models. They were also twin-cam straight eights, with a capacity of 2.3 litres and supercharged. The large-capacity unblown Bugattis and smaller, blown Alfas actually had very similar power outputs, both in superb chassis. Whether they had the stamina of a Bentley remained to be seen.

Above: there was only one German car in 1931, the huge supercharged SSK of Stoffel and Ivanowski, but like Caracciola's the year before it made a fine race of it. Here the SSK is pursued by Howe and Birkin's Alfa. At the end the positions were reversed, with the Alfa winning while Ivanowski took fastest lap.
Right: Mme Odette Siko was the first female driver at Le Mans, but in 1931, in her second appearance, her Bugatti was disqualified.

'The day when the [Bentley] name passed into the keeping of Rolls–Royce Ltd, many were the enthusiasts who mourned the inevitable evolutions of commerce within the industry ...'

The Motor

In 1935, MG's seven cars included a three-car team within the team, all with female drivers. The three 850cc PA Midgets were managed by Captain George Eyston, and driven by Doreen Evans (left) and Barbara Skinner, Joan Richmond and Mrs Gordon Simpson, and Margaret Allan and Coleen Eaton. They all finished, within a couple of laps of each other, in 24th, 25th and 26th places.

Above: following in the footsteps of a famous father, Vanina Ickx at the 2001 test day in the Belmondo Viper she was to share with Paul Belmondo and Carl Rosenblad.

They were the first all-female team at Le Mans, but not the first female drivers. That honour went to two French women, Mmes Marguerite Mareuse and Odette Siko, who finished seventh in 1930 in Mme Mareuse's 1.5-litre Type 40 Bugatti. They did rather better than the other cars in the 1930 race with a female connection: the 'Blower' Bentleys entered by the Hon Dorothy Paget. Neither of the supercharged Paget cars finished, although Birkin's early battle with Caracciola's Mercedes was fiercely fought. Mmes Mareuse and Siko were disqualified for refuelling too early in the 1931 race, but in 1932 Mme Siko took a fine fourth place overall, and the 2-litre class win, sharing her own Alfa 6C with 'Sabipa'.

That remains the best overall result by a female driver at Le Mans. It was also the final appearance for Mme Siko, who had a miraculous escape the following year when she had a huge accident with her Alfa approaching Arnage corner. The car broke several large trees, overturned and caught fire. Mme Siko walked away with a broken wrist and minor burns, and never raced at Le Mans again – but she had proved that female drivers could run with the best.

0 KIL 000   13 KIL 626   0 KIL 000   13 KIL 626   0 KIL 000   13 KIL 626   0 KIL 000   13 KIL 626
ÉPART   ARRIVÉE   DÉPART   ARRIVÉE   DÉPART   ARRIVÉE   DÉPART   ARRIVÉE

LE MANS 24 HOURS

By the early 1930s the circuit had already changed, and the updating has never stopped. In 1972 (above) the circuit was completely re-routed from Arnage to the start, bypassing the notoriously dangerous White House.

In the event only two Alfas started, the car for Campari and Marinoni being withdrawn on the morning of the race. Both Birkin's own Bentley road car and *The Motor*'s famous aeroplane had been pressed into collecting new pistons from Paris, but only two of the Alfas could be finished in time. And the question of Alfa versus Bugatti wasn't really answered, because the Bugattis, too, were withdrawn even before night had fallen, in rather sad circumstances. The Type 50 driven from the start by Rost, swapping places in the leading group, had a tyre tread detach at around 130mph on a straight part of the circuit and wrap around the brake gear, locking the wheel and causing the tyre to burst completely. Rost was pitched off the circuit, over the ditch and through the light fencing into an area with marshals and spectators. Rost and several marshals were badly injured, one spectator was killed. The Type 50 driven by Achille Varzi and Louis Chiron had already had problems with throwing tyre treads, and Jean Bugatti, managing his father's team, immediately withdrew his other cars.

That just left the Alfas to fight with the big Mercedes, which had shown considerable pace from the start – agility versus power, a classic confrontation. In spite of tyre troubles of its own, the Mercedes survived to take second place. But seventy miles ahead was Howe and Birkin's Alfa – the combination of experienced British drivers and brilliant Italian engineering victorious at an average of 78.1mph. Zehender, having led, had crashed the other Alfa, which he shared with Marinoni, and finally it was Rose-Richards and Saunders-Davies in the British Talbot who finished a respectable third. Further down the field, as *The Light Car* reported, 'The two MG Midgets created a wonderful impression among the French, who had never seen anything quite so small move quite so fast.' But neither officially finished.

This, in a way, was the end of the beginning for Le Mans. Following changes in Rudge-Whitworth's business interests, the Rudge-Whitworth Cup, although still with the same sponsors, was renamed the

Biennial Cup of the Automobile Club de l'Ouest. But there was a more fundamental difference at Le Mans, too. The circuit was about to change again, this time more drastically, as the race began to attract even more spectators. As well as a challenge to the drivers, the new section would soon become a new centre for Le Mans' nightlife.

The changes bypassed the most troublesome part of the early course, the leg from just beyond the pits up to the Pontlieu hairpin (or latterly the Rue du Circuit link) and back to the beginning of the long stretch past Hunaudières to Mulsanne. As well as the cars getting faster, Le Mans town was getting bigger, and swallowing up suburbs like Pontlieu, so the link between the two long sides of the circuit was moved south, away from the town boundaries. The Automobile Club de l'Ouest bought a tract of land, about 75 hectares, between the main pit and grandstand area and the Ligne Droite des Hunaudières, the modern Mulsanne Straight. They built a new section of road, in the area of the modern Dunlop Curves, sweeping gently right beyond the pits, over a gentle brow, down through a tricky new sequence of S bends and hard right again back onto the shortened straight. Shortened, but at almost six kilometres it remained quite fast enough for any car to reach its maximum speed and hold it for a very long time.

The new section was called Tertre Rouge, 'the red hillock', after the distinct rise that it crested – now the most pronounced hill on the circuit. The left-right flick at the bottom of the drop was labelled The Esses, and the corner onto the long straight was also called Tertre Rouge. The new corners were fast and difficult, but crucial for making up time, overtaking, and most of all for getting the fastest entry onto the all important Mulsanne Straight. All this reduced the lap distance by just under two miles, to 8.38 miles, and this circuit survived with very few changes into the late 1960s, when the first serious chicane was added just before the finish line.

Below: nowadays the big landmark between the pits straight and the Esses is the Dunlop Bridge, but in 1932 the Champion Bridge took spectators over the track.
Overleaf: Marinoni attempts in vain to lever his Alfa 8C out of the ditch at the White House with a fence post.

The links between the infield and outfield sections made the new area a natural place for the growing 'village' of cafés and bars, sideshows and fairground rides – which remain to this day.

The section also became a natural focus for Le Mans' growing social scene for ordinary spectators – perhaps not as sophisticated as the Hartford Hotel of the 1920s, but a key element in what makes Le Mans so vibrant and unique. From the start there were two pedestrian bridges over the circuit on this stretch of road. The first was right at the beginning of the new link, and originally carried advertising for Champion spark-plugs; later it would move to the brow of the hill and become famous as the tyre-shaped Dunlop Bridge. These links between the infield and outfield sections made the new area a natural place for the growing 'village' of cafés and bars, sideshows and fairground rides – which remain to this day.

The first race to use the revised circuit was another Alfa Romeo success – and a remarkable performance by one man in particular. Alfas made up seven of the 26 cars in the now traditional Le Mans start, and the six 2.3-litre supercharged 8Cs (the other was a six-cylinder 1750) proved to be a lot quicker than the pair of supercharged 2.3-litre Type 55s that Bugatti had brought this time. There was a hint of a challenge from the big cars, but this time they were all privately entered: a 7.1-litre Mercedes, one of Birkin's 4.5 Blower Bentleys and a Stutz, still hoping to come good. But this year size didn't count, and none of the three made the finish – the Stutz and Bentley out in accidents and the Mercedes sidelined by lubrication problems.

The Bentley's accident, while driven by Trevoux, brought shades of déjà vu. He crashed at the White House curves on his first lap, turning over and partly blocking the track. This year the problem was at least in daylight, but that didn't stop a number of other cars joining in. Minoia in one of the works Alfas, having just taken the lap record, piled in next, followed almost immediately by Brisson in the Stutz – or rather out of it, as he was catapulted into the hedge, without coming to serious harm. 'Putting his hand into his pocket', reported *The Autocar*, 'he found that his cigarettes were crushed beyond use. "you might give me a cig," he remarked to a native who was standing open-mouthed by the side of the road. For reply the astonished farmer uttered one word, made famous by a French general at Waterloo . . .'

Minoia's Alfa was dragged out of the way but there was enough debris to catch Marinoni in one of the private Alfas, and to give the officials some frightening moments as other cars raced through the partly blocked road at what seemed like suicidal speeds. And the race was not yet four hours old.

For a while, there were four Alfas in the first four places, followed by the lone Mercedes (until

Left: another victim of the infamous White House in 1932. Jean Trevoux hadn't finished a lap before he inverted his Bentley directly opposite the point where Marinoni and works Alfa driver Minoia would crash later in the race – all without serious injuries.
Right: a happier finish in 1932 for Raymond Sommer and Luigi Chinetti, leading Cortese and Guidotti to an Alfa 8C 1-2.

'Hundreds of thousands of people line the circuit, and at night the lighting effects of the tribunes and pits, and the dispensation of music, give a wondrous effect.'

The Motor

it crashed, in the early evening), Bouriat's Bugatti, Sommer and Chinetti's privately entered 8C 2300 Alfa, and the rest. It turned into a remarkable performance for Raymond Sommer, and a victorious one. After just one driving stint his co-driver was taken ill and couldn't continue. Sommer did, and drove some twenty hours of the race single handed – and there was nothing in the rules at that time to say he couldn't. He swapped places during the night with the Alfas of Howe and Birkin and Cortese and Guidotti, until the former had engine problems just before dawn and the latter lost a lot of time with minor repairs, while still managing to keep running.

Once the Bugatti of Count Czaykowski and Ernst Friederich had dropped out on Sunday afternoon, the Alfas only raced each other. In the end, Sommer (with more than a little help from Chinetti, who had also prepared the car) won by just sixteen miles – less than two laps on the new, shorter circuit. Cortese and Guidotti were second, Britons Brian Lewis and Tim Rose-Richards were third for Talbot, and Madame Siko was a fine fourth, this year in another Alfa shared with Sabipa. Fifth place went to the Aston Martin of Newsome and Widengren and the ninth Biennial Cup was won by Bertorelli (the designer of the car) and Driscoll in another Aston, in seventh, giving the British enthusiasts at least something to cheer.

The winning average and new lap record were slower than the best on the old circuit, at 76.5mph for Sommer and 88.5mph for Minoia respectively, but the new circuit was generally much liked – not only by the competitors but also by the crowds. The following year it was the scene for both an Alfa hat-trick (again led by Sommer) and one of the closest finishes in the race's history, while the new distance and lap records surpassed anything seen on the old circuit.

The atmosphere of the event was again noted in *The Motor*'s report. 'The event, to use a much abused word, is unique in every respect. It is the greatest race of its kind in the world, one in which the atmosphere has to be experienced to be appreciated. The course, which has a splendid tar-macadam surface, lies some 4½ miles south of the town and in glorious wooded country. There are two long S-bends, the famous right-handed Arnage and Mulsanne bends, and the Mulsanne downhill straight, where speeds of 120mph were attained.

'Le Mans goes *en fête* for this festival, shops being closed during the proceedings. Hundreds of thousands of people line the circuit, and at night the lighting effects of the tribunes and pits, coupled with the dispensation of music, give a wondrous effect ...'

1933 saw 29 starters, seven of them Alfa Romeos again, and among the Alfa pilotes was one of the finest drivers in the world, Tazio Nuvolari – teamed with 1932 winner Raymond Sommer. It would be the only time Nuvolari raced at Le Mans, but he made it count.

Considered by some to be the greatest racing driver of all time, Nuvolari was still to reach the peak of his career but by 1933 he was already regarded as something special. 'The Flying Mantuan' was small, wiry and so tanned that his skin looked almost like leather, but in a racing car he was a giant. He was even Birkin's hero. The year before, in his autobiography *Full Throttle* (dedicated to 'All Schoolboys'), Birkin called Nuvolari 'the finest driver living at the moment'. He described him as 'small, swarthy, dark and agitated, with all the fire of his southern blood in his veins. He does not have a fit of

Tazio Nuvolari only raced at Le Mans once, in 1933, but he won, to add the world's greatest 24-hour race to his tally of wins in Grands Prix, the Mille Miglia, the Targa Florio and the Tourist Trophy.

nerves before a race but is wildly excited instead; and after it he is very modest but still as excited.' Ferdinand Porsche had described him in 1930 as 'the greatest driver of past, present or future', and his great rival Achille Varzi called him 'the boldest, most skilful madman of us all'.

His nickname, Figlio di Diavolo – Son of the Devil – alluded to the rumour that his speed and courage came from a pact with Satan. The truth was Nuvolari simply had no fear, and consummate skill. Having survived childhood adventures jumping off roofs with a home-made parachute, and a fiery crash into a haystack in a Bleriot aeroplane which he had rebuilt from a pile of parts, his early career as a motorcycle racer must have looked relatively safe. He did crash a lot, but he won too, and carried on winning when he switched to cars. He raced anything and everything and through the 1930s won everything worth winning, including the Mille Miglia (twice), the Targa Florio, the Tourist Trophy (twice), and the Monaco, French, German, Italian, Belgian and Donington Grands Prix among others. He frequently raced within days of accidents which had left him encased in plaster, and his machinery often expired under him, but he never gave up.

Like Birkin he was superstitious. Birkin hated anything to do with the number 13 and would never race without his blue-and-white spotted silk scarf or his white helmet with an old St Christopher token attached. Nuvolari always wore a yellow jersey with his TN monogram, a pale blue leather helmet, blue trousers and shoes with yellow laces. He also wore a small silver tortoise, given to him by the poet and politician Gabriel d'Annunzio – 'a symbol of prudence with slowness'.

Nuvolari was not slow at Le Mans in 1933, and added the race to his list of victories on his one and only appearance. It was a hard-fought victory, too, shared with the man who had won almost single-handed a year before.

Below and Overleaf: night-time at Le Mans has its own special atmosphere. While the pit crews work through the darkness towards dawn, with more than half the race still to come, spectators eat, drink and make merry, and maybe stop occasionally to catch up with what's happening on the track just outside – in this case a 24-hour accordion marathon in the 1950s.

Above: Nuvolari and Sommer made a fine team in 1933. Nuvolari, who many consider the greatest racing driver of all, contributed a mixture of unaccustomed caution when it was appropriate and sheer pace when it was needed – helped by the Le Mans experience of his co-driver Raymond Sommer. Nuvolari brought the Alfa home just ten seconds ahead, after a wonderful last-lap duel with Luigi Chinetti in another 8C. **Right:** chasing hard on its way to fifth place overall, first in Index of Performance, and winning the 1933-34 Biennial Cup, the Riley 9, number 36, of von der Becke and Peacock.

Alfa were actually in deep financial trouble. Since 1931 they had been at least partially under government control and in 1933 the company was restructured in what was effectively a liquidation. The racing team would survive in the guise of Scuderia Ferrari, managed by one Enzo Ferrari. There was no sign of weakness in Alfa's Le Mans line-up for 1933, however: the weakness was in the opposition. The few big cars were private entries, one Bugatti, one 'Blower' Bentley, one Model J Duesenberg and not much else – and none of them lasted very long in the race. The smaller cars could race for the other prizes, but the outright distance contest was really an Alfa benefit.

At least they put on a great race between them. The leading driver pairings were Nuvolari and Sommer, Chinetti and Varent, Lewis and Rose-Richards, Chiron and Cortese, and Moll and Cloitre. Nuvolari set the pace, ably backed up by Sommer, fell back with a leaking fuel tank, clawed back into the lead, sprang another leak, and eventually took the race to the very last lap. Cortese had crashed at the new Esses, and it was Chinetti who was swapping the lead with Nuvolari in the last hour, as the Flying Mantuan struggled in the pits with his fuel leaks. Chinetti started the last lap in the lead with Nuvolari just about to leap out of the pits for a final effort. They then swapped places all around the circuit until Chinetti made a mistake at Arnage, letting Nuvolari through to win by just ten seconds in one of the closest finishes in the race's history. Lewis and Rose-Richards were third in another 8C Alfa, and the next three places were taken by smaller British cars, an 1100cc Riley, a 1½-litre Riley and a 750cc MG Midget. Surprisingly it was Sommer, not Nuvolari, who took the lap record, at 90.9mph.

The winning marque wouldn't change in 1934, but other things did, as the circuit facilities continued to grow more elaborate and ever more permanent. This year the highlight was a new two-tier pits building with all-new fuelling arrangements. In the past, fuel had usually been tipped into the cars (by the drivers, as the rules demanded) from petrol cans or latterly milk churns. It was slow,

'Only the
competitors
themselves,
and other
highly scientific
people, who
work it out
for themselves,
are aware
of what is
happening on
handicap.'

The Motor

messy and potentially hugely dangerous, but for 1934 there would be a more elaborate built-in refuelling system.

For the first time, the second storey of the redeveloped pits (which could now accommodate up to sixty cars) featured a facility which is still very much in evidence in the 21st century, 'hospitality' boxes for non-competitors, often with motor trade connections but usually just there for a good weekend party. The more practical purpose of the second storey, of course, was the new refuelling facilities, installed by Shell and Esso and comprising main tanks each feeding groups of four pits by individual hoses. There was still no barrier of any kind to separate the pit lane from the race track, and just white picket fences between cars and pit counters.

The Autocar, as ever, set the scene. 'Glorious hot weather – really it was almost too hot – saw the entire countryside making its way out to the course on foot, on the inevitable French bicycles, or in cars with equally inevitable incessant hooting, such a characteristic of the country. From far and near they rolled in, till even the crowds of past years were exceeded, and car park after car park glistened in serried ranks.

'Much of the circuit, 8.3 miles in length, lies among beautiful pine woods and here tents and caravans were set up, while thousands came prepared to spend a night in the open. Picnic parties spread themselves out, booths sprang up like mushrooms, and lilting French airs from the innumerable loud-speakers greeted the gaily decked throng – women in summery frocks of unmistakable French taste, the men in short-sleeved pull-overs and small round berets.

'This year the pits – always permanent structures fitted with electric light – had been provided with an upper storey, reaching indeed a standard of magnificence unparalleled in motor racing. Beneath them were lined up the cars – seventeen carried the blue of France, twenty-three the English green, and four the Italian red – all arrayed pointing diagonally in the direction of travel at the side of the road, and the vivid advertisements of various accessories, so characteristic of a Continental road race, lent additional colour to the scene. As four o'clock approached a stentorian voice announced "Messieurs les gendarmes, prenez garde à la route", or words to that effect, and the task began of getting the chattering throng off the road. But the French have all the instincts proper to a road race, and soon all was clear.

'Round the stands and along each side of the new road after the start there are avenues or paths marked in picturesque style after famous names connected with the race. One saw thousands of eager spectators pressing to the railings around such signs as the Esplanade Dunlop, the Avenue Bentley, and the Esplanade Guy Bouriat, after the late French driver. . .'

After all this work, and the excitement of recent years, 1934 wasn't a particularly good race, except perhaps for Alfa, who recorded their fourth straight win – this year with a privately entered car. It was driven by Chinetti, adding a 'real' win to his limited driving role in Sommer's 1932 victory, and sharing with Phillipe 'Phi-Phi' Etancelin.

The numbers were good, with 44 cars on the grid, but the trend towards smaller cars was repeated, and the majority of entries were British, reinforcing the notion of Le Mans as a British race on a French circuit. The Brits weren't in the hunt for outright victory, though; that again devolved to the four privately entered Alfas (the familiar 8C 2300s) and not much else, as

'One mechanic only is allowed to assist a driver in adjustments. An assistant must also be provided to fill the petrol tanks, but is not allowed to help in any other way.'

The Autocar

the official Bugattis stayed away again leaving only a few privately entered examples and the ageing La Lorraine to uphold French hopes in the big league.

They really didn't get a look in. Sommer's Alfa was first to lead, from the other three 8Cs, but only until his car caught fire near Arnage during his first driving stint. That left British Alfa drivers Earl Howe and Tim Rose-Richards ahead, battling with Chinetti and Etancelin, but only until nightfall when they were slowed by lighting problems. For several hours they climbed back up the order but another electrical failure and finally a broken clutch brought their race to an end. The other British-crewed Alfa of Saunders-Davies and Clifford were out with engine problems by mid-evening, and Veyron's big Bugatti, the only other car remotely in touch with the Alfas, suffered engine failure around midnight. Chinetti and Etancelin cruised on to victory by the handsome margin of 130 miles at the lowest average speed in the past five years, and even Etancelin's fastest lap broke no records.

Behind the solitary Alfa it was almost all British and almost all small cars. Four Rileys and an MG made up the top six, the leading Riley driven by Sebilleau and Delaroche and the MG Magnette in fourth place. The first French car was the 3-litre class-winning Bugatti of Mahé and Desvignes in ninth place, and France again had nothing to shout about.

The huge field for the 1935 race was perhaps a sign that economies were reviving, and Alfa and Bugatti were again the main challengers to the hordes of British cars which made up the majority of the 58 on the grid. And now, for the first time since the glory days of the Bentleys, although the bulk of the 37 British entries were small cars again, there was a British challenger for outright honours: Lagonda.

Ironically, W.O. Bentley himself was about to join Lagonda, after a short and unhappy time seeing his old Bentleys becoming just an offshoot of Rolls-Royce following his company's problems in the early 1930s. But the pair of Lagonda Rapides at Le Mans in 1935 weren't W.O. Lagondas – his speciality would be the later, luxuriously sporty V12-engined cars. The Le Mans Lagondas were, however, quite in character with the once dominant Le Mans Bentleys: big 4.5-litre straight-six engines, simple chassis, extreme robustness and ample pace.

Enough pace and reliability, as it turned out, ultimately to beat this year's four 8C Alfas, the seven Bugattis of various types and sizes, Prince Nicholas's big but rather old-fashioned Duesenberg and cars from the restructured Talbot company and French newcomers Delahaye.

The Lagondas were driven by John Hindmarsh and Luis Fontes, and Dr Benjafield and Ronald Gunter. From the start they chased the pace-setting Alfas – headed again by Earl Howe and Brian Lewis, who were early leaders before falling back with electrical problems. Chinetti and Gastard's Alfa then made the running, pursued by the Lagondas, the other Alfas of Stoffel/Louis-Dreyfus and Sommer/de Sauge, and the big Bugatti driven by Labric and Veyron. Sommer may have had a touch of déjà vu when de Sauge was taken ill, leaving the Frenchman with the prospect of another mostly solo drive, like his winning effort in 1932.

He led again, but was spared a long stint at the wheel by retirement in the early hours of Sunday. It was unusually wet on Saturday evening and through much of the night, as the Hindmarsh/Fontes Lagonda disputed the lead with the Howe/Lewis and Stoffel/Louis-Dreyfus Alfas. Then the opposition started to fail. The Bugatti broke its back axle on Sunday morning, the Chinetti/Gaston Alfa made one too many visits to the ditch, and Howe's Alfa had an engine blow-up. The remaining Alfa still led, but

Above Left: a modern Le Mans team working in its clinically clean garage would be appalled by the grubby conditions in which the Aston Martin of Auguste César Bertelli and S Clifton Penn-Hughes was prepared in 1934. The tiniest speck of dirt can undo all efforts at Le Mans, but the Aston was eliminated at mid-race for falling behind its required distance.
Above: the winning Lagonda in the pits in 1935. Hindmarsh and Fontes won partly because Alfa Romeo's pit-crew made a last-minute lap-scoring mistake.

Hindmarsh and Fontes overhauled it on Sunday morning and hung on in the closing stages in spite of slowing with failing oil pressure (while the other Lagonda had dropped right back with gearbox problems). Still the lone Alfa might have won except for a mistake by the team. In the final hour, Dreyfus passed the Lagonda while it was in the pits and his own crew signalled that he was in the lead. He wasn't, he was a lap down, and without the time to make up the distance.

So the Lagonda won, at an average of 77.8mph, with less than a lap in hand over the Alfa. The team received a telegram while they were in Paris en-route home from British Minister of Transport Hoare-Belisha – of beacon fame. 'This is really splendid. My congratulations to all concerned.' In 1931 Howe and Birkin's Alfa win had brought a telegram from Mussolini, congratulating them on their 'victory for Italy ...'

All but six of the 28 finishers were British, and again British cars dominated the smaller ranks, with Martin and Brackenbury third in an Aston Martin, winning the 1500cc class and the eleventh Biennial Cup, while Barnes and Langley's Singer won the 1-litre class.

1936, alas, was the Le Mans that never was, not for any problems with the race but for deeper problems affecting all France. The country was crippled by strikes and factory occupations for better pay and better working conditions. The motor industry was particularly badly affected, with both the Renault and Bugatti factories occupied for a time by the workers, while petrol supplies began to run short. The race had received a maximum entry of sixty cars, but it was cancelled just a week before the due date. There was some suggestion of it being run at the beginning of August, but it never happened, and the next gathering at the Circuit de la Sarthe was not until June 1937.

Jean Bugatti came to Le Mans with a beautiful streamlined racing version of Bugatti's supercharged 3.3-litre Type 57, popularly nicknamed the 'Tank'.

For France, it was a race worth waiting for, as the national entry – including Delahaye, the Delahaye-built Delage, and Talbot – was far more respectable than it had been, and the return of the works Bugattis brought the marque its first win, with one of its most spectacular cars.

Jean Bugatti was now running the company and the team and came to Le Mans with a beautiful streamlined racing version of the supercharged 3.3-litre Type 57. It was popularly nicknamed the 'Tank', and had already been successful in the 1936 French Grand Prix, run to sports car rules. That, in fact, was what had given the French sports car makers new impetus. Talbot had a 4-litre contender and Delahaye a fine 3.6 straight-six with electromagnetic semi-automatic gearbox – shades of modern F1!

The Bugatti win was the first for a French car since 1926, and the fine all-French driving team of Robert Benoist and Jean-Pierre Wimille (above) overcame a strong challenge from the seven Delahayes in the race and the Delage D6 Coupé. They also set a new distance record (over 2000 miles for the first time, at 2044 miles) and, with Wimille driving, a new lap record at a very impressive 96.4mph. Once the very fast 2.9-litre supercharged Alfa of Sommer and Giudotti and the leading Lagonda (now with some input from W.O. Bentley) had gone, and once their team mates Veyron and Labric were out, they only really had the fastest of the Delahayes to worry about, and finished comfortably ahead of Paul and Mongin, and Dreyfus and Stoffel.

Sadly, the race was marred by its first fatal accidents since 1925. Within the first hour a multiple pile-up just after the already infamous White House corners claimed half a dozen cars, and the lives of French amateur Bugatti driver Rene Kippeurt and English Frazer-Nash driver Pat Fairfield, who died in hospital on Monday morning.

The French upsurge was set to continue for the final two races of the 1930s. The leading cars were rapidly becoming more two-seater racing cars, often with Grand Prix connections, rather than true production sports cars. Oddly, Bugatti didn't come back in 1938 to defend their title, withdrawing their entry after practice supposedly because they didn't feel they were ready to race. The Talbots, Delages and Delahayes were more than ready, and strongly fancied with their Grand Prix-derived 4.5-litre engines – sixes for the Talbots, V12s for the Delahayes, in purpose-built Le Mans chassis which, like the engines, were closely related to the Grand Prix designs. And while the French marques were only bit players in Grand Prix racing against the new generation Mercedes and Auto Union 'Silver Arrows', they were definitely the class of the sports car field at Le Mans in 1938.

The most obvious opposition again came from the powerful twin-supercharged 2.9 Alfa 8C 2900, with its very slippery closed body. It was a lot prettier than the German Adler coupé driven by Orssich and Sauerwein, making its second appearance and described by *The Light Car* as 'not unlike a bomb-proof shelter'. But, they went on, the Adler 'dropped a mild bombshell of its own by winning the Rudge-Whitworth Cup'.

In the main event it was the year of the Delahayes, which finished first, second and fourth, sandwiching one of the Talbots in a dominant French performance. As *The Light Car* reported, it was watched by the now familiar huge crowd. 'From early on Saturday morning there was a continuous

> 'It was impossible to stop in 150 metres so I tried to find a gap in the twisted heap of five cars but the road was completely blocked.'
>
> *Raul Forestier on the 1937 White House crash*

Left: 1937, another multi-car White House accident, this time with fatal results. René Kippeurt was thrown from his Bugatti as he hit the BMW driven by Fritz Roth, and several other cars piled into them, Tremoulet's Delahaye, Pat Fairfield's Frazer-Nash, Raph's Talbot. **Below and Right:** in 1934 the track was no wider than today's pit-lane, and spectators were protected only by earth banks and wooden fences. The refuelling process still has similarities, though.

Right: night pit call for Rob Walker's Delahaye 135S, en route to eighth in 1939. His co-driver, Ian Connell, did very little driving after burning his feet in the early stages.

exodus from the old city of Le Mans, and long before zero hour (4pm) every seat on the grandstand was occupied, all vantage points on the 8.38-mile course had been taken, flags fluttered, loud-speakers blared, refreshment tents were doing a roaring trade ... in fact the unique Le Mans atmosphere had descended – and would remain until after the last exhaust note had died, over 24 hours later.'

They were treated to a fine race, if an unpredictable one, in sultry weather. The fastest cars were now exceeding 150mph on the Mulsanne Straight, and Le Mans was becoming more of a 24-hour sprint than an exercise in conserving cars and energy. There was great rivalry between the French cars and the Alfas. From the start the race settled into a battle between Sommer and Biondetti in the Touring-bodied closed 8C, Comotti and Divo and Chiron and Dreyfus in the 'Ecurie Bleue' Delahayes, and Etancelin and Chinetti in the single big-engined Talbot. Comotti was an early departure with gearbox problems, followed by Dreyfus with engine failure following overheating, and eventually the Talbot, its engine breaking just as night began to fall.

Through the night, the Alfa continued to pull away as car after car broke behind it. Then, almost within sight of the finish and leading by around a hundred miles, the Alfa succumbed too. Chaboud and Tremoulet's win for Delahaye, followed by Serraud and Giraud-Cabantous' similar car, was unexpected, but at least it was French. And

Left: Anne Itier and Huschke von Hanstein's Adler Rennlimousin in 1937. In 1940 von Hanstein won the Mille Miglia with SS flashes on his overalls, and later became Porsche team manager.

another French victory was about to round out the decade.

This time Bugatti was back, threatened mainly by its French compatriots, the Delahayes and Delages. Those were out in large numbers to challenge the single 'Tank' driven by Veyron and 1937 winner Wimille. But in the event, even ten works Delahayes and Delages, the assortment of British Lagondas, the latest Alfa, even a team of three BMWs making the German marque's first appearance, were no match for the one works Bugatti.

There was a new incentive to win from the front, with a new prize of 1000 francs for the leader at the end of each hour, and Gérard and Monneret in a Delage won quite a lot of that before falling back with engine problems during Sunday morning. With the quickest of the other big cars already largely struggling, the Bugatti Tank slipped gracefully into the lead and stayed there. In its streamlined wake came the Gérard and Monneret Delage, hanging on grimly, and two Lagondas, driven by Arthur Dobson and Charles Brackenbury and the two Lords Selsdon and Waleran. Then came another aristocratic team: Prince Schaumburg von Lippe and co-driver Wenscher in one of the promising streamlined BMWs, which won the 2-litre category, followed by its two team-mates for a 2-litre clean sweep. The 1938 race was to be the last at Le Mans until 1949. A more far-reaching and deadly contest between Germany, France and Britain was looming.

RESTORING FAITH
THE 1940s AND 1950s

Like the rest of Europe, for most of the 1940s Le Mans had more on its mind than motor sport, and the Circuit de la Sarthe suffered like almost everywhere else. Its final race of the 1930s finished on 18 June 1939. Only months later Europe was at war, and although the Axis powers held motor races in Italy and Tripoli during 1940, motor racing was otherwise suspended for the duration.

Early in the war the RAF used the airfield which was already growing up around the Le Mans pits area, on the opposite side of the track, towards the outskirts of town, but it wasn't long before the RAF had gone and the German occupiers moved in. They also used the airfield, and used the Mulsanne Straight as an additional runway. But the German presence inevitably attracted the attention of the Allied forces. The area around the pits in particular, and many other parts of the circuit in general, were badly damaged through the course of the war by Allied bombing. The pits, the new balconies, the recently installed fuelling systems, the grandstands, timing boxes, press office and scoreboards were all wrecked. And what the Allies didn't destroy, the Germans made a pretty good job of before they were eventually driven out – leaving both roads and circuit buildings virtually as ruins, and Le Mans itself not much better.

The town was liberated by American troops of the 15th corps of the Third Army, in August 1944. They were commanded by General Patton, who was later made an honorary citizen of Le Mans. A painting by the French artist Geo Ham, who had painted many happier scenes at Le Mans before the war, showed the track in ruins in 1945. It shows the two roadside markers at the old start and finish line – '0km 000 Depart' and '13km 492 Arrivée'. The adjacent track is scarred by bomb craters, the buildings all but flattened. The paddock area behind is a wilderness of bare mud, columns of smoke and broken trees. Contemporary photographs show nothing standing but the rubble of buildings that had been the ACO's pride and joy.

One thing the Automobile Club de l'Ouest did have left was its old determination, an ambition for its race to be great again. And most of its leading lights had survived the war and were able to make the first plans. Gustave Singher, who had been president of the Club since 1910, was still president, and his committee included the man who would soon succeed him as president, Paul Jamin. Jamin was a former racing driver and winner of the Paris-Dieppe and Paris-Trouville inter-city road races in 1897, although sadly he only had two years at the helm of the Club, before he died in 1952. Georges Berthier was still in evidence, and much admired by Singher, who described him as 'the main-spring of the ACO, the brain which knew every piece of its vast machinery – which had, in fact, put each part in its place'. Berthier wasn't a public figure but he was a vital one in the organisation, and Singher also said of him, 'Georges Berthier has not ceased, since 1923, to consecrate himself to that most ungrateful task – the financial and detail planning. Surrounded by hidden rocks, he has always been able to circumnavigate them in a masterly way.' Yet oddly, Berthier fell out of favour in the early 1950s and was quietly pushed out of the picture by his peers.

Georges Durand, sadly, was no longer around. He had died in Le Mans on 8 May 1941, at the age of 76. Nor was Emile Coquille, whose Rudge-Whitworth connection had given Le Mans its starting point; he had fallen on hard times with ventures of his own and faded from the scene. But Charles

One thing the Automobile Club de l'Ouest did have left was its old determination, an ambition for its great race to be great again.

Above: The start of the 1949 race. The Talbot Lago Coupé of Morel and Chambras is at the head of the numerical-order line-up, alongside Vallée and Mairesse's 'single-seater' Talbot. Neither of them finished, although the Coupé survived until the 24th hour.

Faroux, who had been the third of the pioneering triumvirate and clerk of the course since the first race in 1923, was very much alive and kicking, although already in his early seventies.

In February 1946 Berthier outlined the Club's plans to the press. The Club would continue with its original constitution, and ask its members (around 30,000 of them), local and national government, what was left of the motor industry, and the Automobile Club de France, to help it rebuild the Circuit Permanent, and its famous race.

In fact the first race to be held in Europe after the war was held in France, in the Bois de Boulogne on 9 September 1945. There were other quite major races, too, through 1946 and 1947 in France, Italy and Switzerland, bringing out an amazing collection of prewar machinery, up to Grand Prix level. The Grand Prix revival then went from strength to strength, but for Le Mans, unfortunately, postwar French bureaucracy wasn't as quick to move as the Automobile Club de l'Ouest. It has to be admitted that there was a genuine shortage of many resources, but either way initial plans to resurrect the 24-hour race in 1947 (including reserving a date in the calendar) proved wildly optimistic. The Club had presented its plans to the Ministry of Reconstruction in October 1946 but hadn't received the necessary authority for work to begin by the time it needed to if there was to be any hope of running a race in 1947. By mid 1948 they were still waiting but in December the Club published regulations for a 1949 race – to be held on 25 and 26 June. All they needed now was a rebuilt track and facilities, and an entry list.

By the end of January they had their permissions and their financial grants in place, and by the beginning of June they had an entirely resurfaced track and almost entirely new buildings.

In its 1949 race report, *The Motor* acknowledged the efforts of the Club and revelled in the overdue return of what was now established as one of the great events in the world's sporting calendar: 'This weekend, Saturday and Sunday, June 25-26, a legend came to life again in the realm of motor racing. The classic 24 hours sports car race on the 8½-mile Circuit of the Sarthe was revived after a 10-year interval, and the pages of memory, dimmed by warfare and the post-war years of austerity, were turned back to the spacious days of before the war.'

Elsewhere, racing had re-started on makeshift street circuits and new tracks opportunistically laid out on the barren expanses of now redundant wartime airfields. Le Mans was a different story. As *The Motor* said: 'Where a desolate, war-blitzed expanse existed in February of this year, there sprang up, as if by magic, a modernized version of the permanent installations of the historic circuit just outside the ancient Roman city of Le Mans, once the capital of Maine. At a cost of over £130,000, with Government assistance, the Automobile Club de l'Ouest speedily built a set of modern-style concrete pits, grandstands, timekeepers' pavilion and the auxiliary buildings which go to make a racing circuit in the grand manner.'

Four of the new grandstands on the pits straight (and still standing) were named for the recently deceased club stalwarts Singher and Durand, two more for former French winners of the race, Robert Benoist and Jean-Pierre Wimille. Benoist had died in a German concentration camp and Wimille – one of the greatest of prewar drivers – had died in the Argentine Grand Prix in January 1949. Wimille, winner in 1937 and 1939, was posthumously awarded the Legion d'Honneur, and at an event in Le Mans before the 1949 race the President of France quoted him extensively in his speech.

All this new building would recognisably fit *The Motor*'s description for many years to come: 'The scene on race day rolled away the years between. Once again the quarter-mile line of pits stood alongside the circuit on the ruins of their old site. On the gallery above, 250 flags of the competing nations fluttered gently in the breeze under a blazing summer sun. The pits, unlike our British type, were concrete rooms properly floored in wood and with spacious counters fronted by a safety wall of earth and white-painted fencing. On the other side of the road stood brand-new, gleaming white concrete grandstands, surmounted by a luxurious Press box complete with telephones, foyer and bar. Next door stood a 1000-seater restaurant. A tunnel connected the sides of the circuit at one end, a bridge at the other. Two more covered stands flanked the main stand on each side. Behind them stood a line of buildings containing tourist offices, an art exhibition, tabac, buvettes and magazine stalls.'

Below: 1949, and the second-placed Delage D6S of Louveau and Jover passes the Delahaye 135S of Leblanc and Brault, temporarily stranded in the Tertre Rouge sandbanks on its way to tenth place. The Delage was only a lap behind at the finish, and catching the ailing Ferrari which just hung on to take its debut win.

Le Mans was a natural habitat for Enzo Ferrari the constructor, just as it had been for Enzo Ferrari the team manager in his pre-war years with Alfa Romeo.

In his early days as a car maker (and indeed for most of his life as an individual rather than a company) Ferrari sold customer cars essentially to finance his racing cars. Le Mans gave him everything he wanted, even

beyond what Grand Prix racing had to offer. It gave him the opportunity to race, the opportunity to sell racing cars to customers and, when

Left: Mike Hawthorn in the 250 Testa Rossa he shared with Peter Collins in 1958, taking fastest lap but failing to finish. **Above:** 1954 winners Trintignant and Gonzalez – with friends.

he was successful, the reputation to sell road cars to fund even more ambitious racing activities. After winning at his first attempt, Ferrari quickly took his Le Mans tally to nine wins, including some of Le Mans' finest, fighting off the might of Ford in the mid-1960s. He could undoubtedly have won far more, but Enzo Ferrari had a strange love-hate relationship with Le Mans that on more than one occasion saw him withdraw his cars in protest (or supposedly so) at various rule changes or official decisions. And finally Ferrari walked away from Le Mans altogether.

Above: the British returned in 1949, as soon as the race was revived. Soltan Hay and Tommy Wisdom's streamlined Bentley saloon (which finished sixth) leads Dudley Folland and Anthony Heal's elderly Aston Martin, which retired in the fourth hour.
Right: the winning Ferrari in the Esses, capitalising on the problems of the big French cars which gave it a run for its money in the early stages.
Overleaf: preparing the Rolt and Hamilton Nash-powered Healey for the 1950 race – where it finished fourth.

The faithful returned in force. 'In among these magnificent buildings milled a crowd of many thousands under a steady haze of dust thrown up by the multitude of feet from the sandy soil, which hung in the air throughout the 24 hours of the race, and with the characteristic sand on the Le Mans terrain there was the atmosphere of a plage under the blazing sun and the clear blue sky. Ladies in the longest of New Looks perambulated with others in the briefest of shorts, the most dashing of beach wear or the smartest of 'pedal-pusher' beach trousers, while their escorts sported every form of sun hat known to French imagination. The traditional air of carnival had returned to Le Mans and the 24-hours race was itself again ...'

Less happily, *The Autocar* reported: 'Mind you, the scene is not quite what it was. The course is just the same, though the surface is better and in places seems wider, but for acres round all the trees have disappeared, so there is a certain bareness about the scene where we used to remember very pleasant forest land ...'

The race was started by the Minister of Transport and Tourism, M Pineau, under the direction of Charles Faroux – and, according to *The Motor,* 'duly booed by the serried ranks of French patriots'. The finish was graced by the presence of President of France Vincent Auriol, who was driven around the circuit in a big open-topped Renault cabriolet with motorcycle outriders. It was M Auriol who presented the trophies before giving a speech about the reconstruction of the French motor industry.

Their products made up the majority of the 49 cars on the grid – whittled down from an astonishing initial list of more than a hundred hopefuls. For the first time the regulations had allowed 'prototypes'. In 1949 the new category was prompted by the possible lack of top-class machinery built in sufficient numbers in the austerity years after the war, and actually intended to mean non-series production models in the spirit, at least, of production cars. The category then became more or less a Le Mans fixture – but over the years it came to mean more and more extreme racing designs. Among the 29 French cars in 1949 were Talbot, Delahaye, Delage, DB, the diesel-powered Delettrez (a Le Mans first), Simca, Monopole, Renault and Dyna Panhard. The British were headed by a single 4¼-litre Bentley saloon and included cars from Aston-Martin, Healey, Frazer-Nash, HRG and MG. There was a Czechoslovakian team of front-drive, two-cylinder, two-stroke 750cc Aero Minors. But with hindsight perhaps the most significant entry of all was the first-ever Le Mans appearance of a new Italian marque, Ferrari.

Enzo Ferrari wasn't a newcomer to Le Mans. He had been team manager of the all-conquering Alfa team of the 1930s, but now he was a car constructor under his own name, and rapidly building a reputation. His first Le Mans entry was two 2-litre V12-engined Tipo 166 barchettas – literally 'little boats' for the shape of their pretty open bodywork by Touring of Milan. It would be a debut win. The bigger (but far less mechanically sophisticated) French cars led from the start, headed by Chaboud's 4½-litre Delahaye – driven flat out, according to *The Motor*, 'as in a Grand Prix', until he overdid it on his fourth lap and had to slow with the resulting body damage. He led at the end of the first hour, though, from another Delahaye – and the surprisingly rapid Ferrari of Jean Lucas and Pierre-Louis Dreyfus, nicknamed 'Ferret'. After Rosier's big Talbot, the other Ferrari, driven by Luigi Chinetti and Lord Selsdon, completed the early top five. The leader's 95mph average in the first hour was remarkable – almost 10mph faster than 1939's record race average – and the pace wasn't easing significantly.

After four hours Chaboud and Flahault were clinging on at the front in the same two Delahayes while Chinetti had climbed to third and Dreyfus had dropped to fourth, but it was clear now that the 2-litre Ferraris had the speed to match anything any of the bigger cars could come up with. They were also a fair match for each other until Dreyfus crashed his quite heavily at White House – not long after Chabaud's Delahaye had caught fire near Mulsanne.

As darkness fell, the Chinetti/Selsdon Ferrari led, but although the car was healthy, Selsdon was not, so Chinetti in effect became sole driver, faced with driving around 22 of the 24 hours himself. Nursing a slipping clutch, he won by just one lap, from Louveau and Jover in a 3-litre Delage. At the end Chinetti almost had to be lifted from the car, but the first postwar Le Mans was a Ferrari triumph – the first of an eventual nine, making the Prancing Horse the second most successful marque, after Porsche. The speed and efficiency of the 2-litre 166 also captured the Index of Performance, and the Biennial Cup – for which the 1939 qualifiers had been eligible, ten years on. The race average had slowed after the initial sprint, to 82.3mph, but the fastest lap, at 96.6mph by Simon in the 4½-litre six-cylinder Delahaye he'd shared with Flahault, was a new record – by a large margin. Third place was a good result for the best of the British, Culpan and Aldington's 2-litre Frazer Nash, but the works Aston Martin which might have taken third crashed within a few hours of the finish, killing its driver, Marechal. It was a sad conclusion to a generally upbeat weekend, and a tough decade.

At the end, Chinetti almost had to be lifted from the car, but the first postwar Le Mans was a Ferrari triumph – the first of an eventual nine.

By the beginning of the 1950s, Le Mans, following its postwar rebuild and with a new breed of car emerging, was taking on a subtly different, 'modern' feel. That was summed up by the new Dunlop Bridge at the start of the section towards the Esses and Tertre Rouge – in the shape of half a 'Dunlop Fort' tyre, soon to be one of the most famous landmarks on the whole circuit.

The Automobile Club de l'Ouest were still working hard, as *The Motor* reported: 'The circuit has been so improved that any comparison with previous performances is no longer true. This year the 8.68-mile circuit has been completely resurfaced with an experimental carpet of non-skid and very smooth material, and except for the mile run from Mulsanne hairpin to Arnage right-angle, where the course is still only 15½ feet wide, the entire circuit has been widened so that it is distinctly faster than in 1949 when Chaboud on a Delahaye lapped at 95.4mph or in 1939 when Mazaud's Delahaye went round at 96.71mph.'

Chaboud's speed was what they'd quoted for his first hour's driving in 1949, and Simon had actually set fastest lap last year at 96.6mph, slightly slower than the 1939 record, but the circuit was certainly likely to be quicker now.

So it was, with 1950 seeing the first 100mph-plus lap record and a new distance record, in a race

Above: The beginnings of a long and fascinating association with Le Mans – the Cadillac Series 61 Sedan de Ville entered by Briggs Cunningham in 1950, in town for scrutineering before the race. Driven by Sam and Miles Collier it surprised many people by taking tenth place, less than a lap ahead of the other Cunningham entry, the V8 Cadillac-engined special, nicknamed Le Monstre.
Right: another Cadillac engined hybrid, the Allard J2 of Sydney Allard and Tom Cole, third in 1950.

where the advantage had swung back to France. The strength of Le Mans was demonstrated, too, by a new record of more than 110 entries on the original list, of which the maximum permitted number, 60 cars, were eventually allowed on the grid. The French were in the majority again, with just over half the starters, alongside cars from Britain, Italy and Czechoslovakia (this year represented by Skoda as well as Aero Minor) – plus the first American entries of the postwar era, from a man who would become a real Le Mans stalwart, Briggs Cunningham. And the Cunningham story had just about everything for a classic racing story, starting with the man himself – Briggs Swift Cunningham.

Cunningham was the classic all-American sporting hero, born in Cincinatti in 1907, son of a millionaire meat packer who died when Briggs was only seven. A year later, with the help of the family chauffeur, Briggs had learned to drive his mother's huge Pierce Arrow and by the time he was 16 he owned his own car, a Dodge.

He studied engineering at Yale, and became involved in many sports, from boxing and tennis to athletics, golf, flying, and sailing – his other great passion, which eventually saw him skippering the winning yacht in the 1958 Americas Cup series.

His first awareness of motor racing was when 1915 Indianapolis winner Ralph de Palma took his Miller racing car to the college's engine dynamometer and Briggs made his acquaintance. On honeymoon in Europe a few years later, Cunningham was tempted into what was actually a fairly important two-man bob race, and finished third – which he didn't think was very good. That was quite typical: Cunningham only played anything to win.

Just before the war, Briggs and a friend had built a Mercedes-bodied, Buick-engined special, the Bu-Merc, which was raced before and after the war by another friend from Yale, Miles Collier. After the war Cunningham raced the Bu-Merc, too, and through that met Alfred Momo, who in quick succession became a good friend, then manager of Cunningham's racing pits and a close business associate. Through racing, Cunningham also met Bill Frick and Phil Walters, who specialised in putting big Cadillac engines into more humble cars, such as Fords and Studebakers, mainly for racing. Cunningham, meanwhile, had bought his first Ferrari, a 166, and watched Luigi Chinetti – the US importer who sold it to him – win Le Mans with a similar car in 1949. That was how Briggs S. Cunningham came to be hooked on the idea of winning Le Mans with an American car.

For 1950 Chinetti used his influence to arrange two entries for Cunningham, and when the organisers drew the line at his first thoughts, two Cadillac-engined Ford special 'Fordillacs', he came up with what were ostensibly two standard Cadillacs. One was more or less that, a Series 61 coupé for the Collier brothers, Sam and Miles; the other was arguably one of the ugliest cars ever to run at Le Mans – an open two-seater designed with the aid of the Grumman Aircraft company's wind-tunnel and powered by a 5.4-litre Cadillac V8. When the French saw it they quickly dubbed it Le Monstre.

The Cunningham story had just about everything for a classic racing story, starting with the man himself – Briggs Swift Cunningham.

Above: Through the 1950s and 1960s, Briggs Cunningham dedicated huge efforts to chasing the first American win at Le Mans. He tried first with Cadillac power, then Chrysler's V8 Hemi in his own sports racing cars, latterly with private Maseratis, Ferraris and Jaguars, always patriotically liveried in American white and blue. He never won, but his efforts made him a much-loved part of the Le Mans story.

But Cunningham was deeply serious about the effort, and deeply patriotic. Both cars were painted in the American racing colours of white with a blue stripe, and they carried two-way, pit-to-car radios – a novelty for Le Mans, even by the early 1950s. Cunningham would drive too, in Le Monstre, with Phil Walters.

1950 also saw the first appearance of Juan Manuel Fangio, sharing a Simca with fellow Grand Prix driver Froilan Gonzalez, while the French entry saw the return of the diesel Delettrez plus another French diesel, the massive, supercharged 5-litre MAP. The MAP was doubly novel for having a mid-mounted engine, but far more technically advanced were the works Talbots – in effect versions of Talbot's 4½-litre six-cylinder twin-cam Grand Prix cars converted to low-slung, two-seater, cycle-winged sports car form. As a Grand Prix car the Talbot had been too heavy to run with the fastest (even though it did score some unexpected wins); as a Le Mans car it was not only fast but also very durable. It showed how the new 'prototype' category was allowing much more exotic machinery than the original modified production models. But *The Autocar* was sceptical about the coming of the prototype class, and worried about what it meant for the future. 'This year, as last, manufacturers were permitted to enter 'one-off' designs, on the understanding that they were prototypes, presumably being considered for eventual production. Events suggest that the sooner this state of affairs ceases to exist the better, and the sooner the race will resume its original role of a supreme reliability test for sports cars. Over-laxity will tend to spoil the event entirely.'

That was a forlorn hope – the prototypes had come to stay.

Ferrari arrived in force, with five of their barchettas, including two of the latest evolution with larger 2.3-litre V12s. During practice, one of those, driven by Raymond Sommer, came close to turning Le Mans' first 100mph lap, and while leading the early stages of the race Sommer raised the record tantalisingly close to the magic 'ton' with a lap at more than 98mph. But it was his fellow Frenchman Louis Rosier who finally did it, with a lap at 102.8mph in the 4½-litre Talbot, en route to a famous win shared by his son Jean-Louis. Or at least nominally shared, because Rosier père actually drove all but around twenty minutes of the 24 hours.

The Ferraris, having again shown race-leading pace, struggled. Every one of them eventually retired, with a variety of electrical and mechanical problems and an accident for the car shared by Lucas and Lord Selsdon. The exotic Talbots had anyway been their equal for speed, and with superior reliability. From early evening on Saturday the Rosiers led, and relinquished the lead only briefly on Sunday morning to Meyrat and Mairesse, whose Talbot finally took second place, little more than a lap adrift. The third Talbot, a more conventional sports car driven by Chambas and Morel, plodded round to 13th – while the places in-between were dominated by the British.

All but two of the 16 British entries finished. The dropouts were one of the three works Aston Martin DB2s and one of the nominally private but actually works-supported Jaguar XK120s. The three 3.4-litre six-cylinder XKs were racing versions prepared for selected private customers to establish the new marque's sporting credentials among the racing fraternity. They were managed by Jaguar engineer 'Lofty' England, who had a fine decade at Le Mans ahead of him. Leading all the British entries, though, in a unexpected third place, were Sidney Allard and Tom Cole – their 5.4-litre Cadillac V8-engined Allard J2 showing that even with just the tallest of its three gears left for much of the later stages, there was no substitute for cubic inches.

Allard also won the 8-litre class, Abecassis and Macklin's Aston the 3-litres. Completing a great weekend for Britain, Mathieson and Stoop's Frazer-Nash topped the 2-litres while the flat-four-engined Jowett Jupiter (driven by the neat pairing of Wisdom and Wise) took 1½-litre honours. That left the French with the 1100 class (for Renault) to add to Talbot's outright win. Fourth overall was taken by the 3.8 Nash-engined Healey driven by Tony Rolt and Duncan Hamilton – who had greater Le Mans glory to come a couple of years hence. The leading Aston was fifth, another sixth. The Cunningham Cadillacs had rumbled on to tenth and eleventh, the Collier's coupé ahead of Briggs and Walters in the spectacularly ugly Monstre, the latter offsetting time spent in the Mulsanne sandbank early in the race, and a loss of gears later on, with the advantage of a 50-gallon fuel tank which allowed them to run around four hours between fuel stops.

It was the start of a real love affair for Cunningham and Le Mans, which in the end was blighted by bad luck, but which could just as easily have given America its first home-grown winner. Another love affair was beginning, too. After their 'private' 1950 debut, Jaguar, like Bentley before them, took to Le Mans with a vengeance. For 1951, Jaguar boss Sir William Lyons had agreed that chief engineer Bill Heynes could develop a sports racing version of the XK120, with a particular eye on Le Mans and its unique demands. Heynes delivered a tubular chassised, alloy bodied car powered by a special development of the twin-cam 3.4 six, giving about 200bhp. The car was dubbed XK120C, or C-type. The C stood for Competition, and the car's smoothly streamlined bodywork (designed by aerodynamics specialist Malcolm Sayer) reflected the fact that Jaguar had recognised even more than most the growing importance of the long Mulsanne Straight, while the brakes were also uprated in line with the added performance.

Jaguar's presence with a real chance of winning stirred memories of the Bentley years of the 1920s. As *Autosport* said, 'Never before has such a large crowd from the UK arrived for the race. The Place de la Règublique is full of GB plates and Gruber's [a favourite café in the square] looks like an enlarged version of the Steering Wheel Club.

'On race day cars pour into Le Mans from every corner of Europe. The routes to the Circuit Permanent de la Sarthe are solid with vehicles of all descriptions. Despite the threat of rain, the crowds

Left: Jaguar's first winner, the XK120C of Peter Walker and Peter Whitehead, in 1951. The Jaguar name had evolved from the old SS marque after World War II, and to Jaguar founder William Lyons, Le Mans was the perfect show-place for his new sports cars. The first Jaguar entries, in 1950, were mildly modified XK120 production models. The 'C-type' was the first of Jaguar's more specialised racing models, with a strong emphasis on high-speed aerodynamics.

are reported to be larger than ever before. Truly nothing can daunt the enthusiasm of the Continentals.'

William Lyons was a firm believer in the principle of 'win races on Sunday, sell cars on Monday', and Jaguar were out to win here. The three works cars had a strong driver line-up, led by the experienced Jack Fairman with Le Mans newcomer Stirling Moss – a British rising star to match the marque. The others were driven by Whitehead and Walker, and Johnson and Biondetti, but it was the young Moss who stamped his and the C-type's authority on the early stages of the 1951 race. Gonzalez's much bigger 4½-litre Talbot led briefly but once Moss was past he stormed away from the rest of the field, lapping the whole lot within the first couple of hours and eventually leaving the lap record at 105.2mph. Behind him the other C-types took station for 1-2-3, with the slowest of the Jaguars pursued doggedly by the fastest Talbots and Ferraris – the latter now including the first of the bigger V12-engined Americas.

It became a nail-biting test of speed and reliability, especially for Jaguar. Once they had lost both the Biondetti and Moss cars with oil feed problems they could only sit and watch the clock tick away as Peter Whitehead and Peter Walker in the surviving C-type hung on ahead of the Meyrat and Mairesse Talbot and the rest. As the flag fell at precisely 4pm on Sunday afternoon they were still there, for Jaguar's first win at only their second attempt. They had raised the distance record to 2244 miles and won by a comfortable 64 miles, or almost eight laps – with Moss's lap record as a bonus.

Behind them, the other Talbots had been fast but mechanically suspect, and the Ferraris hadn't been fast enough, and fragile. The other British front runners, Aston Martin, had a pretty good weekend, with third and fifth places for the lightweight DB2s, managed now by John Wyer – another man with a great Le Mans future ahead of him. The third-placed Macklin and Thompson DB2 won the 3-litre class and deserved particular credit as the first of the genuine 'production' cars. Jowett won the 1500 class again, while Fitch and Walters' Chrysler-engined Cunningham C2-R (which had run strongly in the early stages) took the biggest class.

This year, Cunningham had entered three C2-Rs, which were considerably more sophisticated (and rather prettier) than his first sports car entry. They were powered by the outstanding Chrysler 'Hemi' V8, and again the Cunningham effort was deadly serious. This time the team had brought three race cars plus a spare, a large team of personnel, some 17 tons of spares and equipment, a caravan for the drivers to rest in, and a well-equipped mobile workshop – all finished, like the cars, in America's blue and white colours. They had been quick but not very lucky. The cars driven by Cunningham and George Huntoon, and George Rand and Fred Wacker, had crashed early on, in heavy rain. Fitch and Walters had been as high as second before suffering engine and transmission problems, but the car had been timed at more than 150mph on the Mulsanne.

In a slightly lower key effort than Cunningham's, tucked away in 21st place, driven by French privateers Veuillet and Mouche, was the first German car to run at Le Mans for many years. It was the first appearance for the marque that would go on to win more Le Mans victories than any other. It was a Porsche 356.

There was another German return in 1952, and this one had a far greater impact than Porsche's first appearance, at least in the short term. Their first appearances at the beginning of the 1930s had been only partly successful, and very low key, but when Mercedes-Benz came back to Le Mans in 1952 they came heavily armed.

Their recovery from the war was well under way, but not quite well enough to re-enter motor

Right: The Cunningham C4-R of Briggs Cunningham and Walter Spear during the 1952 race, where it finished fourth. The C4-R was powered by the superb Chrysler V8 'Hemi' engine, and alongside the two open C4-Rs, Cunningham produced a coupé version, the C4-RK, designed by famous aerodynamicist Wunibald Kamm. The coupé went out with engine problems in the eighth hour, a couple of hours after the other open version.

racing at Grand Prix level, so they looked at the next most prestigious area – and that was Le Mans. In June 1951 a small delegation from Stuttgart had attended the race, and seen Jaguar take their first win. Led by the portly, autocratic but hugely respected team manager Alfred Neubauer (who had also masterminded Mercedes' tentative prewar efforts at Le Mans), the group included drivers Karl Kling and Hermann Lang. Back in Stuttgart they reported to chief designer Franz Roller, to technical director Dr Fritz Nallinger, and to the new head of the newly re-formed racing department, Rudolf Uhlenhaut. In March 1952 the company announced its postwar return to racing.

Nallinger described the programme as 'opening the little window on motor racing'. The company had already started testing its new competition car, in the winter of 1951, barely six months after they had watched Jaguar's debut victory. The car was initially known as the W194, and it was tested by Uhlenhaut, an exceptional driver as well as an exceptional engineer. It became better known as the 300SL racer – forerunner of the famous 300SL 'gullwing' road car.

With both time and resources short, by Mercedes' standards at least, it used a lot of components derived from production cars – even though in Le Mans terms it would be unashamedly a prototype. It used a 3-litre single overhead camshaft straight-six, four-speed manual gearbox (all-syncromesh, which was a luxury for a serious Le Mans driver), coil and wishbone front suspension, coil and trailing arm rear suspension, and uprated brakes with big, finned drums. All this went into a light multi-tube chassis, the engine tilted to one side to reduce the height of the bonnet and the wheelbase considerably shorter than the saloon's. The depth of the chassis side members meant the driver had to climb over them into the cockpit, and the only way to have the regulation opening doors for Le Mans was to make them open upwards, from the centre of the roof – which made them look rather like a gull's wings.

The 300SL racer (the SL stood for Super-Licht, or Super Lightweight) made an impressive debut with second place in the Mille Miglia in May and a win in the sports car race at the Swiss Grand Prix soon after. Mercedes-Benz came to Le Mans with five cars (three race cars, the luxury of a complete spare vehicle, plus an experimental car with a roof-mounted moveable air-brake). They also brought a reputation which in effect cost Jaguar the 1952 race before it started.

Jaguar knew their 1952 versions of the C-type were fast, and knew their new disc brakes were an advantage, but they believed the Mercedes would be faster. Moss, in particular, had told Jaguar after the Mille Miglia that they couldn't hope to beat the Mercedes at Le Mans without more straightline speed. They responded by modifying the C-types' bodywork to wring a little more on the all-important straight – with long noses and long tails. The new bodywork probably had only a marginal effect on the C-types' maximum speed but had a disastrous effect on their cooling, and although they modified the radiators after realising the problem in practice, it wasn't enough.

Ironically, Neubauer was planning to sacrifice a little outright speed for reliability, and to make the most of his legendary tactical skills. The engines were mildly detuned, by maybe 5bhp, the experimental car with its airbrake remained an experiment, and Mercedes took a deliberately cautious approach. They would run to their own schedule, and leave the opposition (which included seven highly threatening works Ferraris, led by Ascari in a 250S similar to the one with which Bracco had beaten the 300SL in the Mille Miglia) to run their own races. Mercedes' philosophy worked.

The cars were driven by Kling and Klenk, Lang and Riess, and Helfrich and Niedermayer. Each had a clock on the dashboard, and a list of times for refuelling and other pit stops. There were air vents in

Like a real tyre, the Dunlop bridge has changed its profile over the years – as well as its precise location. **Right:** Mercedes' 1952 winner, the 300SL of Lang and Riess. **Above:** 1991, the Mercedes of Mass, Schlesser and Ferté, heading for retirement.

the roofs to make the comfortable cockpits even more user-friendly in the expected heat of the Le Mans day. There were even huge Mercedes stars over the pits to allow the drivers to identify their own pit quickly and easily while passing at speed.

From the start, Ascari stormed away in the much more powerful 3-litre V12 Ferrari, setting a new lap record of over 107mph before expiring with clutch problems within three hours of the start. The Jaguars had already gone, their engines failing one at a time within an hour or so of the start, after the almost inevitable overheating. The Mercedes drivers had watched, and kept to their dashboard schedules – and ironically their cars had been slower than the C-types.

They still didn't have the race won, but one by one the faster Ferraris went out and Neubauer kept to his plan. There were other hares. A 2.3-litre Gordini was a surprising leader until it ran out of brakes. Then there was a remarkable personal effort. The lead passed to a 4½-litre Talbot, driven by Pierre 'Levegh' (actually a pseudonym for a 42-year-old Parisian garage proprietor, Pierre Bouillion) and René Marchand. Or rather, driven by Levegh. He was in the car when it took the lead, had been from the start, and decided that he would be until the finish – as the rules still allowed.

It wasn't an entirely rash decision, as he was comfortably pulling clear of the Mercedes. After 16 hours, although he was getting slightly untidy and was clearly tiring, he had a four-lap lead. With barely an hour to go he was still comfortably ahead. Then he made a mistake, probably through sheer tiredness. He selected a wrong gear in the preselector box and broke the engine. His epic run was over.

Kling and Klenk (initially fastest of the Mercedes and regularly lapping marginally quicker than Moss's 1951 lap record) were also out of the race by now, with electrical problems, but the other two silver 300SLs cruised on. With Levegh gone, Lang and Riess inherited the lead and stayed there. They covered 2320 miles at an average of 96.7mph and led Helfrich and Niedermeyer by just under nine miles. It wasn't a dominant win exactly, but it was a Mercedes 1-2.

Johnson and Wisdom were best of the British with their 4.1 Nash-Healey in an excellent third place, and Cunningham scored their best result to date with fourth. This year's three-car entry had been two open C4-Rs and one C4-RK – the K for Wunibald Kamm, the legendary aerodynamicist who had designed its low-roofed coupé body. Power was up to 325bhp and weight down to 2400lb, so they were again very quick, and the coupé, driven by Walters and Duane Carter, led briefly from the start, but the team was let down by reliability – largely the result of the engines and transmissions doing too much of the work that ought to have been done by better brakes. Appropriately, it was Briggs Cunningham himself who did most of the driving in the fourth place car he shared with Bill Spear – almost 20 hours of the 24 in all. There were only 17 finishers from the 60 starters, but Veuillet and

Left: the Mercedes pits in 1952, dominated by the rain-coated figure of larger-than-life team manager Alfred Neubauer. Neubauer had led the pre-war Silver Arrows in their all-conquering Grand Prix programme, and when the team returned in the 1950s, via sports car racing and the 300SL, he was there to pick up where he had left off – winning again.
Overleaf: refuelling stop for Duncan Hamilton and Tony Rolt's winning C-type in 1953.

Mouche were among them, and scored Porsche's first Le Mans class win, in the 1100 ranks.

Having won, albeit luckily, in 1952, Mercedes didn't return to offer Jaguar a rematch in 1953, but there was plenty of opposition for the British team to be going along with until its next head-to-head confrontation with the Silver Arrows, which would have to wait until 1955. In fact Le Mans was as important a race as it had been for many years, as the third round of a new world championship for sports car manufacturers, and that brought yet another maximum grid of 60 cars, the overall quality getting better all the time.

This year Jaguar weren't about to make such a fundamental mistake as they had in 1952, and while others spread their efforts across the whole championship, Jaguar concentrated almost exclusively on this jewel in the sports car crown. Their three cars had reverted to the earlier, short-nose, short-tail bodywork but were lighter, more powerful and better braked. They now used triple Weber rather than SU carburettors, and most famously they adopted Dunlop disc brakes – a major departure from the almost universal drums and quoted almost ever after as the classic example of 'motor racing improving the breed' for the ordinary motorist.

In the absence of Mercedes their most obvious challengers were Ferrari, leading the championship and fresh from victory in the gruelling Mille Miglia. Ferrari's V12s continued to grow, and in 4.1 or 4.5-litre form they had substantially more power than the Jaguars, but the efficiency of Sayer's C-type aerodynamics was evident in the fact that the Ferraris were no more than a couple of miles per hour faster than the Jaguars on the Mulsanne, while the C-types also had fine handling and the advantage of their new Dunlop discs.

This classic confrontation was joined by potential front runners from Cunningham, Aston Martin, the French Gordinis and Talbots (the latter making a big effort with a three-car team of very smooth-looking open two-seaters), and the usefully quick Nash-Healeys. Italy had four of the Targa Florio-winning Lancia D20 coupés with supercharged 2.7-litre V6 power, and most spectacularly the team of Alfa Romeo 'Disco Volantes' – or flying saucers. They gained the nickname from their aerodynamic coupé bodies, but the engineering underneath was pretty impressive, too. With tubular spaceframes, around 230bhp from their 3.5-litre six-cylinder engines, and five-speed gearboxes, they were among the fastest cars of all on the long straight, at almost 153mph. It didn't do any harm to have drivers of the calibre of Fangio, Kling and Marimon on the driving strength either. Further down the capacity ladder came a pair of the new Austin Healeys, a pair of Frazer Nashes, and two ugly but aerodynamically efficient Bristols, all from Britain, as well as the usual catalogue of even smaller machinery.

Any one of perhaps six makes looked to have a real chance, and on paper the big Ferraris should surely have been the favourites, but as the great technical writer Laurence Pomeroy had observed the year before, 'Ferrari ... had both

It was a classic confrontation, size versus science — and in the first round at least, size won. Ferrari won.

open and closed bodies, and it was two of the latter driven first by Ascari and secondly by Simon who led the race for the first four hours. Unfortunately, from the Ferrari viewpoint, there were a further 20 to come after this and sports-car racing up to now has shown that cars which leave the factory at Maranello can go far, or fast, but not both.'

In 1953 the Ferraris' demise was slightly more complicated, but the result was the same. Sadly, the only private entry overturned at the White House on Sunday morning and Tom Cole was killed. The big-engined 375MM of Ascari and Villoresi set fastest lap at 112.9mph, led briefly in the opening laps but soon fell back to second, and eventually went out with clutch failure. The Hawthorn/Farina car also held fastest lap for a while but was disqualified after only 12 laps for refuelling before the allocated distance (still a Le Mans rule). So in the end there was just one Ferrari among the leading finishers, the Marzotto brothers who brought their 4.1 car home in fifth, 74 miles behind the winners.

Other front runners dropped out fairly steadily. All the Alfas, having proved very fast, were out by dawn on Sunday and none of the Lancias saw the chequered flag, neither did the Aston Martins. The Talbots and Gordinis never got close to the pace of the leaders but patience netted eighth place for Levegh and Pozzi in a Talbot and sixth for Trintignant and Schell in a Gordini. Cunningham had a mixed outing, but for the second year running showed they weren't at Le Mans just to make up the numbers. They again had three Hemi-powered cars, and all three finished. The Cunningham/Spear open car and Morgan/Gordon-Bennett in the coupé managed respectable seventh and tenth places, but the first Cunningham home, in third place overall, was Walters and Fitch in the slab-sided open C5R. The French had dubbed this one The Shark for its gaping 'mouth' and streamlined shape – a slightly kinder nickname than Cunningham's first Le Mans entry, Le Monstre. The Shark was officially fastest of all on the Mulsanne, at 154.8mph. It also won its class, and it was the only car to split the triumphant Jaguars. Many people reckoned that had the Cunninghams stopped as well as they went, the result could have been even better.

But this would be the Jaguars' race – and the first 100mph Le Mans. Moss, as was his way, had been the first to lead, but when he had carburation problems it was the Rolt and Hamilton car which chased and caught the briefly leading Ferrari, and they never lost the lead again. They covered 2535 miles and the winning average was 105.8mph – faster than Moss's C-type lap record of only two years

earlier. Moss and Walker finished second, not quite three laps down, and Peter Whitehead and Ian Stewart were fourth. A private C-type run by Ecurie Belge and driven by Laurent and Tornaco gave Jaguar another top ten placing, in ninth, with all the C-types finishing. In Coronation year, it was just as popular with the massive British Le Mans following as many of the Bentley wins of the 1920s.

Those who thought Jaguar would now rest on their laurels were very wrong. There were no Mercedes again in 1954, and none of the promised Maseratis, whose transporter had crashed en route to the circuit – although there was a single privately entered Maserati A6G driven by de Portago and Tomasi. There were no Lancias, the Talbot effort was a shadow of former years, and there were no Alfas.

There was a strong Aston Martin entry, and further British entries from Bristol, Frazer-Nash, Lagonda, Kieft and Triumph. Donald Healey had withdrawn the Austin Healeys, and in a letter to *Autosport* he explained why: 'The Austin Healey cars under preparation for this year's event were basically production models, but, if we were to keep pace with our competitors, I found they would have to have such radical alterations as special high compression cylinder heads and multiple non-British carburettors, multi-pad-type disc brakes with complicated servo system

and special wheels to suit close ratio gearboxes and ratios quite unsuitable for normal use. The bodies would have to be converted to virtually single-seater shells. The resulting car would bear no resemblance to our production model. Its expensive specification brakes alone would cost more than a complete production car ... I therefore decided to stop their preparation and to withdraw my entries as a protest against regulations which admit such changes and virtually change a great sports car endurance test into a race of hand-built prototype racing cars.'

Jaguar had no problem coming to terms with the prototype rules, neither the technical side nor the spirit. They had built the C-type as a customer car (based on a genuine production model, the XK120) and they would also offer their new car as a customer model – exotic and expensive as it was. Logically enough, it was called the D-type, and it was a masterpiece – one of the most advanced racing sports cars ever seen up to the mid-1950s. It still had the engine in the front, of course, but it was laid over, Mercedes 300SL style. It had disc brakes, naturally, used aircraft thinking in the structure of its aluminium 'monocoque' centre section, and most of all it had superb low-drag aerodynamics – again the work of Malcolm Sayer.

But Jaguar's main opposition for their third win undoubtedly came from Ferrari and the ever-threatening Cunningham. The D-type had a new, low-line version of the 3.4-litre in-line six, producing around 250bhp. The latest Ferrari V12s were within a whisker of 5 litres and 350bhp. The Cunningham's Chrysler V8s were 5.4 litres and probably over 325bhp – and to make things doubly difficult the third 1954 Cunningham entry was a modified and re-bodied Ferrari 375LM, with water-cooled brakes (they were learning).

It was a classic confrontation, size versus science – and in the first round at least, size won. Ferrari won. Alongside the super-sleek Jaguars, the big Ferraris had barn-door aerodynamics and relatively crude tubular chassis – because Enzo Ferrari was far more interested in engines than in what to put them in. But for this year, might was right. The D-type was extremely fast on the Mulsanne, with Moss now nudging towards 175mph, but the Ferrari's massive flexibility and top-end power allowed it to stay in touch.

In the early stages, in the dry, it was the Jaguars' turn to chase three leading Ferraris, led by

Left: the 1954 winner, Maurice Trintignant and Froilan Gonzalez's Ferrari 375, powers through the Esses ahead of one of its less successful 375 team mates. **Above:** part of the 1955 crowd unaware of the scale of the tragedy which had unfolded opposite the pits. The organisers reasoned that telling the crowd of the disaster would have caused a mass exodus from the circuit and made it impossible for ambulances to remove the many casualties to hospital.

Gonzales and Trintignant's car, then Marzotto and Maglioli's. But it wasn't dry for long, and when it rained the Jaguars' superior handling had the edge, allowing the brilliant Moss into the lead. Now it became a race of stamina and reliability. Marzotto and Maglioli were out before midnight with gearbox problems. The Jaguars began to suffer fuel-feed problems, then Moss had brake problems, Wharton and Whitehead (having clawed up to second place behind Gonzalez and Trintignant who were back in the lead) had gearbox problems, and early on Sunday morning so did the third front-running Ferrari, of Rosier and Manzon.

Now it was Rolt and Hamilton's D-type chasing Gonzalez and Trintignant's Ferrari, briefly overtaking it, being delayed at the pits with minor body damage, then with rain falling again in the last couple of hours, hauling the Ferrari in again as it suffered mechanical problems of its own and spent a long time stationary in its pit. It was nail-biting stuff, but as the rain eased off and both cars were running something like properly again it was the Ferrari which held on at the front. Gonzalez and Trintignant won by just two and a half miles, and Gonzalez and Marzotto shared a new lap record at 117.5mph. It had been a hard-fought battle in the rain.

It promised so much for a head-to-head rematch in 1955, spiced by the return of Mercedes-Benz, stronger and more single-minded than ever, but any dream of a 1955 classic turned into a nightmare. The record book shows that 1955 was Jaguar's year, but nobody wanted to win the way the Coventry team did here.

With the race only two and a half hours old, three cars approached the pits area. Lance Macklin's Austin Healey was ahead, but the two cars closest behind, Hawthorn's Jaguar and Levegh's Mercedes, were very much faster. Levegh had been given the plum Mercedes drive on the strength of his near solo effort of 1952. Macklin appeared to be allowing them room to pass. Hawthorn did come past, on the left, then turned towards his pit, raising his arm to say that he was doing so. Macklin, either unsettled by the passing manoeuvre or with problems of his own, began to swerve into the middle of the track, into the path of Levegh, who was still travelling at full speed, not intending to peel off into the pits. Fangio's Mercedes, which was also among the group, squeezed through the chaos, almost touching Hawthorn's car in the pit lane. But Levegh's Mercedes hit the sliding Austin-Healey and its sloping tail acted as a launching ramp.

Macklin crashed into the earth and wood barriers, and although his car was badly damaged, he survived. Levegh didn't. He hit the barriers opposite the pits, directly in front of the main stands, virtually on the startline. He was probably killed instantly, but the huge impact also broke the engine and transmission and various other heavy components from his car. The flying debris scythed into the crowded open standing areas, and magnesium parts burst into intense white flame. It was clearly a major disaster, but for a long time no one knew just how great a disaster.

The race went on. The organisers had apparently decided (and probably correctly) that stopping it would send the crowds away, blocking all the roads that were desperately needed for the fleets of emergency vehicles. For the moment, Mercedes continued too.

For what it was worth, the race saw a fine duel between the Jaguars, the Mercedes and the Ferraris until the remaining Mercedes were withdrawn at 2am on Sunday. It was a tantalising contest, and would have been even more so had it gone to its normal conclusion. All three major contenders were open cars. The latest works D-types had longer, more aerodynamic noses and more power from modified engines. Ferrari had apparently gone backwards to go forwards. In place of its long-favoured V12s it now had straight-six engines, in this case of 4.4 litres but with probably 80 or 90bhp more than

The record books show that 1955 was Jaguar's year, but nobody wanted to win the way the Coventry team did here.

the 3.4-litre Jaguars. More important, they were smaller, lighter, and at last a bit more aerodynamic. The Mercedes were the most sophisticated of all, closely based on the dominant W196 Grand Prix car, with a technically brilliant fuel-injected 3-litre straight-eight, splitting the Jaguars and Ferraris in terms of power output. That was mounted in a very stiff but lightweight tubular chassis with all-independent torsion bar suspension and inboard brakes all round. The Mercedes 300SLRs also had the option of a large air brake, following on from the 1952 experiments, in the form of a large panel behind the driver which opened from a rear hinge. Such technology was relevant as overall aerodynamic drag continued to fall.

The other regular front runner, Cunningham, had an odd mix of machinery for 1955. The Hemi-powered cars were no more and Cunningham offered the C6-R with a 3-litre four-cylinder Indianapolis-type Offenhauser engine adapted to run on Le Mans regulation-issue petrol rather than its usual diet of alcohol, plus a white and blue D-type and another white and blue Ferrari. For the first time in Cunningham's Le Mans forays, none went the distance.

Nor did the Ferraris. Castelloti led from the start, and Maglioli and Phil Hill briefly stayed with the leading group, but the three works cars and two leading private entries would all be put out by mechanical failures early on, as Mercedes and Jaguar forced the pace. The duel at the front was between two Grand Prix world champions in the world's quickest sports racing cars, Fangio in the Mercedes and Hawthorn in the Jaguar, partnered by Stirling Moss and Ivor Bueb respectively. And it was Hawthorn and Bueb who had to take the fight to Mercedes as the other two works D-types fell out, Beauman and works tester Norman Dewis after an accident, Rolt and Hamilton (who would be second for a time after Mercedes' withdrawal) with a split oil tank and transmission failure.

It's pure conjecture to say who would have won. Fangio and Moss were in the lead at two o'clock on Sunday morning when team manager Neubauer withdrew his two surviving cars as a gesture of respect to Levegh and the 80-plus spectators it was now known had died with him. The Jaguars continued, with Hawthorn and Bueb leading, followed by Rolt and Hamilton until their retirement.

Hawthorn and Bueb won quite comfortably, and in spite of the disaster off the track the performances on it were quite remarkable, with five new class records for overall distance. The winning Jaguar took the 5-litre class. The open Aston Martin DB3S of Peter Collins and Belgian journalist/racer Paul Frère which had finished an unexpected second overall took the 3-litre class. The open Bristol of Wilson and Mayers took seventh overall and 2-litre honours, and Porsches took both 1500 and 1100cc class wins, at record averages. But it was a race which will always be remembered for other reasons – as the greatest single disaster in the history of motor sport. And the implications would soon begin to emerge ...

The number usually quoted for the death toll at Le Mans in 1955 is 88 people, including Pierre Levegh. There are other numbers, but what is absolutely unarguable is that it was a tragedy, and there were massive repercussions. They echoed around the world. Many countries temporarily banned all motor sport while they assessed its future. Switzerland in effect banned circuit racing for good. And Le Mans itself, of course, had to come to terms with the options of extinction or major changes.

There was little to be gained from levelling specific blame, but it was

Below: the least satisfying win in the history of the race. Hawthorn and Bueb go through the motions of celebrating, twenty hours or so after Hawthorn had been at the centre of the accident which killed Mercedes driver Pierre Levegh and more than eighty spectators.

obviously necessary to establish causes, and to guard against any possible repetition. Both Jaguar and Mercedes issued official statements immediately after the 1955 race, more in self-defence than in accusation. 'In view of the fact [Jaguar said] that all the circumstances surrounding the Le Mans disaster are in course of official investigation by the French authorities, we would not have thought it incumbent upon any firm or individual to make any comments which seek to fix responsibility or aportion blame for the tragic occurrence. Nevertheless, certain statements have been quoted in the Press implicating one of our drivers and, in fairness to him, we have no option but to make it known that, as a result of close questioning of the Jaguar pit personnel and others who witnessed the occurrence, there is no evidence to establish that Hawthorn acted in any way contrary to accepted racing practice.

'In the course of our own enquiry, Hawthorn made the following statement: "After passing Levegh's Mercedes at Arnage, I passed the Austin-Healey between White House Corner and the Pits and, having given the necessary hand signal, I braked and pulled into my pit in accordance with pit instructions given during the course of the previous lap. In my judgment I allowed sufficient time for the driver of any following car to be aware of my intentions and for him to take such action as might be required without danger to others."

'In view of the foregoing statement [they concluded] and the evidence of the Jaguar pit personnel who witnessed the occurrence, the company is of the opinion that any adverse criticism of Hawthorn's driving is without justification.'

Mercedes gave their statements at a press conference. Dr Koenecke said that leaving the remaining cars in the race for so long after the accident was to avoid the risk of causing panic. That was pretty much the line also taken by the organisers in not stopping the race completely. He said he was satisfied that Mercedes were not responsible for the disaster. Dr Nallinger suggested that spectators had been injured and killed by debris, not by burns from exploding components. He claimed that because of the narrowness of the road, all Mercedes' drivers were warned to pull to the right in plenty of time when intending to come into the pits. And he came as close as anybody to blaming one driver, suggesting that Hawthorn's pit-stop had caused a chain reaction which forced the Austin-Healey to turn to the left, brake sharply and finally skid. This caused Levegh's Mercedes to collide with it and run into the embankment. Fangio agreed, and said his car had just brushed past the stationary Jaguar.

Team manager Neubauer confined himself to suggestions about making pits stops safer, by controlling overtaking in the pits area, and by massive changes to the circuit. Two of his suggestions were that the road be made considerably wider and that a ditch between track and spectators would create better protection than just an earth bank or concrete walls. The organisers were listening.

The old pits, a quarter of a mile long and only six years old, were demolished. New pits were built further back towards the White House, and further back from the roadside into the paddock area, leaving room for a 'deceleration lane' between track and pit counters – although there was still no wall to separate track and pits. The whole area between pits and grandstands was excavated well below the original level. On the opposite side of the road, between track and spectator areas and grandstands, a deep 'service road', or 'ambulance road' was sunk, protected by a deep bank and concrete wall. New

spectator terraces ran down to the lower trackside, and the new pits had three tiers – the working pits with 'hospitality' stands above them, and open viewing balconies above those. The Dunlop Curve after the pits was eased slightly, and the famous Dunlop Bridge moved further along to its present location.

Pit signals would no longer be allowed from these main pits as they were considered a dangerous distraction to drivers on one of the fastest parts of the course. Instead, new 'signalling pits' (linked to the main pits by individual telephone lines) were built on the exit from Mulsanne Corner – one of the slowest areas of the course.

It was a difficult and expensive programme, but the Automobile Club de l'Ouest had done everything in its power to make real changes – not just token ones. As *Autosport* reported, 'Cost of the improvements to the Sarthe circuit total something like 300 million francs; 70,000 cubic metres of earth have been moved, and 2500 cubic metres of concrete, and 161 tons of iron have been used in the various constructions. Installations of the telephone lines between the pits and the signalling stations alone cost 12 million francs.'

Above: The immediate aftermath of one of the worst moments in the history of motor sport. Lance Macklin's Austin-Healey is across the track in the right foreground, Kling and Simon's 300SLR is in the pits. The remains of Levegh's sister car are burning in the background, where it had hit the barriers, broken up and burst into flames, scattering debris into the crowded terraces.

If the public had any fears about going back, they weren't immediately obvious, and come race day the new grandstands and terraces were packed as tightly as ever. To allow for the building work to be finished the race had been put back by a few weeks, to 28 and 29 July 1956, where the hours of daylight were slightly shorter – but to many spectators that only meant the party hours were longer.

Autocar noticed little change in the pre-race atmosphere.

'The hundred-and-one attractions of the 'Village' within the circuit – one-make motor shows, rifle ranges, cafés and all – have been patronised by the wandering crowds as they wait in the growing excitement. It is Le Mans in the true tradition – flags, multitudinous banners, striped marquees and colour everywhere.'

But the past wasn't entirely forgotten. Immediately before the start there was a short address and a minute's silence for the victims of 1955. Then at 4pm on Saturday, Le Mans burst back into raucous life.

In some areas, Le Mans wasn't seen to have moved forwards. Maximum capacity for prototypes had been limited to 2.5 litres, and the permitted number of starters was reduced, from 60 to 52. Further new rules, including larger windscreens and smaller fuel allowances had been intended to reduce outright speeds, and did so – but they attracted a lot of criticism in the process, and the discrepancies between Le Mans' rules and everyone else's meant the race had lost its world championship status. It wouldn't be the last time that that happened, but in or out of the championship, Le Mans has always proved strong enough to go its own way.

From a manufacturers' point of view the race had something of an interim feel. Jaguar and Ferrari arrived in strength, Cunningham stayed away and so did Mercedes, who had withdrawn from all motor sport after their two-year domination of Formula 1. The works Ferraris, Maseratis, Gordinis and Maserati-engined Talbots all complied with the 2.5-litre prototype rules, as did the prototype Aston Martin DBR1. The 3.4 D-types (three works cars and one each from Ecurie Ecosse and Ecurie Francorchamps) were as technically sophisticated as anything in the field, but didn't have to suffer the prototype capacity limit because Jaguar showed they had built enough customer cars (more than the required 50) for them to qualify as production sports models. And Aston could do the same with their two 3-litre DB3Ss, while most of the other entries of any pedigree were in the smaller capacity classes – which nevertheless were still an intrinsic part of what made Le Mans unique.

Another area that created problems in 1956 was the road surface, which seemed to be particularly slippery in the wet, and was blamed for an inordinate number of accidents. One, sadly, claimed the life of Panhard driver Louis Héry; the others were less serious but caught more than a dozen cars, including several potential winners. On the second lap two works Jaguars (Paul Frère's and Jack Fairman's) and de Portago's works Ferrari tripped over each other in the Esses and went no further, and later in the

race Aston's prototype plus one of the DB3Ss crashed, as did the quickest of the Talbot-Maseratis.

The third works D-type, of Hawthorn and Bueb, stayed on the road but lost many laps with fuel-line problems, spent hours playing catch-up, and did well to claw back to sixth at the end – helped by fastest lap for Hawthorn, at 115.8mph. But it was the privately entered D-type from the Scottish Ecurie Ecosse team, driven by Ron Flockhart and Ninian Sanderson, which won. It had disputed the lead with the DB3S of Moss and fellow Grand Prix driver Peter Collins, who eventually finished second by just over a lap – but the rest of the field, headed by Trintignant and Gendebien's Ferrari, were a long way adrift. The Belgian Jaguar was fourth, the leading Porsche fifth, and Lotus and Cooper seventh and eight. It was one of Le Mans' less exciting races, but it was a miracle that there was a race at all.

1957 saw both the 50th anniversary of the Automobile Club de l'Ouest and the 25th running of the Vingt-quatre Heures – and brought a renewal of the status quo, as Le Mans eased its limits on

Above Left: 1956, and Ron Flockhart and Ninian Sanderson take a famous victory for Ecurie Ecosse. **Above:** a happy Ecosse team shares its celebrations with the second-placed Aston Martin squad. Aston drivers Collins and Moss are on the left, winners Flockhart and Sanderson in the centre, and Ecosse boss David Murray and his chief mechanic 'Wilkie' Wilkinson on the right.

prototype capacities and fuel consumption, and returned to the world sports car championship fold. That transformed the race, and in one move took it right back to the pinnacle of the sport. High on the list of likely winners were the two Italian sports car masters, Ferrari and Maserati, both with the latest developments of their championship contenders. Ferrari's biggest works cars were its four-cam 4-litre V12 engined 335s. Maserati's were the 4.5-litre V8 450Ss – whose 400bhp-plus was more even than the near-400bhp Ferraris. Ferrari drivers included Hawthorn, Gendebien and Collins; Maserati had Moss, Behra – and Fangio in reserve! Both marques had lesser cars backing up their biggest guns, Ferrari's ten entries ranging through the 3.8-litre V12 315s to the 3-litre V12 250 Testa Rossa, a brand new open car testing ideas for the next proposed change in world championship rules, to a 3-litre limit. The Biennial Cup, incidentally, reached its 23rd running, and the nine qualifiers for this year's final included Aston Martin, Cooper, two from DB, and one each from Ferrari, Jaguar, Lotus, Porsche and VP.

The works Jaguar team had withdrawn from racing at the end of 1956, but there were new developments of the still-competitive D-type for last year's surprise winners Ecurie Ecosse, and for Ecurie Belge. And Ecosse's experiences at Le Mans 1957 are a fine example of how the race could run back in those halcyon days.

Ecosse, although already a Le Mans winner, was a small team, and a fairly new one. It was founded in 1952 by former racing driver David Murray and engineer Wilkie Wilkinson. Murray, a chartered accountant turned wine merchant, had given up racing after a big accident in a private Maserati while practising for the 1951 German Grand Prix at the Nürburgring. He already knew Wilkinson well through Reg Parnell, the Maserati's entrant. Ecosse was based in Merchiston Mews in Murray's native Edinburgh, and patriotically named at the suggestion of *Autosport* editor Gregor Grant – another Scot.

They would have liked to have gone Grand Prix racing but couldn't afford it. As Murray wrote in his fine book *Ecurie Ecosse*, the least the team could spend for three cars contesting the European Grands Prix would have been £25,000. Insurance would have cost at least £125 per car per meeting (with an excess of £300 per accident) and racing tyres could cost as much as £27 each. Happy days ...

Grand Prix racing's loss was sports car racing's gain, and from the start Ecurie Ecosse (running in the strictly unofficial national colours of dark blue with a white St Andrew's Cross) had extensive experience of racing Jaguars, starting with an XK120. Murray, with true Scots thinking, maintained he went to Le Mans in 1956 only to qualify for the 1957 25th anniversary race, which he had heard would have a large gold trophy in addition to the normal prize money.

Winning in 1956 was by far the biggest thing that had happened to the team in its so far short history, and it earned a lot of future support from Jaguar. For 1957 the works in effect gave them its now supposedly retired 1956 cars, as Murray put it, 'at financial arrangements which were, to put it mildly, generous'. One of Ecosse's two cars was apparently sent straight to Le Mans from Jaguar and its British Racing Green livery changed to dark Scottish blue at the circuit. The other car, XKD606, the eventual winner, was prepared at Merchiston Mews and only made it to scrutineering by the skin of its teeth. Wilkie normally stripped and rebuilt each car in the week before a race, but XKD606 had had an adventurous couple of seasons. As a 1956 works car, built early that year, it survived one small accident during Le Mans practice and was transferred to Ecosse, fully rebuilt, in 3.4 spec, in November. Early in 1957 it was crashed fairly heavily by Ron Flockhart, rebuilt by Jaguar (the stressed shell wasn't easy either to repair or to modify) and returned to Edinburgh more or less ready to race, and with one of

'I have heard it said that to win at Le Mans you need, first and foremost, luck. I do not think that is true; but I am convinced that neither the car nor the drivers must suffer from bad luck. The distinction is important.'

Olivier Gendebien, four times winner, speaking in the 1970s.

Right: 1957 brought Ecurie Ecosse's second win. The victorious Bueb and Flockhart D-type passes the unfortunate Aston Martin DBR1 of Tony Brooks and Noel Cunningham Reid. Brooks inverted the Aston into the sand at Tertre Rouge just before half distance after holding second place, and was hit by Maglioli's Porsche. Both drivers were taken to hospital but neither was seriously injured.

Below: After the 1955 disaster Le Mans was clearly in need of major changes to cope with the increasing speeds of the current generation of cars. The start-finish area was almost completely rebuilt.

the new 3.8 six-cylinder twin-cam engines. The extremely precise Jaguar engine records show it produced 297.5bhp at 5750rpm and 297lb ft of torque at 4500rpm – almost 100bhp less than the big 1957 Ferraris and more than 100bhp shy of the V8 Maseratis.

During practice it developed a misfire, which Wilkie eventually cured. Murray checked it out on the public road at 4am on race morning. He ran the car to its full 178mph potential, and only narrowly avoided being detained by the local gendarmerie, who were normally very friendly, but not necessarily that friendly.

The team travelled in two transporters converted from old single-decker buses. They had their two cars and four drivers. David Murray and his wife flew out a week early, via Paris. He was team boss, she was chief timekeeper. Wilkie was chief mechanic with his 'regular' Le Mans mechanics Stan Sproat and Ron Gaudion each in charge of their own car. With the small band of assistants it was a compact team which stayed at M Ricordeau's Hotel Ricordeau, in nearby Loué. Certainly more compact than the might of Ferrari and Maserati.

But they were a thoroughly professional organisation. As Murray wrote, 'How long does it take to change all four tyres on a car, refill its petrol tank and check the engine oil level? In Ecurie Ecosse the answer is 65 seconds, stopwatch timed.' They practised for hours before the race, choreographed every split second, even made a cine film of their practice routine to hone it to perfection. One thing they didn't have to worry about in the way today's teams do, though, was tyre choice. The D-types would run on off-the-shelf Dunlop racers – the same pattern for practice, qualifying and the race, rain or shine.

It really shouldn't have been enough to beat the Italians – or maybe even the fastest Aston Martins, the DBR1 and DBR2. But the Goliaths played right into David's (Murray's) hands. *Motor Sport* summed up the 1957 race. 'As a free-for-all the event was virtually finished by 7pm on Saturday, and it was an excellent demonstration of a number of things. A driver who has the flair for Grand Prix racing seldom has the ability to control himself for a 24-hour endurance run; the Italians seem to have little idea of just how long 24 hours really are; the British, and Jaguars in particular, have got the art of "racing" at Le Mans well and truly sewn up; and reliability with speed is a difficult thing to attain, even in a sports car engine.'

The Italian cars had torn away from the start as though this were a Grand Prix. Within three hours all the early leaders had failed. The Jaguars raced on, fast and steady, to take five out of the first six places. Ecosse were one and two, Flockhart and Bueb in the 3.8, Sanderson and Lawrence in the 3.4. The winners had covered 2732 miles at an average of 113.8mph, to win by almost eight laps. Le Mans had seen its first sub-four-minute lap, and Hawthorn's Ferrari left the lap record at 126.9mph. Lotus, completing a fine day for the British, took first and second in the Index of Performance.

The Ecurie Ecosse D-types crossed the line to the strains of 'The Road to the Isles', while a light aeroplane flew overhead scattering a million rose petals over the crowd. It was Ecosse's second win, Jaguar's fifth, and a hat-trick for the D-type.

David Murray had sneaked a box into the pits without telling the crew. It contained a few bottles of champagne, 'just in case'. Murray telephoned news of the win to Jaguar boss Sir William Lyons back in Britain, who celebrated by going out to play golf, and losing. The 1957 purse was the biggest Ecosse ever won, but it hardly covered their expenses. The 'gold trophy' David Murray had coveted turned out to be a crystal bowl with a narrow gold rim. But a second Le Mans win was beyond value.

It would prove to be Jaguar's swansong, at least for another 31 years, but as Jaguar stepped back from the top, another British marque, Aston Martin, was closing in on outright victory. They might have won in 1958, maintaining the British winning streak, but this year it was the Britons who failed and the Italians who triumphed.

Maximum prototype capacity was back to 3 litres, which was good for Aston Martin's already pretty well developed DBR1, but good too for Ferrari and the Testa Rossas – the nickname 'redhead' deriving from the distinctive red crackle paint used on their camshaft covers. In 1957 Colas and Kerguen's near-standard DB3S had scored Aston's fifth consecutive 3-litre class win, and the far more exotic DBR1 had already beaten Ferrari in 1957 at the Nürburgring 1000 Kms, but form is rarely that clear cut at Le Mans, as events proved.

There were no works Maseratis as the company had major financial problems, and no works Jaguars again – but there were five private D-types, including two from Ecurie Ecosse, with the latest short-stroke, carburettor engine. Ferrari had ten Testa Rossas, including three works examples – but Aston had three DBR1s, and they had Stirling Moss. Moss was never any great fan of Le Mans, but he was always very, very fast there. In the early stages in 1958 his DBR1 simply stormed away from the hordes of Ferraris, until the engine let go, still 22 hours short of the lap that counts.

Both Ecosse D-types had piston failures – attributed to problems with the officially supplied fuel. The 'official' fuel was a regular bone of contention at Le Mans when there was nothing else left to blame, and sometimes almost certainly a genuine problem. Aston couldn't blame it for the demise of its other two works DBR1s in 1958. The Salvadori/Lewis-Evans car ran out of road and the Brooks/Trintignant one ran out of gears. Heavy rain from late evening added to the problems of the

Below: Lotus and Lotus boss Colin Chapman had a turbulent relationship with Le Mans, mixing success with political in-fighting. This is one of the happier moments – Chapman, second right (with Graham Hill on far right) celebrates an Index of Performance win and 750cc class win with drivers Cliff Allison and Keith Hall, who also finished fourteenth overall in their Lotus XI.

survivors, but it was settling down to be a Ferrari race, with the main opposition, for a while, taken up by Hamilton and Bueb in another private D-type, whose power and speed disadvantages were offset by the wet. One of the other D-types unfortunately did crash on the run towards the Esses, Kessler's closely following Testa Rossa couldn't avoid hitting it, and Jaguar driver Jean-Marie Brousselet, 'Mary', died from his injuries.

The three works Ferraris dominated initially, Hawthorn and Collins, Gendebien and future American world champion Phil Hill, and von Trips and Seidel running 1-2-3. But having set fastest lap at 122.2mph Hawthorn's went out with clutch problems while Seidel put the third place car in the ditch at Arnage just after midnight. That left Gendebien and Hill, and once the Hamilton/Bueb D-type had spun off around midday on Sunday, another victim of the weather, the race was theirs. Second place fell to the probably surprised Aston Martin crew of the two Whitehead brothers in their privately entered DB3S – albeit almost precisely 100 miles behind the winning

Above: Gendarmes line the pit lane and Belgian Olivier Gendebien hitches a ride from American co-driver Phil Hill after their Ferrari had won the 1958 race. It was one of only three Ferrari finishers from a dozen starters, in a race made difficult by dreadful weather, and marred by the death of French driver 'Mary' Brousselet, whose D-type Jaguar had collided with Bruce Kessler's Ferrari at the Dunlop Curves.

Ferrari. They had a reasonable buffer to the remarkably quick 1.6-litre Porsche of Jean Behra and Hans Herrmann, with two other Porsches (Barth/Frère and de Beaufort/Lange) fourth and fifth.

In 1959, Aston Martin had their revenge, thanks to an Englishman with an Italian name and a Texan in farm overalls, Roy Salvadori and Carroll Shelby. Salvadori was a car dealer turned racer, Shelby was a flamboyant adventurer, sometime flier, sometime chicken farmer turned racer. Salvadori had already shown considerable promise as a Grand Prix driver. Shelby had been brought to Europe by Aston Martin team manager John Wyer. He raced at Le Mans for the first time in 1954, sharing an Aston with Paul Frère. Shelby brought the car into the pits complaining that the steering didn't feel right. The crew jacked the car up and one front wheel fell off, and the hub with it.

He had none of those kind of dramas in 1959, and perhaps his biggest concern was driving with a nitroglycerine capsule under his tongue – an emergency back-up in case he had heart problems, a recurring condition that he probably forgot to mention to the team. In classic Le Mans style, Shelby and Salvadori didn't set out to be the fastest pairing in the race, but they hung around going just fast enough while the quickest of all gradually eliminated themselves.

Moss in one of the three DBR1s was as fast as ever, and as he powered into an early lead the Ferrari drivers were as incapable as ever of resisting the chase, with all too familiar consequences. Gendebien and Hill pursued Moss first, followed by Allison and da Silva Ramos. Then slow-starting Behra and Gurney found their true pace (six years after disc brakes had first appeared on the Jaguars,

notoriously conservative Enzo Ferrari fitted them to his works
Testa Rossas) and clawed back from halfway down the field.
They took second, then the lead, as the Moss/Fairman Aston
started to feel the engine problems which were to put it out
of the race. Behra and Gurney followed soon enough, with
transmission failure; Allison and da Silva Ramos had already
gone, so had the single D-type of Ireland and Gregory –
which was still capable of putting on something of a show, if
not of threatening the way they had a few years earlier.

Around one-third distance Shelby and Salvadori had a
two-lap lead, from the sole surviving works Ferrari, Hill and
Gendebien, fighting hard to catch up. Just before half
distance the lead was down to less than a lap. By early
morning the Ferrari had turned the deficit into almost a
three-lap lead, as the leading Aston had lost a considerable
amount of time with what appeared to be a chassis problem
but which turned out to be a shedding tyre tread. The
Trintignant/Frère Aston was doing a classic quick-but-steady
job to stay comfortably in third place, once the demise of the
two fastest Porsches (Bonnier and von Trips, and Barth and von Hanstein) had put it there around
breakfast time. Most uncharacteristically the other two works Porsches also dropped out on Sunday
morning, for once leaving them with little to show for the year's efforts.

The Astons weren't going to catch the Ferrari on pace alone, but the team stuck with its strategy
and proved it correct. Just before midday on Sunday, with a little over four hours to go, the Ferrari was
into the pits every few laps. When it retired Ferrari cited fuel problems; really it had been overheating.
Shelby and Salvadori cruised into the lead and stayed there, a triumph of tactics over bravado.
Trintignant and Frère were an equally conservative second, trailed at some distance by four privately-
entered 3-litre Ferraris.

Britain had excellent 2-litre and 1500 class winners from AC and Lotus. It's just possible that Carroll
Shelby, tousle-haired, happily swigging champagne from the bottle, hugging the girls and dressed in

his famous chicken-farmer
striped dungarees, took a
good look at the AC. A few
years later a similar car
would be the basis for his
classic Shelby Cobra. That
would have the support of
the Ford Motor Company –
and the Ford Motor
Company were going to be
a big influence at Le Mans
in the decade which was
about to start.

In 1959, Aston
Martin had their
revenge, thanks to
an Englishman
with an Italian
name and a Texan
in farm overalls.

Left: Roy Salavadori in the
Aston he shared with Texan
Carroll Shelby to win in 1959.
Above: the team celebrates,
Shelby in the car, in chicken-
farmer's dungarees, Salvadori
on the back with David
Brown – the DB of Aston
Martin. **Overleaf:** Maserati
transporter in 1957, with the
non-finishing 200S of Léon
Coulibeuf and José Behra.

PRANCING HORSE, BLUE OVAL
THE 1960s

The 1960s was one of the great decades at Le Mans. Only two winning marques shared the whole ten years between them, but their stature and their rivalry were on such a level that this was all-out war. The 1960s was the decade of Ford versus Ferrari – blue oval and prancing horse.

Ford would be the latecomer, not taking a huge amount of notice of Le Mans until 1963, and not really stamping their authority until a while after that. Ferrari were already experts and, for another few years at least, that gave them the chance to build their score.

In 1959, as well as defeating them at Le Mans, Aston Martin had beaten Ferrari to the world sports car championship, of which Le Mans had again become a part. In 1960 Aston relieved Ferrari of the challenge of winning the title back in a head-to-head fight as they withdrew the works team from racing. But Ferrari were faced with another old adversary when Maserati found a new lease of life. And for the next ten years there would be plenty more new blood to keep both Ferrari in Maranello and Ford in Dearborn on their toes.

To the teams themselves, let alone to outsiders, the detailed Le Mans regulations were as complicated and confusing as ever, but for 1960 the basic structure at least reflected what applied elsewhere. The main divisions were now for sports cars and GT cars – in effect what had previously been known as prototypes and production sports cars. Within those categories were the usual extensive sub-divisions based on capacity. And naturally, beyond all that there were still all Le Mans' own arcane races within the race, including the various 'Indexes', based on combinations of capacity, weight, fuel efficiency and speed, versus a target figure. Then there was the Biennial Cup. That had been part of Le Mans virtually from day one, was abandoned briefly in 1957 and 1958, but now returned as an intrinsic part of the event – until

Previous Spread: a Ferrari rule-stretcher, the 250 GTO – not quite a simple evolution of the 250 GT SWB. This is Elde and Beurlys' GTO, third in 1962, behind Noblet and Guichet's similar car and Hill and Gendebien's winning Testa Rossa. **Above:** Mulsanne corner in 1960, Rodriguez and Pilette's Ferrari and Salvadori and Clark's Aston – second and third respectively. **Below:** Frère and Gendebien, 1960 winners for Ferrari.

it was replaced by other indexes of consumption and efficiency in the fuel-conscious 1970s when motor sport had to show a conservationist conscience.

As ever, Le Mans began the 1960s with infinite variety. Because the rules allowed both, there had never been any absolute preference for either closed or open cars (and in the twenty-first century there still isn't). There was never any fixed pattern for the ratio between production cars and prototypes, and capacities had run from the sub-750cc class to the diesel-engined MAP of 1950, whose 5-litre capacity plus supercharger gave an official capacity of 10 litres.

In 1960 the biggest cars were the 4.6-litre Chevrolet Corvettes, the smallest the 741cc Stanguellini. The winner would be a 3-litre open Ferrari 'sports car', the Testa Rossa driven by the Belgian pairing of Olivier Gendebien and Paul Frère. It was a promising race rather than a particularly exciting one. The promise was of a battle between the Ferraris and the Maseratis – back on the racing scene through the American Camoradi team, even though the Italian company still had serious financial problems. The reality was that Ferrari won as much by outlasting as by outpacing the opposition.

Including four works cars, Ferraris counted 13 entries – the works Testa Rossa open 3-litres and a small army of short wheelbase 250GT coupés. Four of those were from the North American Racing Team, and they were part of the biggest American presence to date at Le Mans. After an absence of five years, Briggs Cunningham was back, and still very much a favourite of the Le Mans crowds. For 1960 he had an intriguing two-pronged attack, three of the four Corvettes and a Jaguar. The Corvettes were works cars in all but name, and Briggs Cunningham himself shared one with Zora Arkus-Duntov. Belgian-born, Russian-raised, German-educated, American-domiciled Arkus-Duntov was the brilliant General Motors engineer who developed the Corvette from slow-selling, underpowered six-cylinder posers' car to commercially successful and highly potent all-American V8-engined sports car. He gave General Motors its first production engine to deliver 1bhp per cubic inch (the first fuel-injected V8 for the Corvette) and he developed the racing engines for this 1960 Le Mans effort. In between, he occasionally found time to go racing himself, although 1960 would be his last competitive year.

Cunningham's other car should also by rights have been a works effort – the Jaguar E2A. It was the link between racing D-type and production E-type, developed from the former and in effect a prototype of the latter. On loan to Cunningham from Jaguar, it was to be driven by Dan Gurney and US sports car star Walt Hansgen. In all there were 24 American drivers at Le Mans in 1960 and, although none of them won, they played a large part in the action.

So did 'Lucky' Casner's Camoradi team, which ran the fourth Corvette as well as the three highly fancied Maseratis. Lloyd Casner was the team patron at the time, a former airline pilot in his mid-thirties who raced himself and was rarely far away when there was a

'What does Le Mans mean to me? It is much more than a race, it is a place to which you come and spend a week during which you share almost everything with your team, with a single aim: do as well as possible in the last 24 hours of the party, which starts on the Tuesday with the scrutineering formalities. During race week, Les 24 Heures is the only thing that matters in Le Mans, the race becomes the centre of the world and you are part of it.'

Paul Frère, June 2001

Right: A pit stop for the Ferrari of Gendebien and Frère, en route to victory in 1960. Tall windscreens obeyed the letter of the rules, at the expense of lower top speeds and increased fuel consumption.

American interest was going through another strong phase in the early 1960s, both with domestic machinery and with European sports cars run by American entrants. **Above:** the T61 'birdcage' Maserati entered by Camoradi for Masten Gregory and Chuck Daigh in 1960, out by one third distance with electrical problems. **Overleaf:** a very mixed bunch heads for the Dunlop Curve at the start in 1962, Porsche mixing it with Sunbeam and Ferrari – the real essence of Le Mans.

dollar to be made, in whatever way. Sadly, he would die in a Maserati at Le Mans in 1965. This year his three cars were to be driven by Gregory and Daigh, Munaron and Scarlatti, and Lucky himself with Jefford.

The Camoradi cars were one of Maserati's most famous models, the Tipo 61, nicknamed 'Birdcage' for its complex spaceframe of very small, lightweight tubes. The first versions had 2-litre four-cylinder engines, but for Le Mans capacity was up to 2.9 litres. Although the Maseratis weren't as powerful as the 3-litre V12 Ferraris, they were lighter and, in one way at least, cleverer. Confronted with the rule requiring a ten-inch high full-width windscreen, most manufacturers had simply erected big plexiglass affairs that were as aerodynamic as a wall. Maserati tried harder to minimise the barn-door effect and with the Gregory/Daigh car took its solution to extremes by having a screen that was the requisite ten inches deep but which stretched almost to the front of the car, with a smooth sloping profile. It may have looked odd, but in spite of its power disadvantage this 'Birdcage' was almost 10mph quicker than the bluff-screened Testa Rossas on the Mulsanne straight.

Fastest lap of all in practice went to the Jaguar E2A, and that car would also be fast in the early stages of the race, but it went out with engine failure after around nine and a half hours. The Ecurie Ecosse-entered D-type lasted another four hours before its engine broke too, its retirement marking the end of an era for the D. The early race leader was the Gregory and Daigh Birdcage, but two hours in the Maseratis began to run into trouble. The leader made a pit stop and lost an hour with a starter motor problem before getting out again, then didn't quite survive to midnight before retiring with engine failure. The Munaron/Scarlatti car also had starter motor problems after the third hour, and never did restart. The third car, Casner and Jefford's, went off into the sand, escaped, but eventually suffered transmission failure – probably sand-assisted.

Two of the works Ferraris had failed to go even as far as their first pit stops. Von Trips and Scarfiotti both ran out of fuel on the circuit, not because of fuel consumption rules as in the past but from simple miscalculation – and the lack of any reserve system.

All this allowed the two remaining Testa Rossas, Gendebien and Frère, Mairesse and Ginther into first and second, ahead of the first of the private Ferraris, driven by Rodriguez and Pilette. The only other car to give any serious challenge was the Aston Martin DBR1 driven by 1959 winner Roy Salvadori with up-and-coming Grand Prix driver Jim Clark. And when the generally awful weather of the first half of the race was at its worst, Clark was at his brilliant best, splitting the Maranello cars and briefly taking third place with the demise of Mairesse and Ginther when a driveshaft failed.

Other than that, there wasn't much change and at four o'clock on Sunday the chequered flag duly fell on Gendebien and Frère, ahead of Rodriguez and Pilette, Clark and Salvadori, then a fleet of Ferraris. Only one of the Corvettes finished, Fitch and Grossman in eighth place, a long way behind the GT-winning Ferrari of Tavano and Loustel. The British did well in the smaller classes, with the twin-cam MGA heading the 1500s, a Lotus Elite the 1300s and a very special Austin-Healey Sprite the one-litres. Tucked away among the also-rans was a Lola, driven by Vogele and Ashdown. Nobody knew it at the time, but it was the first step to the big confrontation of the decade.

Enzo Ferrari wasn't a man to avoid confrontations: he was more likely to engineer them, especially to make political points. He liked to do things his own way, even when his own way was out of step with the rest of the world. Accepting the rear-engined revolution in racing was a classic example of Ferrari's stubbornness. By the end of the 1950s Cooper had showed that a mid-engined

Grand Prix car could make up in handling and roadholding a certain amount of deficiency in power – one thing the British teams usually did have in comparison with Ferrari. Very soon, the rest of the Grand Prix grid had followed Cooper's example, and moved their engines behind the driver. Ferrari alone stuck with tradition, and was frequently beaten on the strength of his pig-headedness. In his memoirs, *My Terrible Joys,* he stated his philosophy that engine power was 80 per cent of winning, not 50 per cent as most would say. That cost him the 1959 and 1960 Grand Prix world championships, and although Ferrari eventually built a rear-engined Grand Prix car, and indeed won the 1961 championship, the knock-on effect was that he spent much of the 1960s playing catch-up behind the British teams which had become dominant. In sports car racing he proved to be less intransigent. In 1961 Ferrari arrived at Le Mans with his first mid-engined sports car.

He was not alone. Hedging his bets no doubt, only one of Ferrari's four works entries was a mid-engined car (both engine and chassis derived from the nostril-nosed F1 car), but this year three of the leading Maserati entries were mid-engined – 3-litre V12 Tipo 63s, again with 'Birdcage' multi-tubular chassis. Like the mid-engined Ferrari they were F1-related. And again they were run privately rather than by the troubled works, two of them by Briggs Cunningham, the other by Scuderia Serenissima. Cunningham's cars were driven by Walt Hansgen and Bruce McLaren, Augie Pabst and Dick Thompson. Briggs himself was back to share a 2-litre 'birdcage' with Jim Kimberley, in a tough class where the obvious favourites were three works Porsches. At the head of the field it would clearly be a race between Ferrari and Maserati, with an outside chance for the latest Aston Martins. Those were a pair of open 3-litre DBR1/300 sports cars from the Border Reivers and Essex Racing teams, plus three 3.7-litre GT cars – a 'normal' DB4 and two of the pretty Zagato-bodied DB4GTs, the latter also entered by Essex.

They didn't get a look in against the Ferraris (none of them even finished, and in any case they had never been on the pace; not even Clark could work that much magic for Aston this year). Neither did Maserati offer any serious challenge, even though they managed eventually to get Pabst and Thompson home in fourth place.

Le Mans, as *The Autocar* observed, remained a unique challenge. 'Shorn of its sideshows, its fairground atmosphere and its colour, the Le Mans 24-hour race would be no more than the fourth round in the battle for the Sports Car Championship for 1961; yet, in fact, it is the most glamorous, the best publicized, and perhaps the best attended event of the racing year. Other races are fought and won in an afternoon, or a day at most; but Le Mans itself involves a full day and night with, above all, the thrill of racing in darkness; and if you care to lose yourself completely in the atmosphere that builds up beforehand, there are the four days of preparation and practice before ever the race begins. Somehow in an age of unquestioned reliability, when the most mundane car driven by an average driver can cover great journeys without uncertainty as to its safe arrival, Le Mans has retained, and continues to provide the romance and glamour of great distances covered against the clock, and of travel in the mode of the 'heroic age' of motoring.'

'Unquestioned reliability' was not a feature of many of the potential front runners of Le Mans 1961. Two of the Tipo 63s were soon gone. Hansgen had briefly held third place but crashed on a wet track just after the three-hour mark; the other V12s suffered overheating, with only Pabst and Thompson driving their way around the problems. So, with Maserati and Aston faltering, the fight was between the Ferraris themselves, and on that level it wasn't a bad one. For much of the race the first four places were a permutation of the 2.4-litre V6 mid-engined car driven by American Richie Ginther and German aristocrat Count Wolfgang 'Taffy' von Trips, the 3-litre front-engined V12 Testa Rossa of Pedro and Ricardo Rodriguez, and the similar cars of Mairesse and Parkes, and Gendebien and Phil Hill.

The front-engined 246SP proved the point that a good chassis and compact packaging can make up for modest power, and stayed with the leaders all the way, until it ran out of fuel on Sunday morning. Ferrari obviously hadn't learned from the year before. The front-engined troopers survived to save the day, and Gendebien and Hill led home from Mairesse and Parkes, and Noblet and Guichet – GT category winners in their 250GT. The latter Ferrari hadn't been nearly as quick as the similar car of Stirling Moss and Graham Hill, but were still running when it counted; the British pair were gone by Sunday morning. And Moss was gone from Le Mans forever; before the 1962 race he suffered the accident which ended his career, at Goodwood on Easter Monday 1962. He had never much liked Le Mans, anyway.

The 1962 24 Hours turned out to be much like the 1961 race but with somewhat different cars – similar storyline, similar cast, new costumes. The rules had changed again. The change was down to the world championship organisers, who (with the best intentions) had tried to discourage the proliferation of 'sports cars' (for which read prototypes) and emphasise 'experimental' cars, of up to 4 litres – which they had intended to mean GT cars. The manufacturers being more creative than the rule makers, their thoughts turned towards creating 4-litre sports cars. Or at least Ferrari's did ...

In 1962 their Le Mans entry experimented in all directions. With both Ferrari and Maserati the jury was still apparently out on how to make a big rear-engined car work, so from both camps there were smaller mid-engined cars and big front-engined ones. From Ferrari there were open and closed front-engined 330s, 2.4 V6 and 2.6 V8 versions of the mid-engined 246SP, plus various versions of the ubiquitous 250GTs, including half a dozen examples of a new, more aerodynamic version, the 250 GTO – or Gran Turismo Omologato.

This was a fine piece of rule interpretation on Ferrari's part, and the car which Ferrari used to steamroller his way to three consecutive world championships for GT cars, in 1962, 1963 and 1964. The regulations said that cars in this category had to be usable on the road, and strictly speaking the 250 GTO was, so long as you weren't too picky about comfort, or cost. Another part of the 'homologation' requirement was that to be eligible for the GT category a car must be built in specified numbers, in this case 100 examples – not huge numbers, but the intention was to specify more cars than any manufacturer could afford to build purely to go racing, so cars would have to be sold to everyday customers. But the rules, sloppily perhaps, allowed the 'evolution' of an existing car which already satisfied the homologation requirements. Ferrari had already built more than a hundred examples of the highly successful 250GT SWB, and so far as he was concerned the 250GTO was simply a modified version of the SWB. The rule-makers, the Federation Internationale d'Automobile, had intended evolution to mean such things as minor bodywork changes; Ferrari's definition of minor was obviously more flexible. The GTO began to evolve a series of highly aerodynamic shapes – increasingly the key to performance on this level – and the additional spaceframe chassis elements were obviously only there to support the new bodywork. In total, from 1962 to 1964, Ferrari actually built just 39 GTOs, the FIA shrugged its shoulders, and by the end of 1962 it had won its first title.

The GTO didn't win Le Mans in 1962, but it did take second, third and sixth, for Noblet and Guichet, Elde and Beurlys, and Grossman and Roberts, all after fast and reliable performances. They were beaten by Ferrari's similarly liberal reading of the rules in the form of the open 4-litre V12 front-engined 'experimental' Testa Rossa driven by Phil Hill and Olivier Gendebien. Hill and Gendebien knew they had the pace to win the race but with marginal transmission reliability they had to treat the car gently, and they were far enough ahead of the opposition to do just that. Their main challenge came from the 2.4 V6 mid-engined Testa Rossa driven (with considerably more aggression) by the Rodriguez brothers. That swapped the lead with the big front-engined car several times before it expired near the halfway mark, with transmission failure. The larger 2.6 V8 mid-engined Testa Rossa also ran second for a while, and also had transmission failure after around 17 hours.

Maserati's interpretation of the 'experimental' rules had been just as liberal as Ferrari's, and they

'Le Mans is an amazing event with a terrific atmosphere, but it wasn't the sort of thing that I enjoyed. I supect it's different now, but in my day I wasn't allowed to race – and I'm a racing driver, so I found endurance driving very boring. I enjoyed the time with Mercedes, because I was with Fangio, and in my opinion he was the greatest racing driver that ever lived.'

Stirling Moss, June 2001

Left: The Ferrari 250GT entered by the North American Racing Team and driven by Stirling Moss and Graham Hill leads the Aston Martin DBR1 entered by John Ogier and driven by Roy Salvadori and Tony Maggs. Neither car finished in 1961, and Moss was of the school that thought Le Mans was a fine race that lasted far too long. Overleaf: the Ferrari garage in the run-up to the 1964 race, the year in which Ford arrived. Ferrari won, with Guichet and Vaccarella in the 3.3 275P, car number 20. 21 and 22 are the team cars of Scarfiotti and Parkes, and Baghetti and Maglioli.

turned up with three front-engined 4-litre GT coupés, two entered by Cunningham, the other by Maserati France. All failed without making a great impression, although they were fearsomely fast in a straight line. The French car had tyre problems, as did one of Cunningham's cars before its engine failed around dawn on Sunday, long after the other one had crashed. Both 3.7-litre Aston DB4 GT Zagatos blew up, and the 212 GT prototype driven by Graham Hill and Richie Ginther led very briefly on the opening lap, stayed on the pace for a while, but expired with engine problems at only quarter distance. Jaguar, attracted back by what it thought were real 'GT' rules, proved the only other cars capable of splitting the Ferraris, snatching fourth and fifth places with two of their three lightweight E-types, driven by Cunningham and Salvadori, Lumsden and Sargent – the latter in spite of transmission problems in the later stages of the race.

Demonstrating their usual perverseness, the Le Mans organisers had caused a lot of bad feeling in the British ranks by refusing to admit the little Lotus 23s, which they said didn't satisfy the 'spirit' of the rules – interpreted by most people as a definite likelihood of them beating their French class opposition. Lotus did beat the French when David Hobbs and Frank Gardner took eighth place and the Index of Thermal Efficiency with the Elite. And having refused Morgan an entry in 1961 on the grounds that the car was too old-fashioned, they let it in for 1962 – whereupon Chris Lawrence and Richard Shepherd-Barron promptly won the 2-litre class, while taking a very steady 13th place overall, of 18 finishers.

1963 was another year of chaotic rule changes, another year of Ferrari victory, the first win for a mid-engined car, the first year when the overall distance exceeded 4500km, the second biggest winning margin ever, and the beginning of a great chapter in Le Mans history – although that may not have been obvious at the time.

Of the 48 (plus one) starters 26 were 'prototypes' and 22 GTs, although the distinction was becoming increasingly blurred. The plus one was a gas turbine-engined Rover BRM, invited to run as car 00 in a special category of its own. In the main field there was another world title for GT prototypes, alongside those for various sizes of 'production' GTs. But there was no limit on capacity for prototypes, and no minimum production number. That was as good as telling someone like Enzo Ferrari to build whatever he wanted to build.

In fact his 1963 winners were Scarfiotti and Bandini in the 3-litre V12 250P, a handsome, fast and strong open car, first of the mid-engined V12 Ferraris, and the first mid-engined car ever to win at Le Mans, in the 31st year of the race. Remarkably perhaps, it was also the first all-Italian win, both drivers and car.

They won by 134 miles, after setting a record distance of 2835 miles, with fastest lap for Surtees' similar car at exactly 129mph – another record. Surtees wasn't around for the finish, though. Having led at 4, 8, 12 and 16 hours, the car he shared with Mairesse went up in flames on the circuit, after a messy pit stop which had left fuel spilling around the exhaust area. Mairesse was obliged to bail out of the car before it had even stopped moving, but escaped with only minor burns – which is more than can be said for the car. Parkes and Maglioli in the third of the 250Ps started in the leading bunch, fell back with electrical problems during the night, fought

Below: A classic example of the old adage that you shouldn't judge a book by looking at the cover. In 1961 the Le Mans organisers rejected an entry from Morgan because they said the Plus 4 Supersport (a current model, of course) was too old-fashioned to compete. In 1962 Chris Lawrence and Richard Shepherd-Barron came back with the same car, were accepted, and finished 13th overall, winning the 2-litre class.

back to second, then slowed, virtually within sight of the finish, with a misfire – dropping them to third. It was largely academic, of course, as Ferraris of one sort or another took the first six places – including second, fourth and sixth for GTOs and fifth for the first of the 4-litre 330LM GT prototypes, driven by Salmon and Sears.

Much of the significance of Le Mans 1963 would only become clear with hindsight. The single Maserati entry was by no means the last Le Mans Maserati but their cars were looking increasingly outmoded. This ugly 5-litre V8 version of the front-engined 151 GT coupé was monstrously fast in a straight line for Simon and Casner, but only until its gearbox broke. Then there was the far more effective Rover BRM – a BRM chassis with a 'lightweight' Rover gas-turbine engine in the days when the British firm were exploring such engines as a production possibility. It whispered round for 24 hours with no problems whatsoever and comfortably beat the distance target the organisers had set it for a 'Special Award'. Had it been an official competitor it would have finished in eighth place.

Most significant of all was a clutch of Ford-powered entries, from both sides of the Atlantic. Carroll Shelby, 1959 winner with Aston Martin, had retired from racing in December 1960 and was now a constructor, with the Shelby Cobra – a hybrid of European sports car chassis and big but uncomplicated American muscle. The Cobra's chassis was derived from the AC Ace, which had already had considerable Le Mans success as a 2-litre car; its 289cu in, 4.7-litre lightweight V8 was from Ford of America. Together they made a

Above: Even as Ferrari grudgingly joined the ranks of the mid-engined sports car generation, he hedged his bets with the last of his front-line front-engined cars – and in 1962 it was the front-engined 330 Testa Rossa of Olivier Gendebien and Phil Hill which took the honours. They survived the distance, while none of the mid-engined Ferraris lasted beyond the 18th hour. But this was the end of the front-engined era.

mighty roadgoing sports car, and on shorter tracks a formidable race car. At Le Mans the unlimited capacity rules let them in, but aerodynamics hampered their GT battle against the Ferraris, the Aston Martins, the Cunningham-run lightweight E-types and the rest. Seventh place, however, was promising.

The other Ford-engined challenger was a British Lola with Ford V8 power – a mid-engined coupé with modern monocoque chassis and sophisticated suspension design. It was designed by Eric Broadley, was only just finished in time to appear, and almost didn't get into the race because the organisers demanded modifications so that the drivers could see out of the rear window. Only one of the two cars could be made ready for the start, for Hobbs and Attwood. It had all kinds of gear selection problems in the race, and finally crashed (around dawn) when Hobbs arrived at Tertre Rouge in neutral and rolled it into retirement. At the end of *Autosport*'s 1963 technical analysis, John Bolster wrote, 'Let us end by repeating the lesson of Le Mans. To compete against twelve cylinders you need twelve cylinders. It's as simple as that.' Ford obviously didn't agree ...

Ford was about to reinvent itself, changing from an admirable but dull image typified by the Ford Safety Campaign to a programme they would call Total Performance. At the dawn of the 1960s Ford didn't have much by way of performance models. Since 1957, in common with other major American manufacturers, Ford (officially at least) had followed the Automobile Manufacturers' Association 'recommendation' not to participate in motor sport. But Lee Iacocca, head of the Ford Division of Ford Motor Co. since 1960, thought Ford needed to be seen from a more sporty perspective.

When Le Mans was conceived, one of its most important aims was to improve certain aspects of everyday motoring – such fundamentals as

effective lighting, brakes and mechanical reliability.

In later years, Le Mans, at least to some extent, became a test bed for new ideas that might have some relevance to an everyday motorist – the most famous being disc brakes, as pioneered by Jaguar in the early 1950s. But there have been many less obvious benefits, and one or two dead-ends.

In 1963 the Ferrari 250LM of Bandini and Scarfiotti (right) was the first mid-engined winner at Le Mans, and a layout which many roadgoing supercars would soon echo.

Le Mans has always favoured low drag aerodynamics – a function of the special demands of the long circuit with its crucial element of the Mulsanne Straight. Again the benefits ultimately filtered down to far more mundane cars, with benefits not only to performance but also to fuel economy. Le Mans has played its part in improving fuel efficiency for the real driver in other ways too, and not only in the years when its fuel regulations were controversially tight. It's an intrinsic part of the race that going further and stopping less often is a big advantage, and the less fuel you use, the less often you stop.

Supercharging and turbocharging have both had their day at Le Mans, because efficiency, not just power, is vital here. The Le Mans categories emphasise that, by relating performance to capacity and other factors. Le Mans has occasionally been brave enough, too, to open its doors to real innovation, where Grand Prix racing and other areas of sports car racing have been far more conservative. Le Mans has, at various times, not only allowed but encouraged 'alternative' fuels and power sources. In the early days there were cars like the Delettrez diesels, in the early 1980s the option (albeit poorly supported) of 'mixed' fuels. And, most famously, classes for turbine-engined cars, originally as a special category led by the Rover-BRM (above) in 1963, and later with a formal equivalency, which attracted the American Howmets in the 1970s. But most of all, Le Mans favours cars which last the distance ...

Right: Carroll Shelby's great creation, the Cobra, brought together American V8 power with European chassis abilities. On short circuits it was hugely effective, but aerodynamics weren't the Cobra's big thing and at Le Mans that was a major disadvantage. In 1963 the Peter Bolton/Ninian Sanderson Cobra, entered by AC Cars, made a token gesture with the tack-on hard-top, and showed the car's potential by finishing seventh overall, and winning the 5-litre class.

In 1962 Henry Ford II pre-empted the other major manufacturers in announcing that Ford would no longer follow the AMA's line, and was officially back in motor sport. They came back first on home territory, through NASCAR racing, but Iacocca's vision for Total Performance included Europe as well, and virtually every area of top-class motor sport, from rallying to Indianapolis, Grand Prix racing to saloon cars. And of course, the jewel in the sports car crown, Le Mans.

Ford weren't interested in racing purely as a sporting activity. They saw it as a way to sell cars in an era when the market was getting younger and more attracted by a performance image. As one Ford executive said, 'Our racing programme is a prudent business investment. Our product improvement and sales record can be attributed to many factors, but we have no hesitation in saying that racing is one of them'. So, 'racing improves the breed' and 'win on Sunday sell cars on Monday' were as compelling as ever.

By the late 1960s Ford would have won everything worth winning – the Indy 500, the Formula 1 world championships, multiple saloon car and rallying titles, and Le Mans. They formed powerful partnerships in their pursuit of Total Performance, with people like Lotus, Cosworth and, not least, Carroll Shelby. But even for Ford, winning at Le Mans proved to be a tough call. They had to do it the hard way, after the 'easy' way eluded them. Put simply, early in the 1960s Ford tried to buy Ferrari – planning, essentially, to create a family of Ford-Ferrari road cars and Ferrari-Ford racers. But $15 million and the promise of a continuing role in the racing programme wasn't enough to make the famously stubborn Enzo Ferrari sell. So having failed to join Ferrari, Ford started plotting how to beat them.

They wanted to be at Le Mans in 1964, but didn't have much time. The Ford-engined Lola from 1963 became the key. By the time that car appeared, Roy Lunn at Ford's Dearborn R&D facility had done preliminary work on a Le Mans car, but without completing anything. In the summer of 1963 Ford turned to Eric Broadley, Lola's founder and designer of the Lola Le Mans car, to help them. To cut a long story short, within less than a year the best elements of Lunn's concepts and Broadley's mid-engined Lola GT had metamorphosed into the first generation Ford GT40. And while they were developing the car at a new facility (Ford Advanced Vehicles, in Slough), Ford found one of the best men in the industry to manage the whole programme – former Aston Martin team manager John Wyer.

The cars' first Le Mans appearance was a disaster. The first two were ready just in time for the very wet Le Mans test days in April. Neither proved very quick, both had endless minor problems (most worryingly high-speed instability) and both were crashed – one heavily (but without personal injury) by Jo Schlesser at Mulsanne Corner, after being caught out by standing water on the track.

Ford had at least sorted out the aerodynamic problem before the car's first race appearance at the Nürburgring in May 1964 – by the addition of a small tail lip which increased downforce but actually reduced drag. The single car entered at the Nürburgring (for Phil Hill and the GT40's main test driver, Bruce McLaren) was reasonably competitive with the Ferraris, but had rear suspension failure. The cause was a chassis-welding fault, it wasn't an isolated one, and before Le Mans Ford had virtually to rebuild everything ...

There was to be no fairytale ending for the GT40's first Le Mans, but there was glory in the opening stages. Whatever else it was, the 4.2-litre four-cam Indianapolis V8-powered GT40 was super quick on the Mulsanne, where it topped 190mph in qualifying. After Ferrari led the opening lap, the Fords showed they had the speed to lead, and not just briefly but for much of the next four hours. Ginther and Gregory led by a growing margin, but in the fifth hour the Attwood and Schlesser GT40, still in touch with the leading Ferraris, caught fire on the Mulsanne and retired. Ginther and Gregory lost the lead with a slow pit stop, then succumbed a transmission problem. Hill and McLaren had made up many places after a disastrously slow start and early fuel maladies, were up to third place by Sunday morning, but were finally sidelined by further gearbox problems.

Ferrari raced on as the Fords failed, and for the fifth year in a row (and the eighth overall) it was a Ferrari first past the post – the 3.3-litre 275P driven by Jean Guichet and Nino Vaccarella, ahead of the 4-litre 330Ps of Graham Hill and Jo Bonnier, John Surtees and Lorenzo Bandini. There was consolation for Ford in a new lap record (Phil Hill at 131.3mph) and for the car which took fourth overall and won both the GT category and the 5-litre class. That wasn't a GT40 but the new Cobra Daytona coupé, a more aerodynamic derivative of the open Cobra, aimed right at Ferrari's GT dominance. The story goes that, in one of several arguments, Enzo Ferrari offended Carroll Shelby while they were talking about a possible drive. Straight-talking Shelby promised that one day he would be back to 'whip Ferrari's ass'. The Ford-powered, Ford-backed Daytona achieved it, not only with its Le Mans success but winning the 1965 World Manufacturers' Championship for GT cars.

It was Shelby, too, who helped turn the GT40 into a winner, but not quite yet. In 1965 Ferrari had

'A party of top Ford management, including Henry Ford himself, had visited the Sebring 12-Hours race in the hope of seeing a Cobra victory. Ferrari had run away with the race ... and Mr Ford was reported to have said "That's the way to go racing, why don't we buy those red cars?"'

John Wyer in The Certain Sound

one more win in them, and this was it. For Ford, losing was not for want of trying; the head-to-head battle between Maranello and Dearborn (or Slough) was smouldering.

Ford arrived at their second Le Mans expecting to win. They came with at least some finishes, and one 1965 victory to their name – after not scoring a single finish during 1964. Miles and Ruby had won at Daytona, McLaren and Miles had been second at Sebring and third at Monza. Ferrari won Monza, the Targa Florio and the Nürburgring 1000 Kms. No one else had won anything. Prototypes dominated

Above: In 1964 Dan Gurney and Bob Bondurant finished fourth at Le Mans in this Daytona – first of the non-Ferraris, GT winner and 5-litre class winner.

the Le Mans entry, and Ferrari dominated the prototypes, with no fewer than ten cars from the works and semi-works teams. They included the new 4-litre 330P2s, and the beautiful 250LM – which Ferrari had tried to pass off to the FIA as a production car, but this time they weren't convinced. Ford had six prototypes including four completely revised original type GT40s, now with production-based 'small-block' pushrod V8s rather than the exotic Indy-type four-cam race engines of the previous year. Those had been developed on Ford's behalf by a new operation run by Shelby, while John Wyer produced an open version of the original car. Ford also brought two 'Mark IIs', run by Shelby, developed by Roy Lunn and powered by NASCAR-derived 7-litre V8s in the hope that might should be

right. And the Fords were indeed mighty, but not for long enough.

After a thunderstorm and floods had wiped out the first practice session and cost all the front-runners fine-tuning time, the 7-litre Mark II of Phil Hill and Chris Amon was fastest in qualifying at 141.5mph, fastest in the race with a lap record 139.2mph, and lasted longer than any of its teammates. But that was for less than eight hours of the 24. For both Mark IIs the power (around 475bhp) and torque of the 7-litre V8 was too much for the gearbox. Early leads for both the Amon/Hill and Miles/McLaren Mark IIs disappeared, and so, one by one, did the smaller GT40s, with a mixture of engine and gearbox maladies. For Ford this was deeply humiliating, but for Ferrari it was the opening to score another win that they almost certainly couldn't have hoped for on pace alone.

Even Ferrari seemed to make some effort to throw this one away. What had been the first five places for the P2s after the demise of the GT40s ebbed away, as all but one of Ferrari's fastest prototypes failed, variously with engine, brake and transmission problems. The surviving P2, driven by Rodriguez and Vaccarella, finished a distant seventh; the win went to Jochen Rindt and the bespectacled Masten Gregory in the controversial 250LM entered by NART, followed by the similar car of Dumay and Gosselin in Dumay's own car – a great result for a real private entry. Mairesse and 'Beurlys' in a 275GTB production coupé completed the top three for Ferrari, with 2-litre Porsches stealing fourth and fifth. Remarkably, this was only the second time a closed car had won at Le Mans (Mercedes were first in 1952), but it marked the start of seven consecutive coupé wins. The much revised Rover-BRM gas-turbine car ran again, and was allowed to compete properly, in the 2-litre class against the dominant Porsches. It finished, but was slowed by engine problems.

Ford knew that they threw the 1965 race away with a mixture of rushed preparation, too many

Above: Another of Ferrari's rule-testing creations, the winning 275LM from 1965, driven by Masten Gregory and Jochen Rindt. Evolved from the 250LM, this was Ferrari's counter to newcomer Ford. He had originally tried to have the mid-engined car accepted as another 'production' evolution of the front-engined 250GT.

variations, and arguably a touch of arrogance about their prospects. They had now won Indianapolis, and Total Performance was paying dividends virtually everywhere else, but in two years at Le Mans they had spent vast amounts of money and effort without getting one of their nine entries to the chequered flag. In rainy April testing at Le Mans in 1966 Walt Hansgen had been killed when his GT40 aquaplaned off the end of the start-finish straight. Ford were having a bad time and before the 1966 race a memo circulated in Dearborn – 'Henry expects you to win...'

Moments after four o'clock on the horribly wet afternoon of Sunday 19 June 1966, three GT40s splashed across the finish line in close formation. Finally, Ford had beaten Ferrari and conquered Le Mans. The performance had been so dominant that the team was able to stage manage what was supposed to be the race's first ever dead-heat, between Chris Amon and Bruce McLaren in the black and silver Mark II and Ken Miles and Denny Hulme's sister car. The Le Mans organisers, sticklers for detail and never keen on being manipulated, deemed that because it had started further back in the line-up, the Amon/McLaren car had travelled further. About 20 yards further in a record 3009.5 miles. It would have been a nice touch, but with Bucknum and Hutcherson next up in the third Mark II, Henry (Ford II) was probably as happy with 1-2-3 as with 1-1-3. He could also celebrate that new distance record and a new lap record – the latter at almost 143mph for Dan Gurney in another 7-litre Mark II.

No fewer than eight Mark IIs had started, run by Shelby, the Holman & Moody team from America

and Alan Mann Racing from Britain. Ford also had five 4.7 GT40s as their 'second string' – the Mark I now having been built in sufficient numbers to qualify for the sports car class (with a production requirement of 50 cars), alongside Ferrari's 275LM. One of those GT40s was driven by a young Belgian making his first appearance at Le Mans: Jacky Ickx.

Having won the American season openers at Daytona and Sebring, Ford concentrated on Le Mans to the exclusion of all other European races in 1966. But, while Ford were stronger than ever, Ferrari were weaker. Industrial problems in Italy had affected motor racing as well as other industries, and Ferrari's preparations had been badly compromised. They also lost their Grand Prix star John Surtees immediately before the race in a row over team politics.

150

Whatever, Ferrari's P3 coupés, the lighter, more powerful evolution of the P2, would have been hard pushed to match the Fords in 1966. These were the fastest cars yet seen at Le Mans. In the April trials Ken Miles's Mark II was data-logged; on the start-finish straight it reached 183mph, at the Dunlop Bridge it was doing 160mph, through the Esses 82mph and at the almost right-angled Tertre Rouge 65mph. On the Mulsanne it reached 205mph, lifting slightly to 190mph through the Mulsanne 'kink' – a daunting corner at these speeds. Mulsanne 'hairpin' was the slowest point on the circuit at 35mph. Between there and Indianapolis Miles reached more than 180mph again, 60mph through Indianapolis, 107mph towards Arnage, 40mph through there, and a scary 121mph through the slowest part of the notorious White House corners. And that lap was some 12 seconds slower than Gurney's race record.

One car that might have threatened Ford and Ferrari was the 5.4-litre Chevrolet-engined Chaparral, a technically advanced car with a semi-automatic transmission and composite chassis developed by Texan Jim Hall. It had won at the Nürburgring, but only lasted a few hours at Le Mans before retiring with electrical problems.

The Fords' pushrod engines were very powerful but relatively simple and lightly stressed; the smaller Ferraris were mechanically more sophisticated, but no faster and no more reliable. In a tough race only 15 of the 55 starters finished. Ford's 1-2-3 finishers were the only survivors of the eight Mark II starters, the rest suffered a variety of engine, transmission and suspension failures. Fords in various permutations led at every four-hour intermediate check, but until midnight Rodriguez and Ginther's Ferrari P3 was consistently in the top three, with at least one other Ferrari in the top half-dozen. After midnight Ferrari never appeared on the leader board again: the Parkes/Scarfiotti P3 had crashed,

Bandini's and Guichet's had overheated. Of 14 Ferrari starters only a pair of 275GTBs made it to the finish. But Ford had problems too, and from having the first six places at half distance they lost cars steadily as the race went on. And it was Porsche who picked up the crumbs, not Ferrari – to take fourth, fifth, sixth and seventh with the 2-litre six-cylinder Carreras, which were the most reliable squad in the race.

1966 had been a special year, a turning point in the character of Le Mans which had been coming since Ford first looked to the race. There had been serious team efforts before, from Bentley, Alfa Romeo, Mercedes, Jaguar, Cunningham and Ferrari among many others, but the Ford-Ferrari battle had taken the investment, organisation and machinery to new heights. Speeds on the Mulsanne had passed

200mph, lap averages had topped 140mph, race distance had gone beyond 3000 miles, mid-engined cars were now de rigueur for overall honours. More than anything there was a new atmosphere of big bucks professionalism about a race which only a few years before still had an unmistakably sociable feel, even among the front runners. To an extent that atmosphere never totally disappeared, but more than ever Le Mans was becoming big business. Having discovered how to win, Ford would make a habit of it for the rest of the decade.

Eric Broadley, having severed his connections with Ford, returned to Le Mans in 1967 with a Lola prototype, the stunning-looking T70 coupé with 5-litre Aston Martin V8 power. Ford's other GT40 progenitor, John Wyer, had teamed up with John Willment to create JW Automotive, and JW had created a special 5-litre, narrow cockpit version of the GT40, the Mirage. Those were sponsored by Gulf Oil and introduced the company's famous pale blue and orange colour scheme. But neither Lola nor Mirage would last long, and Le Mans 1967 would have a familiar look. Previewing the race, *Autocar* said, 'Although the entry list for Le Mans is a lengthy one, embracing many capacity classes, the real issue is outright victory. This is likely to resolve into a battle between Ferrari and Ford, with Chaparral as a likely outsider'. They had it almost right, except that the ultimate showdown was between Ford's 'teams within the team', with Ferrari around only fortuitously to pick up the pieces.

'If there's one thing I admire it is the way the organisers of Le Mans hammer home their determination to maintain their own particular style of competition, come what may.'

Jackie Ickx,
after his first win.

The organisers were looking nervously at the speeds of the modern generation of big bangers, but hadn't changed the rules yet, so this was another contest of muscle versus sophistication – Ford versus Ferrari, with Chaparral combining elements of both.

The two Chaparral 2Fs had composite chassis and semi-automatic transmissions, plus all-alloy 7-litre Chevy V8s and even cleverer aerodynamics, including a huge, high wing. That acted directly on the rear suspension and was driver adjustable. Running it almost flat on the straights maximised speed; tilting it in corners increased downforce and grip, and in echoes of the Mercedes 300SLR more than a decade earlier it gave a degree of air-braking. In the hands of Phil Hill and Mike Spence the 2F was quick enough to challenge the latest 7-litre Fords for pole, but just missed out to the Shelby car driven by Bruce McLaren and Mark Donohue. That was a special lap by McLaren in an ill-handling car stripped of all possible weight, including the inner safety cells of its Goodyear tyres.

Ford's big guns were all-new cars, the angular, narrow-cockpit Mark IV, still with 7-litre V8 power but now in a lighter, stiffer aluminium honeycomb chassis. But while the Ford team was publicly all smiles, the drivers were less than happy with the new Mark IV monsters, which were very unstable at over 200mph and all of which broke their windscreens in first practice. Lloyd Ruby said his car was so bad that a ride around Le Mans in it would wake a dead man; another asked 'what good will it do to get the chassis right if the bloody windshield blows in and cuts your head off?'

The Fords were more user-friendly by race day, but Chaparral reliability never did match the 2F's speed. The slower car (Johnson and Jennings) was never on the pace and went out early with electrical problems. The quick one, after a dreadful start, was really quick, carved its way back to the leading group, lost a long time with transmission problems and finally retired on Sunday morning. That removed the only real threat to the Fords, because although the Scarfiotti/Parkes and Mairesse/Beurlys Ferraris had rarely been out of the top group they had never really threatened the massively fast Fords. Or so it seemed, until the Mark IVs, dominating the race since they had overhauled the fast-starting

Above: Ford's massive effort finally rewarded, as Bruce McLaren and Chris Amon's GT40 leads home its sister cars in 1966. Ford intended this to be a staged dead-heat, but the organisers had other ideas. **Overleaf:** the follow-up, Dan Gurney and A.J. Foyt win with the Ford MkIV in 1967. **Left:** Backing the big MkIVs in 1967 were smaller GT40s in various forms, including JWA's Mirages – in this case the Ickx and Muir car, which broke its engine.

Bucknum and Hawkins Mark II, began to threaten each other and fall by the wayside.

A single incident took three GT40s from the leading pack just before dawn, and half distance. Andretti, having been as high as second, crashed heavily at the Esses. Schlesser and McCluskey in two of the 7-litre Mark IIs were close behind and both crashed – three lost Fords in just moments. Others had mechanical problems, and their own off-track excursions. Ruby hit the sand, McLaren and Donohue had transmission problems. Ferrari had their failures too, losing both the Amon/Vacarrella and Klass/Sutcliffe works cars. But the remaining P4s capitalised on Ford's woes, and when the flag fell Scarfiotti and Parks were second with Mairesse and Beurlys third, a long way behind the victorious Mark IV of Gurney and Foyt but comfortably ahead of the sister car of McLaren and Amon. Porsches finished 5-6-7-8, and with what came next, that was an omen.

In 1968 the rules changed again, quite drastically. To the FIA the ultra-fast unlimited capacity prototypes were an accident waiting to happen, and neither the world championship circus in general, nor Le Mans in particular could live with that possibility. Le Mans itself had changed slightly with the building of the Ford chicanes just before the pits complex, to slow cars on the start-finish straight. Ford had financed it, most probably looking back at Walt Hansgen's unfortunate accident of 1966. For 1968 the capacity limit for prototypes was slashed to only 3 litres, and over the next few races, that changed the face of Le Mans yet again.

Ford probably weren't hugely disappointed as they were likely to retire the big works cars anyway, and the 4.7 and 5-litre GT40 Mark Is now qualified as 'production' sports cars, with a maximum capacity of 5 litres balanced by a slightly heavier minimum weight requirement than the 3-litre prototypes. The GT40s included Wyer's cars – Gulf GT40s, pending the completion of 3-litre versions of the non-homologated Mirage; and although Ford and JW had their differences, so far as the outside world was concerned a Ford was a Ford, and the blue oval was pretty much in a no-lose situation.

They didn't lose in 1968, but it was a slightly unexpected win. Political unrest in France saw the race put back to late September, the furthest it had ever strayed from its traditional mid-summer date, and late enough to mean a rather longer night compensated for by an earlier start, at 3pm instead of the usual 4pm. And it also gave a little longer for the teams to prepare. Not long enough, though, for Ferrari, who had chosen to withdraw from sports car racing and try to regain lost ground with his Grand Prix cars. To date the Prancing Horse has never won Le Mans again, never really challenged seriously even – a sad state of affairs. But in Ferrari's place the 3-litre regulations would bring a whole new generation.

This was also the era of the 3-litre Grand Prix formula. So there would be considerable crossover in engine technology from the likes of Matra, Ferrari and especially Ford with the Cosworth-developed DFV V8, but for the moment their successes were in the future and there were interesting twists to come before the new order. In 1968 the prototype entry included six 2-litre V8 Alfa Tipo 33s, four Renault-Gordini V8-engined Alpines, a single 3-litre Matra with F1-derived V12, and four 3-litre flat-eight air-cooled 908 Porsches. There were also two Howmet gas-turbine cars from the USA, classified as 3-litre prototypes but far from competitive.

The long-tailed, lightweight works Porsches were the quickest cars in the field, fastest in practice, and a dominant 1-2-3-4 in the early stages of the race while the leading Ford languished in tenth behind assorted other prototypes. But Porsche already knew they were unlikely to go the distance, and only one did. As the other early leaders fell out with mechanical and electrical problems, and as several of the other prototypes followed them, the Rodriguez and Bianchi GT40 stole the lead, and held on to it. Several cars played pass-the-parcel with second place, including the Hobbs and Hawkins GT40 until its engine failed, and the Matra of Pescarolo and Servoz-Gavin until it

Above Right: Dan Gurney with champagne at the ready in 1967. **Below:** General Motors' strictly unofficial flirtation with Le Mans was their support for the technically innovative Chaparral, in this case Phil Hill and Mike Spence's 2F – which retired in 1967 when its semi-automatic transmission failed.

was put out by punctures caused by accident debris on the track. When the music stopped at 3pm on Sunday the Stommelen and Neerspach Porsche 908 had clung on to third place, but second went to the slower but more consistent 2.2-litre 907 of Steinmann and Spoerry, while the impressive 2-litre Alas

Above: Ford's 1968 hat-trick winner, the JW GT40 shared by Pedro Rodriguez and Lucien Bianchi. It was the only Ford finisher, an unlikely winner as Porsche began to close in on absolute victory.

took fourth, fifth and sixth. It wasn't the result most people had expected, but for Ford it was a hat-trick, and if it was courtesy of John Wyer, no problem.

1969 was the end of another decade, the end of Ford's winning streak, and the start of another new era – the Porsche 917 age. One of the most remarkable racing cars of all time, the 917 showed exactly how much Porsche wanted to win, and although it would do duty in the world sports car championships everything about it – its aerodynamics, its extreme power – screamed Le Mans. What is most remarkable about the 917 is that it wasn't a prototype. Porsche already had the prototype category well covered with the 3-litre 908s, which now had the reliability as well as the speed to take the world title from Ferrari. They were also probably capable of winning Le Mans, as the Matras and Alpines were still working on race-winning pace and the GT40s had now passed their fifth birthday. There was the threat of the new Ferrari 312P coupé, with its F1-based 3-litre V12, but there was no doubt at all that the mighty 917 would have that covered too. Because when Porsche lined up 25 examples of the 917 in the factory in Stuttgart for the FIA inspectors to approve, they satisfied the latest required figure for homologation as a production model. The twist was that although the 917

The 917 was so much quicker than anything else at the circuit that it was almost laughable.

was a production model, it was near the minimum weight limit, with a 4.5-litre air-cooled flat-12, some 585bhp, a thoroughbred spaceframe chassis bred for racing, and performance which made even the 7-litre prototypes of a couple of years earlier look almost ordinary.

The main reason it didn't win Le Mans in 1969 was that it was barely ready to race, let alone for 24 hours. It was so much quicker than anything else at the circuit that it was almost laughable. And to add insult to the prototype builders' injury, after much argument about aerodynamic devices, the 917s were allowed to run with movable tail flaps while the real prototypes could only have fixed flaps. But the early 917s needed all the help they could get, because their evil handling characteristics and savage power delivery were no joke for the drivers, and it took a special mix of skill and massive bravery to explore anything like its hair-trigger limits. That was demonstrated only too starkly at the start of the 1969 race. Before lap one was over the first of the 'customer' 917s got away from its owner, John Woolfe, on the infamous White House section, splitting into two, bursting into flames and killing Woolfe instantly. Chris Amon's Ferrari caught fire as it hit one of the disintegrating 917's fuel tanks, and Jabouille's Alpine and Gardner's GT40 were also damaged by the flames.

While this tragedy unfolded, the other 917s stormed into the lead as though they were in a race of their own – and in effect for the next twenty hours or so they were. But they weren't there at the end. With barely four hours to run the first and second-placed 917s, driven by Elford and Attwood, Lins and Kauhsen, suffered transmission failures. Into the lead slipped Jacky Ickx and Jackie Oliver, in the JW Gulf GT40 – the same car that had won in 1968. It duly crossed the line for its own second and Ford's fourth successive win, just metres ahead of the Porsche 908 of Hermann and Larrousse in the closest genuine finish yet seen at Le Mans. Hobbs and Hailwood completed a great day for JW with third place, and 3-litre Matras were fourth, fifth and seventh. Their day would come, too, but for now the awesome potential of the 917 was only too obvious.

Above: the long-tail 917 of Vic Elford and Dickie Attwood in 1969. It set the fastest lap and led but retired three hours from the end. **Left:** the end of a tradition. The 1969 race saw the last dash across the track at the start.
Right: Mario Andretti, a Ford man in 1967, with Lucien Bianchi in the Holman and Moody Ford MkIV. He crashed after brake problems during the night.

THE OUTER LIMITS
THE 1970s

The demise of the big Fords, Ferraris, Maseratis and Chaparrals in the late 1960s may have looked like the end for the Le Mans heavy metal, but not to Porsche. When they unveiled the 917 at the Geneva Show in March 1969, as a customer car costing 140,000Dm, there wasn't much doubt about their ultimate target.

Their Le Mans record was already impressive. Today, no marque has had more entries, no marque has won more times. That single 1951 entry for French Porsche dealers Veuillet and Mouche brought Porsche's first class win. By 1970 they had racked up almost 120 entries, and more than fifty finishers, scoring thirty class wins, four Index of Performance wins, an Index of Thermal Efficiency, a Biennial Cup, and success in every category from GTs to sports cars to prototypes. In nineteen visits Porsche drivers had only gone home empty-handed once, in 1959 when all six Porsches failed to finish. To date their best overall results had been second and third in 1968 and second in 1969, with the 907 and 908. In 1969 they had lost out in the closest finish yet seen at Le Mans. But in 1970 Porsche looked to crown twenty years of effort with outright victory.

The 917 shocked the FIA, but they had left the loophole. A call for only 25 cars might have sounded a lot to a rule-writer in Paris; to Porsche (who had already built similar numbers of pure racers like the 907 and 908) it was just another logical, if massively expensive, progression. So the 917 revealed their ambitions, and in 1970 they arrived with the biggest armada yet seen at Le Mans.

They brought 24 cars, including seven 917s in various guises – plus a supporting cast of 907s, 908s, 910s, eleven 911s, and a six-cylinder 914. One 908, driven by Linge and Williams, was equipped as a camera car for Solar Productions' film *Le Mans*, starring Steve McQueen and shot around this year's race. Three short-tailed 917s, two 4.9s and a 4.5, in pale blue and orange Gulf colours, were entered by John Wyer on behalf of the factory. Porsche had been impressed by the way the JW Automotive team (led by Wyer, David Yorke and John Horsman) had beaten them in 1969 with the outdated GT40. Porsche team manager Rico Steinmann had approached Wyer with a proposal that JW should run Porsche's official racing effort, and having discussed the offer with his Gulf Oil sponsors, Wyer agreed terms.

Ferry Porsche made it clear they would support JW to the full, but not without limits, both financial and technical, as racing was tying up a disproportionately large part of Porsche's resources. Wyer told Gulf he believed the introduction of the 917 spelled the end of an era, and as he could no longer see the prospect of beating Porsche, they should join them. At Le Mans, after much testing, he stamped his authority by rejecting the factory's favoured long-tail body (which he described as having 'the aerodynamics of a grand piano with the lid open') for his own 'low-drag' version of the short-tail 917 – having calculated that the 'John Wyer tail' more than made up for a 14mph Mulsanne speed deficit with better handling.

The works also supplied a 4.5 long-tail to Martini Racing, plus a 4.9 long-tail and 4.5 short-tail to Porsche Salzburg (in effect a second factory team, run by Louise Piech, daughter of Ferdinand Porsche, sister of Ferry, mother of Ferdinand Piech – prime mover behind the 917 programme).

The final 917 for the 1970 effort was a short-tailed 4.5 for David Piper and Gijs van Lennep. Ferry Porsche was to flag the race away. This was Porsche's show ...

> 'It was a bloodbath, that picture. It was the most dangerous thing I'd ever done and I'm lucky I'm still alive.'
> *Steve McQueen on filming* Le Mans, 1970

Previous Spread: actor Paul Newman, second in 1979. **Right:** actor Steve McQueen, filming in 1970. **Left:** the real thing in 1970, Hermann and Attwood's race-winning Porsche 917, coming into Tertre Rouge.

163

Le Mans was more than just another film about motor racing. For Steve McQueen, the driving force behind it, it was an opportunity first to get even closer to the sport he loved, and second to promote it to a wider audience.

It had its story of romance, relationships and political in-fighting, of course, and it had its spectacular staged accidents, but the true star of the film was the race itself, and the atmosphere that McQueen recognised as unique.

A huge amount of real action footage was shot during the 1970 race, where Solar Productions even ran a camera car during the race proper – the same Porsche 908 McQueen had earlier driven to second place at Sebring with Peter Revson. It was driven by Herbert Linge and Jonathan Williams, both top flight racing drivers in their own right. McQueen would dearly have loved to have done the race himself, but not surprisingly was forbidden from doing so by the insurance company, and unlike his friend Paul Newman he never did race at Le Mans.

The rest of the movie was shot around the circuit before and after the race, in wet conditions and dry, with as many real cars as the production company could lay their hands on plus a large fleet of skilfully crafted lookalikes. And as well as the Porsche 908 camera car they had a GT40 with the top chopped off and a cameraman perched in the passenger side. The film employed more than forty real racing drivers in its production, many of them Le Mans regulars, several of them Le Mans winners. One of the drivers, Englishman David Piper, lost his right leg when he crashed his Porsche during filming. Thirty years later though, he is still racing, and in 2001 he took an emotional win in the historic event before the main race, in the Ferrari LM he has owned since the 1960s.

As a piece of motor racing history, the film is superb; as a technical achievement it was a masterpiece. It was even fairly successful commercially, but the plot really was very thin and the reviews were a disaster, which hurt McQueen badly.

Previous Spread: The 917 of Jo Siffert and Brian Redman, filmed during the 1970 race and driven by Steve McQueen in the movie *Le Mans*.
Above: First start of the 1970s, and a new procedure, with drivers belted into their cars, waiting to start their engines and join battle.
Above Right: French rally champion Marie Claude Beaumont with her Corvette, one of just three front-engined cars in 1971. She was the first woman to race at Le Mans since the early 1950s, but went out with engine failure at half distance.
Below Right: the Ferrari of Americans Sam Posey and Ronnie Bucknum, which finished fourth in 1970.

Of the supporting players, the most important were the 3-litre Matra and Alfa Romeo prototypes (Matra having changed its mind about facing the bigger cars with its more conventional prototypes) and the big but dated Lola T70 Chevrolet. But in reality this was a straight fight – and opposite Porsche was Ferrari.

Like Porsche, Ferrari had taken advantage of the unlimited capacity, specified production rules. With Fiat's support, they had built the requisite 25 examples of their 917 challenger, the formidable 5-litre V12 512S. It faced the latest 4.9-litre 600bhp versions of the air-cooled flat-12 Porsche with around 575bhp. Ferrari entered eleven 512s – so more than a third of the grid were either 917s or 512s. In qualifying, the long-tailed 512s were faster on the Mulsanne than all but Elford's super-quick long-tail 917, and Vaccarella's 512 split the Porsches – by tenths of a second. The line-up was Porsche, Ferrari, Porsche, Ferrari, Porsche, Ferrari.

The race was mainly wet, often wild, occasionally dull. Seven finishers from 51 starters was the worst score in Le Mans history. But Porsche's all-out blitz paid off. They started from pole (at more than 150mph average), took a 1-2-3 victory, established a new outright lap record while the track was briefly dry, won every capacity class, plus Sports, GT and Prototype categories, the Index of Performance and Index of Thermal Efficiency. It was a unique clean sweep which also clinched the World Championship of Makes.

Safety was a concern again. There were miles of new barriers and a new-look start. The cars lined up in echelon along the pit lane but instead of running across the track and leaping into them, drivers were belted in, ready to start their engines when the flag fell. In 1969 Jacky Ickx had made his own protest at the traditional start by walking slowly to his car and conspicuously fastening his belts before he followed the field away. Ironically, not only did he win but driving home after the race, in a 911, he survived a major road accident because he was again wearing belts – something not all drivers would have been doing in the late 1960s.

The pattern was set early when two of the works 512s were eliminated by an accident (yet again at the White House), and all three Matras had engine problems by quarter distance. That left the 917s in command. At four hours, long after Vaccarella's 512 had gone with a broken engine, they held the first five places: Siffert and Redman, Elford and Ahrens, van Lennep and Piper, Attwood and Hermann, Larrousse and Kauhsen, with Ickx and Schetty's 512 sixth. Already, that was the sole surviving works Ferrari; when it crashed in the wet (killing a marshal) the Ferrari challenge was done.

Porsche had problems too, and the Rodriguez and Kinnunen JW car, having been as high as second, was out before four hours. None of the JW 917s finished. Hailwood and Hobbs' crashed, long-time leaders Siffert and Redman's failed shortly before half distance. Wyer had just suggested to Dr Piech and his mother that the JW and Salzburg teams would achieve more by not racing each other. Soon after, Siffert, in a comfortable lead, came up to pass two slower cars in front of the grandstands, made a flourish of the move, missed a gear and destroyed the engine. Piper and van Lennep's private entry lasted into the eleventh hour, Elford and Ahrens were sidelined by 17 hours, but the two 917 survivors kept plugging away.

Hermann and Attwood, slowest 917 in practice and slow in the opening stages, took the lead after eleven hours and stayed there – a great result for Hermann in particular after his agonisingly near miss of 1969. Martini's Larrousse and Kauhsen were second, almost five laps down after a race which had been more exciting for Porsche than for the sodden crowd. Third overall, first prototype, first 3-litre, first on Index of Performance was Martini's Lins and Marko 908 spyder. Pushing Bucknum and Posey's 512 down to fourth, that only rubbed in Porsche's superiority.

After the 1970 race, the Automobile Club de l'Ouest published some fascinating statistics. Three hundred separate commercial concessions, mostly bars, cafés and fairground attractions. Trade takings of more than 6.5 million francs, admission and advertising revenue of more than 7 million francs – which barely covered running costs. 300,000 spectators, around half of them actually paying to get in! A further 40,000 pass holders, from officials, to policemen, doctors, firemen, journalists, guests and trades people. 450 journalists, more than 250 photographers, the race broadcast live by satellite to America and televised across Europe.

There were 337 acres of car parks, 100 acres of spectator enclosures, 11,000 seats, 25 acres of funfair. The average age of spectators was 26, half were younger than 23, fewer than a quarter were female. During the race the circuit used as much electricity as a town of 80,000 people, the Le Mans telephone exchange handled two and a half million international calls, the airfield around a hundred aircraft. Between five and ten per cent of the crowd were 'foreigners', mostly British, Swiss and

Belgian. Around twenty miles of roll-film were exposed during the race; ten tons of extra meat left the Le Mans stockyards; beer, wine and cider sales were up by as much as ninety per cent on a normal weekend.

But the age of giants was ending. By 1971 teams knew the 5-litre monsters would be superseded by a return to a 3-litre formula in 1972. Still, the not-so-old guard had a sting in its tail. 1971 was, and remains, the fastest Le Mans ever, thanks to the combination of the super-quick 917s, the fastest form of the modern circuit, good weather and a hard-fought race. Although Ferrari's non-factory

Above: 1971 and another new starting procedure – first try-out for the rolling start which is still used today. Larrrouse and Elford's 917 leads away, followed by Rodriguez and Oliver's long-tail JW car. Neither finished.
Below Right: 'The Pig' – the wide-tracked, short-tailed 917 entered by Martini and painted to look like a butcher's chart.

effort was highly serious, the 917 would go out with a flourish, with another 1-2 finish and a catalogue of spectacular records.

Porsche set one record before the flag fell, with 33 of the 49 starters – an extraordinary proportion dominated numerically by 911s but for outright speed by one 4.5 and six 4.9 917s. The small-engined 917, a private entry for Dominique Martin and Gerard Pillon, would survive longer than some of the more fancied 917s, but having been up to fifteenth it succumbed to gearbox problems four hours from the end. JW Gulf again had three cars, a short-tail and two long-tails – very different long-tails from the originals, prepared in Slough, not Stuttgart, and now with JW approval.

Wyer was less happy with internal politics. Porsche Salzburg had disappeared as Wyer had insisted that running what looked like two works teams was compromising both. But other 917s were now run by Martini, and prepared by the works. Porsche Salzburg had in effect become Martini-Porsche. For 1971 they had one long-tail, one short-tail and one experimental car, the 917/20.

Its wide, ugly bodywork was painted pink, marked with various 'cuts' like a butcher's display chart. It was quickly nicknamed 'The Pig'. The short-tailed Martini 917 which went on to win had a magnesium spaceframe and many other experimental parts. John Wyer hadn't been offered access to them, and apparently didn't even know that they existed.

In testing, Oliver lapped the long-tail JW 917 at an average of 155.6mph, nudging 240mph on the Mulsanne while reporting that the car was absolutely stable. Wyer noted that the long-tail 917s topped 200mph four times on each lap – on the Mulsanne, between Mulsanne and Arnage, between Arnage and the White House, and 'incredibly' (his word) between White House and the Ford Chicane.

Ferrari's 1971 counter-attack was the 512M, a

lighter, slippier version of the 512, run by private entrants as Ferrari concentrated on developing 3-litre cars for 1972. There were nine 512Ms, the fastest run by Roger Penske for NART, but they couldn't match the pace of the 917s in practice, and Rodriguez took pole, with the leading NART 512 of Mark Donohue fourth quickest.

For the first time, Le Mans used a rolling start. Even the pace car was a Porsche. The early stages were fast and close, between the 917s and the 512s. But patience triumphed. Rodriguez and Oliver led the first eleven hours, except while Siffert and Bell led during the pit-stop cycle. Both those 917s retired, though, the first during the night, the other on Sunday morning, with transmission and electrical problems. The Pig became dead meat around half distance, in an accident; the Larrousse and Elford Martini-Porsche was already gone, with a cooked engine. The single 3-litre V12 Matra had been quick enough to hang on in the top six (and briefly claw into second) but expired around breakfast time. By half time the Vaccarella and Juncadella Ferrari led, but only lasted another couple of hours before its gearbox broke. Whereupon the short-tail Martini 917 of Marko and van Lennep inherited the lead and motored steadily home.

Their winning 3334.6 miles and average of 138.9mph remain outright records, as does Oliver's fastest lap, at 152.7mph. Attwood and Muller, charging in the late stages, took second in the short-tail JW Gulf 917, again majoring on steady pace after the other JW cars had suffered time-consuming problems. Posey and Adamowicz's NART 512 was third, Craft and Weir's fourth. The formidable 917 had rewarded Porsche's sledgehammer approach.

Above: the winning 917 from 1971, the year when all records were broken before rule changes spelled an end to the age of cars like this. Marko and van Lennep won by being conservative as others dropped out.
Below: debris from the Lola in which Jo Bonnier died after colliding with a slower car and flying over the barriers.
Overleaf: lively celebrations after the finish in 1973.

It was sad that John Wyer, who had done so much to make the 917 work, didn't win with the big Porsche. Wyer wrote in his autobiography *The Certain Sound* that this was a poignant moment: '1971, which saw the end of my own active involvement in motor racing, was also to mark the termination of something far more important. By coincidence, it was the end of an era in sports car racing.'

Le Mans, as ever, rose haughtily above such issues and although the detail inevitably changed again, the appeal remained potent as ever. If anything, there were hopes of a return to more open racing – after the Porsche-Ferrari battles and the megabucks Ford-Ferrari wars before that. One thing was for sure, the 3-litre rules looked likely to give French makes a realistic chance of outright victory again, 22 years after the last French win, by the Rosiers' Talbot in 1950. Matra had become favourites to deliver. Porsche had turned to Can-Am racing, while Ferrari's withdrawal barely two weeks before the race, plus JW's decision to withdraw the not fully developed Gulf-Mirages, made Matra's chances even better.

They hedged their bets with three new MS670s and an older MS660 'back-up' car, each with different body shapes to cover various race-day scenarios, and much endurance testing to ensure they worked. Rules which allowed a manufacturer in effect to build a Formula 1-based sports car suited Matra, with their 3-litre 450bhp V12 F1 engines. Their driver line-up was strong, with Graham Hill and Henri Pescarolo, François Cevert and Howden Ganley, Jean-Pierre Jabouille and David Hobbs, and Jean-Pierre Beltoise and Chris Amon. And unlike their big rivals, they concentrated everything on Le Mans.

When Ford won in 1966 Henry Ford II had waved the starting flag; when Porsche won in 1970 it was Ferry Porsche; for 1972, with French hopes so high, the *Tricolore* was dropped by Georges Pompidou, Président de la République Française. Before the start he had paid tribute to the Automobile Club de l'Ouest, and the Club (since 1952 under the presidency of Jean-Marie Lelievre) indeed continued to make huge efforts at Le Mans. This year there were more big changes to the circuit. While retaining its road race character, Le Mans had long outgrown its public road origins. The stretch by the White House in particular was ludicrously dangerous for modern cars like the long-tail 917s, which could approach it at almost 200mph. So the road section from Arnage to the pits was finally bypassed, with a new 3km stretch of dedicated race track, including a further corner into the recently added Ford chicane, to slow the cars considerably before the start-finish area.

This section reportedly cost the ACO some £600,000, partly from the club, partly from regional government. It was supposed to be followed within a couple of years by even bigger changes, creating a purpose-built straight parallel to the public-road Mulsanne and ending in a new Mulsanne corner. Starting just after Tertre Rouge, it would reduce the total length of the Mulsanne stretch from 3.5 to 2.8 miles, while leaving the length of the straight virtually unchanged. From Mulsanne the track would be rerouted towards Indianapolis, again slowing the cars from those worrying 200mph approaches.

The further changes never happened. The 1972 alterations added about 170 metres to the lap, while the combination of slower corners and less powerful cars put more than thirty seconds on the fastest averages compared with 1971's record-breaking times.

Matra made hay. The toughest opposition came from Alfa Romeo, but their 3-litre cars weren't fast enough, all struggling with transmission problems. The other main opposition was from Lola, and a new British challenger, the Cosworth-engined Duckhams-Ford. That was based on a Brabham BT33 F1 car raced the previous year by Alain de Cadenet, who would share the sports car with Chris Craft. It held a cautious sixth place for many hours until a minor accident with barely two hours to go dropped it to eleventh.

Below: Graham Hill and the bearded Henri Pescarolo after winning for Matra in 1972. By 1999 Pescarolo had competed in 33 Le Mans, more than any other driver, before giving up driving to manage his own team, Pescarolo Sport. By that time he had also won the race four times, following up this win with further victories in 1973, 1974 and 1984 – two more for Matra, the last with the Ludwig Porsche 956.

The race was marred by the death of Jo Bonnier, president of the Grand Prix Drivers' Association and long-time crusader for circuit safety. He had just had announced his retirement from GP racing. Around 8.30 on Sunday morning his Lola (painted to look like a Swiss cheese) collided with a Ferrari Daytona while overtaking near Indianapolis and flew over the barriers into the trees.

The two DFV engined Lola T280 spyders had been quickest of all on the Mulsanne, and both Bonnier (fastest of the Lola drivers in practice) and de Fierlant in the other T280 had led, briefly running first and second before assorted minor problems. Bonnier set fastest lap for the new circuit early on, and his co-driver van Lennep raised that to a new record, at 134.5mph. But the de Fierlant/Larrousse/Bagration car (Le Mans now permitted three drivers to a car) had retired even before Bonnier's accident when de Fierlant went off during a shower and couldn't get the car moving again.

With the Lolas gone it was Matra's race, but not without a

Above: the distinctive helmet reveals Graham Hill at the wheel of the Matra-Simca which he and Henri Pescarolo took to a popular win in 1972 – the first win for a French manufacturer since the Rosiers won for Talbot in 1950. The 3-litre Matra was one of the most successful of a generation of early 1970s sports cars which were closely related to the contemporary 3-litre Grand Prix machinery. Hill was the only driver ever to win Le Mans, the Grand Prix world championship and the Indy 500.

few scares. Beltoise, having led, lasted just two laps before his engine broke, and Jabouille and Hobbs lost many laps with fuel problems. The Lolas had their moment of glory, then Matra re-established themselves and by halfway were back to 1-2-3, or 1-2 almost within reach of the finish as the Jabouille and Hobbs car stopped on the circuit with a broken gearbox. The finishing order was Hill and Pescarolo, Cevert and Ganley. President Pompidou was as pleased as every other French fan. A Porsche 908 entered by Reinhold Joest and driven by Joest, Weber and Casoni snatched an unexpected third to keep Porsche's name in the record book. Vaccarella and de Adamich's Alfa limped to fourth, just ahead of five GT Ferrari Daytonas, but the celebrations were more muted than usual.

The Matra win (and the possibility of another) were just what the organisers needed to bring a large, patriotic crowd for 1973, the fiftieth anniversary of the first Le Mans. The parade of previous winners included Matra, but Matra themselves were looking forwards, not back. They had joined the 3-litre title chase, and before Le Mans, Ferrari, Matra and Porsche had two wins each, while Mirage had scored one. The Ferraris, Matras and Mirages all had strong F1 connections, but as *Motor* noted, the shorter races and Le Mans had one big difference. 'The engines that Ferrari use for the shorter sports car races are virtually up to Formula 1 specification. This again underlines the problem with the current Group 5 prototype regulations which allow what are effectively two-seat Grand Prix cars – and Grand Prix cars are not required to race for 24 hours.'

Nevertheless, Ferrari, having pulled out in 1972 claiming worries about reliability, tested 'endurance' versions of this year's flat-12s and at the last minute announced their return. Alfa, on the other hand, withdrew at an equally late stage because their new engine was untried over 24 hours, so they would only be represented by one privately entered T33. The key battle would be Matra versus Ferrari, three extensively revised MS670Bs plus one of the earlier MS670s, versus three works 312PBs. Porsche (with three 908s and two 2.8 Carrera RSRs, running extreme 'prototype' specifications) would be a threat, even against F1-based opposition. And there were outsiders, as Ligier returned with three

'"The Le Mans 24 Hours, the most popular race in the world!" There's a contradiction for you that seems to sum the whole thing up. Le Mans! The race that drivers enjoy least but the one they most wish to win.'

Henri Pescarolo, four times winner, speaking in the 1970s.

Maserati-engined cars while others had the Le Mans equivalent of F1 'kit cars' – the Cosworth engined squad comprising two cars from Gulf-Mirage, two from Lola, and the latest version of the one-off Duckhams-de Cadenet.

It became a great race between two makes and six main cars, each leading at the end of various hours. Ferrari attacked early, sending Merzario and Pace off at what was clearly intended to be Matra-breaking pace, to lead for two hours until fuel problems forced a lengthy pit-stop. The Matras of Beltoise and Cevert and Depailler and Wollek (in the older MS670) then swapped the lead until the first had tyre problems and the second engine failure. That gave the Reutemann and Schenken Ferrari five hours of glory, backed by team-mates Redman and Ickx, chased by the Pescarolo and Larrousse Matra – and for a long time by the steady and decently quick Alfa, driven by 'Pam', Facetti and Zeccoli. The Hailwood/Watson/Schuppan Mirage had been as high as third too, before it crashed just after one-third distance. But once the Alfa slowed on Sunday morning the race was all Ferrari and Matra.

Nearing half distance the leading Ferrari's engine broke, leaving Ickx and Redman fighting off Pescarolo and Larrousse at the front while the Beltoise/Cevert Matra crashed. Behind them the other surviving Ferraris and Matras scrapped with each other against a rash of lesser problems, and the Muller and van Lennep 'Silhouette' 911 Carrera stalked them from not far behind.

Now came the kind of drama that makes Le Mans so fascinating. On Sunday morning Pescarolo and Larrousse snatched the lead back as Ickx and Redman were delayed by a broken exhaust, then the Matra lost most of its lead with brake problems. The Ferrari closed to within seconds but fell back with a fuel leak; the Matra's starter motor jammed in the pits. By midday it was anybody's race. Ferrari turned the screw, risking everything to win. But the Matra (still lapping very quickly) didn't crack, the Ferrari did. Just before 2.30, with only ninety minutes to go, Ickx came in with a broken engine. The Pescarolo/Larrousse Matra was left comfortably clear of the Merzario/Pace and Jaussaud/Jabouille Ferraris and the Muller/van Lennep Carrera. A Ferrari Daytona won the hard-fought GT category from Porsche and Corvette, and just one BMW 3.0 CSL outlasted Ford's Capris in the Touring category – which to many people was far closer to what Le Mans originally stood for, fifty years ago, than the new breed of purpose-built racers. But while the minor categories added spice, those days were long gone.

In 1974 Matra completed a popular hat-trick, untroubled by either Ferrari or Alfa works cars, as both decided they couldn't be ready in time. Or perhaps that they had more to lose than to gain against the proven Matras and ever-improving Cosworth-powered brigade, led by John Wyer's two Gulf-Fords, the renamed de Cadenet-Ford and a Lola-Ford. The biggest threats of all, and the Le Mans shape of the future, were the further developed 911-based Porsche prototypes, with turbocharged 2.1-litre flat-six power and increasingly extreme coupé bodywork covering massive wheels and tyres.

It wasn't a great race, except for Matra, who led from start to finish, and won in spite of big problems for three of their four cars. Beltoise and Jarier, and Wollek, Jaussaud and Dolhem had engine failures. An older model won. It was that kind of race. The de Cadenet briefly reached third before thumping the barriers opposite the pits when its suspension broke. The JW Gulf-Ford GR7 spyders were closest to the Matras on pace (and probably on organisation), but Derek Bell and Mike Hailwood, and Vern Schuppan and Reine Wissell had driveshaft problems virtually from the start – terminally for the

second pair, and time-consuming enough for Bell and Hailwood to lose any chance of winning.

They finished fourth, behind Jabouille and Migault's third-placed Matra (which had struggled with overheating), van Lennep and Muller's ever-improving turbocharged Porsche coupé, and the winning Matra of Pescarolo and Larrousse – Pescarolo adding a personal hat-trick to Matra's. Even that was touch and go; the leader lost lots of time on Sunday morning with electrical and gearbox problems, but was so far ahead by then that it never surrendered the lead, even when the Porsche was reduced to only two gears. A Daytona led the GTs home again as all the Porsches crumbled, and a BMW CSL was again sole survivor of a poorly supported 'touring' category.

It was dull enough for *Autosport* to question where Le Mans was heading. 'Le Mans – "La Plus Grande Course du Monde", the biggest race in the world, is what the advertisements said for miles around the famous French circuit of la Sarthe. Perhaps it was true in past years, but this year, no matter how many roundabouts were erected, police put on special duty, publicity girls publicising, bands playing, airships flying and bright lights flashing, nothing could make up for the cars themselves; or rather the lack of them.

' ... long before the start ..., it felt like a big cheat. With so much fuss that surrounds this classic race one could not help but feel cheated by the miserable 49-car field, of which half were not as good as those you can see wandering around the paddock of a Brands Hatch club race any Sunday afternoon.'

Above: Pescarolo working very hard, powering through the gloom and using every inch of road in the Matra which he shared with Gerard Larrousse in 1974, for his third win in a row and the second in a row shared with his fellow Frenchman. It was Larrousse's last Le Mans win, but Pescarolo added a fourth exactly ten years later, for Porsche in 1984.

The Matra garage at Le Mans in the run-up to the 1973 race, which brought the team's second win of an early 1970s hat-trick with the 3-litre, Grand Prix-based prototype sports cars.

The motor car side of Matra, building both road cars and racing cars, began in the mid-1960s and grew out of France's massive Matra aerospace and armaments company, which had been founded just before World War II by Marcel Chassagny. In 1964 Matra took over the René Bonnet sports car company – long-time Le Mans stalwarts closely associated with André Deutsch to produce the DB, or Deutsch Bonnet. With their new car division, Matra Sports, Matra turned the René Bonnet Djet into the Matra Djet and became a sports car manufacturer under their own name. A few years later Matra introduced their own car, the Ford-powered M530 coupé, and around the same time the company's engineering director Jean-Luc Lagardère was given the job of creating a racing and rallying programme.

Matra's competition debut came with two entries in the F3 race at the 1965 Monaco GP, and right from the start the design and build qualities of the beautifully engineered cars clearly owed a lot to Matra's aerospace expertise. They also started to be successful, and in 1967 Matra moved into F2, and for the next three years they dominated the formula. At the beginning of 1967 they reached an agreement with the French state petrol company, Elf, to start a four-year partnership aimed at creating an all-French Grand Prix challenger – backed by the government in preference to Renault because Matra already had an engine design operation under former Simca man Georges Martin.

The object of the exercise, as well as to promote French prestige, was also intended to promote a planned high-profile production sports car from Matra, but that never really happened. Ironically, Matra's only Grand Prix world championship came in 1969, not for the works but with the Ford V8-powered Matras run by Ken Tyrrell for Jackie Stewart.

Their own V12 F1 engines, though, were wonderful to listen to, highly capable, occasional Grand Prix winners, and a perfect basis for a Le Mans-type sports car in the early 1970s – now under the Matra-Simca banner following a new partnership with the Simca part of the Chrysler France group.

After their three successive Le Mans wins, in 1972, 1973 and 1974, Matra's brand of naturally-aspirated Grand Prix-based car was overhauled by the turbo generation, and Matra left Le Mans behind. In 1978 Matra became part of the giant Peugeot-dominated PSA group, then in 1983 they moved to Renault, where they developed and built the original Espace – a little while after Renault had had their own flirtation with Le Mans.

Right: Famous colours on the winning car in 1975. The powder blue and orange of Gulf Oil, already a Le Mans legend on John Wyer's earlier entries, the Ford GT40s and Porsche 917s, were up front again on the Gulf-Ford shared by the most prolific pair of winners in Le Mans history – Derek Bell (in the car here) and Jacky Ickx.

1975 was, if anything, worse. Le Mans reflected the state of the sports car championship in a period when it should have capitalised on the 3-litre Grand Prix connection but instead lost the likes of Ferrari, Alfa and Matra and became a contest between Porsche and the Cosworth-engined mongrels – good cars, but not manufacturer cars. Out on a limb, Le Mans 1975 contrived another controversial fuel-consumption formula, and lost its championship status. The fuel limit was a well-intentioned acknowledgment of world fuel crises, but didn't do much for the spectacle, as the front runners had to sacrifice hard-won power just to reach the economy target.

It was Gulf-Ford's year, a well-deserved win, but a rather soft victory by Le Mans standards. Gulf ignored the championship to chuck everything at Le Mans – showing that in spite of its debased status this was still the one worth winning. They led the prototype entry with two Cosworth V8-powered GR8 spyders, for Ickx and Bell, and Schuppan and Jaussaud. They were quickest in practice and led all the way – although again the winning team looked capable of snatching defeat from the jaws of victory.

Schuppan and Jaussaud's GR8 led from the start but gave way to Ickx and Bell at the first pit stops. And although the leaders had exhaust problems near the end they held on, while their team-mates stuttered around between second and third places with electrical problems (made worse by wet weather), unfortunately holding third, not second, when the music stopped at four o'clock Sunday.

Splitting the Gulfs was one of a pair of Cosworth-powered, Gitanes-liveried Ligiers which, driven by Lafosse and Chasseuil, closed to within a lap of the winners during their late problems. The other Ligier, driven by three-times winner Pescarolo with François Migualt, might have been well-placed too but was eliminated after it hit the rear bodywork of one of the Lola-Cosworths which had fallen off the car. That Lola was driven by Alain de Cadenet and Chris Craft, and with new rear body it went on to finish fifteenth.

The fuel-economy formula had been part of a plan ... not so much a sop to political correctness as a carrot to the big manufacturers.

There hadn't been many to see it – Le Mans was losing spectators too. The crowd in 1974 had been half the size it was in 1967. In 1975 it was reckoned to be smaller still, maybe only 80,000. This couldn't be allowed to go on, and Le Mans' counter-attack was to try to tempt the big names back with more big changes.

The fuel-economy formula had been part of a plan. According to the Automobile Club de l'Ouest it wasn't so much a sop to political correctness as a carrot to the big manufacturers, who (given the right format) ought to need Le Mans as much as it needed them. The aim was to free the race from the struggling world championships, to remember its roots, with the emphasis on production-based GTs. That, the theory went, would also distance it from Grand Prix racing (which had taken almost all interest away from the sports car championships) and to give major manufacturers a new stage.

1976 was presented as a second 'interim' year, aiming for full rehabilitation for Le Mans in the public eye by 1977. Letting in both prototypes (or in Le Mans terms Group 6 cars) and GTs (the other category catered for by the restructured championships), plus more or less anything else that fitted an FIA-recognised category, was a smart move. While the championship sank lower, Le Mans began to blossom. 1976 had an intriguing look. For the first time since 1949, there was no Ferrari, and only a handful of top 'prototype' front runners – but with a fine mixture strung out behind, including various GT classes, and a small scouting party from America in the IMSA and NASCAR categories, eligible for the first time.

In the 1970s BMW started a series of 'art cars', by famous contemporary artists. **Top:** Roy Lichtenstein works on a model of the 1977 Group 5 320i, the real version of which was driven by Hervé Poulain and Marcel Mignot. **Above:** the same drivers, and Manfred Winkelhock, drove this M1 in 1979, actually painted by Andy Warhol, not just copied from the artist's model as with most of the series.

The production-based Group 5 GTs (heavier than the prototypes, with a minimum production requirement, but no capacity limit) were well represented, and possible outright winners if the prototypes failed. The fastest of those were no longer 3-litre Grand Prix clones but smaller-engined turbocharged cars, taking advantage of the 'equivalency' formula that had existed since superchargers were popular. With mechanical superchargers the 1.4 times equivalency was no longer attractive. But with huge power gains and negligible mechanical losses from exhaust-driven turbocharging, a blown engine of up to 2142cc was a tempting

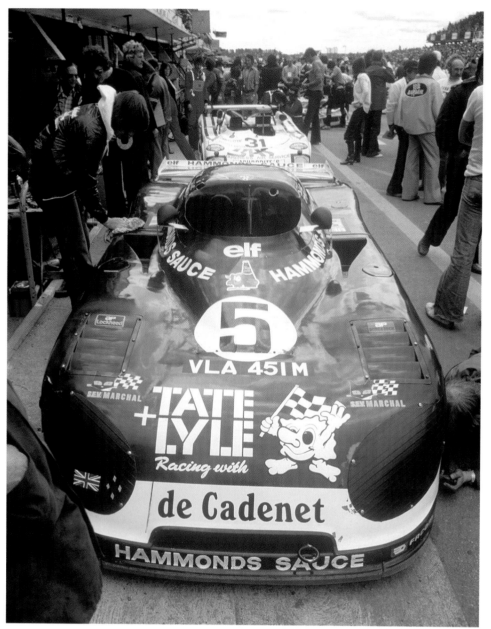

alternative to a non-blown 3-litre. Which brought the latest 3-litre Cosworth-powered machinery, from reborn Mirage, Lola and newcomer Inaltera (a 'GT prototype'), head to head with turbocharged cars from Porsche and Alpine-Renault.

The power and speed of the 500bhp-plus turbo Group 6 prototypes made them clear favourites if they could go the distance. But the 3-litre prototypes and even the top Group 5 GT cars (notably the very strong 911-based Porsche 935s) should be close enough to take advantage of any major glitches. A more than usually exciting possibility and, it transpired, pretty much how it panned out.

The days of multi-car works teams were gone, and although there were 26 Porsches, only two were the turbocharged 936s, in Martini colours, for Ickx and van Lennep, Joest and Barth. They faced just one Alpine Renault A442, driven by Jabouille, Tambay and Dolhem. The Porsches were right on the capacity limit at 2142cc; the Alpine's V6 Renault turbo was 2 litres, but its handling was a match for the 936s, enough to snatch pole – and an early lead, in fierce heat.

It didn't lead for long, before Ickx's Porsche took over, followed by Joest's when the Alpine made an early stop for fuel. When it had electrical problems, then overheating, the Alpine slowed, fought back to third behind the two Porsches, then retired during the night with engine failure. After holding second place well past

half way, the Joest Porsche's transmission broke and the leading Mirage, of Lafosse and Migault, inherited second. The leading Porsche had problems too, on Sunday afternoon, with a broken exhaust. But as its lead had been more than 120 miles at one point, that wasn't enough to deny it victory – Ickx's third, van Lennep's second, and the first ever for a turbocharged car at Le Mans.

The race was marred by the death of André Haller in a fiery crash with his Datsun 260Z on the Mulsanne, but otherwise it was a more successful Le Mans than of late. Craft and de Cadenet, parboiled and with burned feet, brought the Lola home third, a superb result for the shoestring team. Manager Keith Greene told *Autosport*, 'the biggest compliment we had came from the Porsche team manager, who came up and congratulated us ... but then he knows that his lot spent three million Deutschmarks doing Le Mans, and we were only ten laps back, having spent three million farthings ...'

The Stommelen and Schurti Porsche 935 won Group 5, in fourth, ahead of the second Mirage; the Cosworth-engined Inaltera driven by Beltoise and Pescarolo also won its class. One disappointment was the failure of the Americans. The IMSA GTs were too slow (except in a straight line) and too unreliable; the NASCAR cars were far too slow and too unreliable. But by being there they had given Le Mans something back that had been missing for a while.

Le Mans was back on the A-list, as the size and variety of the 1977 entry showed. The rules were essentially as before, with room for just about anything with four wheels, two seats and full bodywork. Porsche had no fewer than 25 of the 55 starters, two 936s in Group 6, the rest a vast army of 911 clones in Groups 4 and 5 and IMSA. Ferrari returned in the shape of a single NART-entered 512BB Boxer, Aston Martin returned for the first time in more than a dozen years with a privately-entered 5.3 V8 amongst the GTs. There were BMW 3.0CSLs in Group 5, a couple of BMW 320s in the Group 2 IMSA ranks (although the Americans were mainly conspicuous by their absence, with no NASCAR cars returning), Inaltera were back, and hordes of more obscure GT cars and 2-litre sports cars all had something worth racing for in the broad new class structure.

For overall honours there would only be two makes in it, yet Le Mans 1977 proved to be a classic. A triumph for speed-with-strategy versus pure speed, the vast experience of Porsche over fast-learning Alpine Renault. Above all it was a stunning victory, his fourth, for Jacky Ickx – who had a very busy weekend indeed.

It was an incredible race. The Jabouille/Bell Alpine-Renault started from pole and took the lead, hounded by Stommelen and Schurti in the 935 that Porsche hoped would push the Alpines to self-destruct. But the 935 failed first, leaving the Ickx and Pescarolo 936 in second place, tailed by its 936 team-mate. Porsche meat in a French sandwich, with two other works Renaults chasing hard.

In the fourth hour the first 936, Ickx's car, shared with Henri Pescarolo, expired with a broken engine. Alpines were 1-2-3, the surviving 936 way down the field after fuel pump problems, in 41st place. Ickx's time had come. The rules allowed not only three drivers to one car but also for a driver to transfer from one car to another. In an inspired move Porsche put Ickx into the surviving 936, with Jurgen Barth and Hurley Haywood. As the team's fastest driver, Ickx's role was simple: drive all out, win or bust.

He started with a three-hour stint, regularly taking ten seconds a lap from the leaders, clawing up the order. But even Ickx couldn't have made it back to the front without the Renaults having problems. And they all did. By midnight he had dragged the 936 back to fourth, ahead of the Renault-engined Mirages, behind the Alpines. Then one by one the Alpines hit trouble; Jaussaud and Tambay a blown engine; Jabouille and Bell engine failure at nine on Sunday morning; Depailler and Lafitte, already delayed by gearbox problems, finally stopped by another broken engine with around four hours to run.

They were well behind, but as things transpired, had they kept running, victory would have been there for the taking. With less than two hours left the now-leading

Above: in 1971, on the pre-chicane circuit and with the hugely powerful JW-run, Gulf-liveried 917, Jackie Oliver set the all-time Le Mans lap record, at 152.7mph – an effort to frighten any Grand Prix car. **Below:** by 1977, when Ickx, Barth and Haywood won in the Porsche 936, both the cars and the circuit had been tamed – if only slightly.

Porsche limped smokily to the pits with a holed piston. It clearly couldn't go much further, but the rules said if it was running at the end, and if its last two lap times were within a percentage of each other, it would be a finisher. Porsche knew its lead was so great that if it finished, even with two slow laps, it would win. So the 936 stayed put until the clock edged towards four o'clock, the second-placed Mirage of Schuppan and Jarier steadily reducing its lead. With barely ten minutes to go it motored gently out of the pits, on five cylinders and a prayer ...

Barth was driving, Ickx had used all his permitted time. Barth did all he had to. Pouring smoke, he crossed the line for the first time at a couple of minutes to four; when he came past again at a few minutes after four they had won. Amazingly they still had eleven laps in hand. The Mirage was second, Ballot-Lena and Gregg third in a 935, Rondeau and Ragnoti fourth for Inaltera, holding off Craft and de Cadenet's fast-closing Lola. Ickx thought it was his best win so far. 'I liked the idea of being 41st and trying to catch up. Not for winning but just so that you can go as hard as possible.'

Renault approached 1978 focused – as focused in the late 1970s as Ford had been in the 1960s, seeing winning at Le Mans as second only to winning in F1. As competitions director Gerard Larrousse said, 'the sales battle in Europe has never been so tough. The commercial fall-out of a race like this is far more obvious than the technical spin-offs, for a victory at Le Mans is one that cannot be doubted ... Le Mans, more than any other race, adds up to the moment of truth for a car builder and his machinery.'

Government backed, highly organised and technically strong, Renault were now as tough a rival as

Below: After Matra's hat-trick run of the early 1970s, French interest in Le Mans was high, and in 1978 Renault took a fine win with their 2-litre turbo car, driven by their Grand Prix regulars, Didier Pironi and Jean-Pierre Jaussaud. They immediately announced that they wouldn't be coming back.

Porsche had ever faced, and both teams brought further developed, more powerful descendants of their 1977 cars. The Renaults (two A442s, a 442B and a 2.1 turbo 443) were still nominally spyders but had extended perspex 'bubble' windscreens. They almost amounted to a coupé roof, added a bit to maximum speed, but even with air slots in front they gave the drivers an oven to work in. Alongside three 936s, Porsche brought an extreme development of the 935 – long-tailed, massively powerful, and nicknamed Moby Dick, because with its mostly white Martini livery people thought it looked like a great white whale.

The fastest 936 in qualifying trim lapped as fast as the mighty 917s at their peak. But while Porsche put on the high-boost show, Renault set up for the long haul. This time they would do it, but again it would be a hell of a script. Nobody had a really clean race, every front runner had problems, and there was a touch of déja vù.

Two 936s, Ickx and Pescarolo, Haywood and Gregg, immediately had engine problems and lost time. Two Renaults, Jabouille and Depailler, Pironi and Jaussaud, led the 936 of Wollek and Barth. Mirage-Renault were best of the rest but off the pace even before electrical problems claimed them after three hours, to the advantage of Moby Dick, driven by Stommelen and Schurti. After four hours Renault were 1-2-3, Jarier and Bell tagging on behind the leaders, with Wollek and Barth's 936 fourth. Then at around 9pm Porsche contrived another game of musical cars, maximising the spectacular speed of Jacky Ickx as an additional driver. This time he joined Barth and Wollek, and by 1.30 in the morning they were in second place.

This year's late-race dramas would be Renault's. Jabouille and Depailler holed a piston, Frequelin, Ragnotti and Dolhem were slowed by gearbox problems. But there would be no second fairy tale for Porsche, as Pironi and Jaussaud's Renault was healthy enough and quick enough to stay ahead of the Ickx 936 – suffering gearbox problems of its own. France's biggest car maker finally won the world's biggest sports car race, while Frequelin, Ragnotti and Dolhem added fourth behind the Haywood, Gregg and Joest Porsche.

One more page of history was to be written before the 1970s ended, again by Porsche. It wasn't that the German cars finished 1-2-3-4; Jaguar had done that in 1957. It wasn't the high placing for a movie megastar, although Paul Newman did finish a deserved second, partnering Dick Barbour and Rolf Stommelen in an IMSA 935. Nor was it a dozen Porsche finishers from twenty starters – they

Government-backed, highly organised and technically strong, Renault were now as tough a rival as Porsche had ever faced.

Right: When Porsche turned the 911 into a Group 5 car in the mid-1970s, they started an era where the 911 clones were always the car most likely to upset the more exotic Group 6 ranks. In 1979 it happened, when Klaus Ludwig and the Whittington brothers won – the only Le Mans win for a genuinely rear-engined, as opposed to mid-engined, car.

Right: The star of the 1979 race, in almost every respect. Ludwig and the Whittington brothers won, but all eyes were on one of the drivers who came second, Paul Newman, film star and genuinely talented racing driver. He shared with team owner Dick Barbour and very quick German Grand Prix and sports car driver Rolf Stommelen, and they all played their parts. If luck had panned out slightly differently in the closing hour they might even have won. As it was, this was still one for the record books.

had better percentages than that. 1979 was the only Le Mans ever won by a rear-engined car, as opposed to a mid-engined (or front-engined) one.

The history maker was Kremer Racing's twin-turbo K3, the most extreme version yet of the 911-based Group 5 935, which either out-ran or out-survived the unusually thin 3-litre Group 6 opposition. Renault stayed away, and so would Porsche have done save for a deal with Essex Petroleum to run two updated 936s for Ickx and Redman, Wollek and Haywood. Renault no longer powered the Mirages, either, as the team (supported by Ford France) had reverted to Cosworths in the latest Ford M10s. DFVs also powered the rest of the big Group 6 ranks, from Rondeau (née Inaltera), Lola (led by de Cadenet, and Francois Migault) and a pair of British-run Anglo-Japanese Dome Zero coupés, as Japan's interest in Le Mans grew.

With a huge horsepower deficit to the 600bhp 936s (and the even more powerful, if heavier, 935s, the best of which had fully 750bhp) the DFV brigade should have been eclipsed. But things are rarely that simple at Le Mans. The Domes had engine problems within an hour of the two o'clock start (there was a European Parliament election on Sunday), the Lolas struggled throughout. Only Rondeau had much to show at the end, with grittily earned fifth and tenth places.

Mirage had their moment. A gearbox change for Schuppan and Jaussaud's M10 led to it being disqualified as behind schedule, but the Essex 936s, while leading for the first couple of hours, also had problems. So for a few glorious hours Derek Bell and Mike Hailwood's Mirage led, just able to resist the 935s where it couldn't touch the 936s. At least until the exhaust broke just after quarter distance, to leave the M10 (with Schuppan joining Bell and Hailwood) playing a vain game of catch-up, hampered by endless problems.

As a wet Sunday unfolded, the 935s adopted the role many had long predicted. The Kremer, Gelo and Barbour cars disputed the top places through the middle stages. Kremer and Barbour had the edge. Their cars took the first three places, while Müller, Pallavicini and Vanoli's 934 beat the next of the Group 4 entries (another 934) by thirty laps to steal a remarkable fourth. First were Klaus Ludwig and the American Whittington brothers, Bill and Don. In the last four hours they had engine problems, but their nearest rival, Barbour's IMSA car, had problems too, including losing 23 minutes with a jammed wheel nut – about six laps at race pace.

They finished seven laps behind, barely rolling – Rolf Stommelen, team owner Dick Barbour and Paul Newman doing for real what Steve McQueen had only filmed. They might have won. Newman, make no mistake, was a fine driver, and through his entire career (as driver and team owner) has made an absolute distinction between Paul Newman actor and Paul Newman racer. Today, inevitably, second place almost stole the show from the winners. As *Motor* reported, 'They had won Le Mans – the Whittingtons in only their second year of car racing – and for a moment the glory was theirs.

'But while Bill deliriously unpicked his victory garland and scattered carnations to the crowd below, back came the cries. "New-man, New-man", they echoed, and after a decent interval for the winners to be feted, the second garlanding ceremony was initiated, with the second place trio of drivers. Leading them out onto the balcony he came. The silver hair, the blue eyes, the slight figure could be no greater contrast than the one with that of his burly entrant, Dick Barbour. Paul Newman, 53-year-old Hollywood star, had done what he came to do: race at Le Mans and finish honourably. He acknowledged the help of Barbour and Stommelen, the "rock" of their driving strength, and modestly embraced them. He permitted himself a quiet smile, possibly the first of the weekend. This will always be remembered as the year of Paul Newman ...'

ALL-POWERFUL PORSCHE
THE 1980s

The 1970s had been a decade of mixed fortunes for Le Mans, starting with one movie star making a film of the race and ending with another one coming perilously close to winning it. In between Steve McQueen's fictional Le Mans and Paul Newman's real one, from the peaks of the fastest cars ever seen at the circuit to the troughs of sports car racing almost self-destructing, Le Mans proved that it could rise above the rest. Le Mans remained special, and it motored into the 1980s with yet another highly emotional script.

This time the hero was Jean Rondeau, not a film star but a local boy who went one better than Newman, and won. Not only won, but uniquely won in a car bearing his own name as constructor, the Rondeau M379B, shared with Jean-Pierre Jaussaud.

Jean Rondeau was born in Le Mans and still lived there. He was an interior decorator, an engineer, and a driver. He had watched his first Le Mans race as a three-year-old, carried by his parents. In 1980 he was 34 years old, and having his fifth tilt at the race. He had been the man behind the Cosworth-engined Inalteras. They were built by Rondeau, in Le Mans, and financed by France's biggest wallpaper manufacturer, Inaltera (the interior decorating connection at work, no doubt). Since 1976 the Inalteras had progressed from GTP to Group 6, and when Inaltera withdrew their sponsorship in 1978 the cars became Rondeaus – as they actually always had been.

Jean Rondeau knew he was no more than a good average driver, but his cars built a reputation for being quick, beautifully prepared and reliable. That attracted big-name drivers from Inaltera's first

Above: one of Le Mans' most popular and emotional wins. For several years the cars built by Le Mans engineer Jean Rondeau in Le Mans had enjoyed a fine record for reliability and speed, even against the big budget works teams. In 1980, Rondeau topped the dream by winning the race – and sharing the winning car himself, with Jean-Pierre Jaussaud. Here the Rondeau of Pescarolo and rally star Jean Ragnotti, which also led but soon retired, chases the eventual winner.

appearance – when the list included past winners Pescarolo and Beltoise, as well as future winners Jaussaud and Rondeau himself. Pescarolo and Beltoise finished eighth on that 1976 debut, Rondeau 21st. In 1977, sharing with Jean Ragnotti, Jean Rondeau was fourth. With Beltoise and Holbert finishing 13th and Lella Lombardi and Christine Beckers 11th, Inaltera had a 100 per cent record.

In 1978 the entry included both an Inaltera coupé and the first car to carry Rondeau's own name – the M378, for Rondeau, Darniche and Jaran. The Inaltera was 13th, and Rondeau in the Rondeau finished ninth, winning the GTP class. By 1979 it was all Rondeau, with three new coupés, two of them in Group 6, the other in GTP. This time Ragnotti and Darniche were fifth (and class winners), Pescarolo and Beltoise tenth. Rondeau and Jaran's GTP retired with accident damage – amazingly, the first retirement for any of Rondeau's Le Mans cars.

So Rondeau arrived at Le Mans in 1980 with two cars (for himself and Jaussaud, Pescarolo and Ragnotti), a growing reputation, and unusually weak opposition. There were no major 3-litre Group 6 factory entries. The single Group 6 Porsche was based on a 936 but politically labelled 908/3. It was entered by Reinhold Joest, sharing with Jacky Ickx. The remaining Group 6 opposition was a handful of Cosworth-powered cars, from Ibec, de Cadenet, ACR (a Lola clone), and Dome. The organisers managed to exclude the Ibec and one of the de Cadenets before the start, in an extremely rancorous row about who had met the complicated new qualifying-time criteria laid out in the latest revised rules. Oddly, no French cars suffered.

The biggest entry was IMSA, followed by the 2-litre Group 6 and potentially front-running Group 5 ranks. Group 5 was dominated by 935s, the Kremer 935 K3s, plus two 1.4 turbocharged mid-engined Lancia Beta Monte Carlo coupés – interesting, but not nearly fast enough to challenge for outright honours. Porsche concentrated its works effort on three front-engined, water-cooled 924 Carrera Turbos in GTP (where Rondeau had another car for Martin, Martin and Spice). This reflected another part of the new rules, which (without being an economy formula) emphasised fuel efficiency by restricting fuel flow at refuelling stops. That made the stops longer, making it advantageous to make fewer of them. The 924s did pretty well to finish sixth, 12th and 13th. There was also the option of running 'alternative' fuels, but only Porsche took it on, with a Group 4 911SC on a petrol/alcohol mixture. It finished a creditable 16th.

The single Group 6 Porsche was fast but troubled. Fuel pump and gearbox problems meant that although it led, on and off, for almost half the race, Ickx and Joest were only second when it counted, at 4 o'clock on Sunday. Several other cars led the mainly wet race – the Wollek/Kelleners 935, the Fitzpatrick, Redman and Barbour 935 K3, and the Rondeau of Pescarolo and Ragnotti (which had been on pole).

When it counted, it was the other Group 6 Rondeau ahead, helped, depending on how you looked at it, by an error of judgement by the Porsche crew or a little help from the gods for Rondeau. Near the end, Rondeau and Jaussaud were in front. Ickx was reeling them in fast. It rained, heavily. Ickx pitted for wet tyres, the Rondeau didn't. The rain stopped, the Rondeau won. It was the first win for a

'Jean Rondeau had accomplished an incredible feat: building and driving his own car to win his hometown race – which just happens to be the biggest sports car race in the world.'

Road & Track

Above Right: local hero Jean Rondeau, the only man ever to win Le Mans in a car of his own making. **Right:** Rondeau and Jaussaud enjoy the spoils of victory after their hugely popular 1980 win.

Right: Jacky Ickx, the man who has won Le Mans more times than any other, with six victories to his name between 1969 and 1982. **Above:** Le Mans' greatest partnership, the 1981 winning Porsche 936 shared by Ickx and Derek Bell, the second most successful driver ever in the 24 Hours, with five wins to his credit – three of them shared with his great friend Ickx.

non-turbo car since 1975, and a fantastically popular one. A driver from Le Mans in a car built in Le Mans, bearing his own name. To complete a spectacular local day, the GTP Rondeau was third, and class winner. The only sad side to the story came some years later, when Jean Rondeau was killed in a freak road accident on a railway crossing. Today his name is honoured at Le Mans in the Jean Rondeau Prize, awarded to a young driver who displays both speed and talent.

For most of the rest of the 1980s, the speed and talent were all working in Porsche's favour, and of the next nine races, seven went Porsche's way – seven in a row, from 1981 to 1987.

The first two went to the same driver pairing, the two most successful drivers in Le Mans history, Jacky Ickx and Derek Bell. Ickx had supposedly retired, but kept coming back, to win his fifth race in 1981, then his sixth. Bell had already won for Gulf-Mirage in 1975, with Ickx. After three wins with his greatest partner Bell won two more, in 1986 and 1987, both for Porsche, taking his tally to five.

Another change of Le Mans rules, removing the 3-litre (or 2.14 forced induction) limit from Group 6 prototypes, brought Porsche back with the forerunner of what would become the new generation sports racing car of choice, Group C. And Group C brought sports car racing back to life, not only with challenging technical rules but also with an unusually long period of stability. Group C didn't impose capacity or weight limits. It allowed closed cars only, but their performance was defined principally by a fuel allowance related to the duration of the race, and a maximum fuel tank capacity. A fuel formula without other restrictions, interestingly, was what John Wyer had long favoured, especially in the bad old days when sports car racing was struggling. At Le Mans the fuel allowance was 2600 litres for the

'Jacky Ickx is quiet, reflective in the Porsche garage, the 1981 Le Mans race before him. He has the best car, he has all the experience he needs. But so much can go wrong ...'

Autocar

race, with a maximum tank size of 100 litres. The new, official gravity fuel rigs had a maximum flow of 50 litres per minute, implying minimum fuelling stop times of two minutes – several times longer than with the old pressure-fed rigs, and obviously playing a proportionally greater part in race strategy. But otherwise, all the designers had to do was to make best use of the fuel allowed, by carefully juggling power with consumption.

The options were relatively large naturally-aspirated engines, or smaller turbocharged ones. For the moment the Ford runners were stuck with the former, but Ford were already looking at the latter. The turbo route was a clear favourite, because turbo engines were both more powerful and more fuel efficient, power for power.

Porsche were already masters of the technology. The 936/81 combined the still effective 936 chassis with a 'low-boost' endurance version of their abandoned Indycar engine – 2.65 litres, turbocharged, air- and water-cooled. It could give 650bhp without breaking sweat, and was so unstressed in this form that it should have all the reliability it would ever need. As would a new four-speed gearbox, derived from the hugely more powerful Can-Am cars, finally addressing one of the '3-litre' 936's weaker links.

In 1981 Porsche brought two cars. The Mass/Schuppan/Haywood car had minor problems from the start, nipped back onto its sister's tail for most of the first half, then fell back with clutch problems, eventually to finish 13th. The Ickx and Bell car (sponsored by Jules, a men's fragrance from Yves St Laurent) had no problems at all. It took pole with ominous ease, stopping the Mulsanne speed checks at 236mph. Porsche let the Joest '908' and the Whittington brothers' 935 K3 swap the lead with the 936 during the first few hours's pit-stop juggling, but from the fourth hour the Ickx/Bell car led as it pleased, to an easy win. It made no stops other than for routine refuelling and maintenance, never so much as had the engine cover raised, and its longest pit call lasted less than four minutes.

Two Rondeaus, driven by Haran, Schlesser and Streiff, and Spice and Migault, took second and third, through impressive reliability more than through real speed – at least compared with the flying Porsche. But there was no celebrating for Rondeau. Another of their cars, possibly after damaging either a tyre or suspension in a minor off-road moment, turned head-on into the Mulsanne barriers at high speed, killing its popular French driver Jean-Louis Lafosse instantly and badly injuring several marshals. Another marshal had died in a separate accident on the Mulsanne, where Thierry Boutsen was lucky to escape almost unharmed from what remained of his WM Peugeot.

Winner Derek Bell collapsed on the podium after the sheer effort of driving the 936 in broiling heat while having to be ultra-careful with backmarkers who were perhaps 50mph or more slower on the Mulsanne. Later he said sadly, 'I have mixed feelings about winning this race. The truth is that it's the long, long straight that's responsible. But if Le Mans was just a matter of going round and round, that would make it just another circuit.'

Nevertheless, he would be back, and back with Ickx and Porsche, for the 50th running of the Vingt-quatre Heures du Mans.

By 1982 Porsche had a real Group C car, the beautiful 956 coupé, with the latest version of the

Left: the Ickx and Bell 956 en route to victory in 1982, Ickx's sixth and Bell's third. **Right:** the winners on the podium, the tiredness showing on Bell's face, exhausted, even though the later stages of the race were something of a cruise.

2.65-litre twin-turbo flat-six, and the latest thinking in underbody aerodynamics, using the airflow to create downforce with the whole car rather than just add-on wings. If you listened to the hype they would be fighting head-to-head with the old enemy Ford, who powered 16 of the cars in the very encouraging 28-car Group C entry, but the reality was different.

Ford now offered larger capacity endurance-biased DFL versions of the 3-litre DFV F1 V8, but vibrational problems could still break both engines and cars. In 1981 only two of the 16 Ford-powered cars finished. Ford's own C100s kept pace for a few hours then succumbed to clutch failure and engine failure. The Lolas, Saubers, Mirage, Dome, Grid, Cougar, de Cadenet, even the Rondeaus all had problems. And even in their biggest, 3.9-litre form the DFLs were way behind the turbo Porsches (and other turbo users) on power and consumption. The 956, anyway, was simply a seminal car, the starting point for a whole generation of Group C cars.

Only Joest's '936C' put up any real fight, staying in the top three overnight while the third works 956 struggled with a catalogue of problems, including losing a door to the high-speed airstream (a recurring Le Mans problem for coupés on the Mulsanne). By the time the 936C blew its engine on Sunday afternoon, the 956s, having recovered from their own minor problems (without ever going faster than they absolutely needed to), were first, second and third, and lined up to take the finish in formation. Ickx and Bell were the winners again, followed by Mass and Schuppan, and Haywood and Holbert, with a little help from reserve driver Barth. According to Bell, fuel strategy had been the big concern, as he told *Autosport*: 'Had anyone been able to push us hard we would have been in all sorts of problems. We had probably enough fuel for another 20 minutes at the end, which is not too great a margin – it would only have been five laps. If we had had to go any faster, or made one fewer fuel stop during the race we would have been in plenty of trouble.

'As it was we were lapping, I would say, 10 seconds off the 956's ultimate pace in the interest of fuel economy, and at times about 15 seconds down towards the end.' But even at that pace, no one could actually push them hard. The next Group C car wasn't a Ford but the overweight Aston-Martin Nimrod of Ray Mallock, Simon Phillips and Mike Salmon. The Hobbs/Fitzpatrick 935 was fourth and IMSA/GTX winner. Richard Cleare, Tony Dron and Richard Jones won Group 4 with their 934; Jim and Doc Bundy took IMSA GT with their 924 Carrera GTR on BF Goodrich road tyres. Another clean class sweep,

Previous Spread: 1982 and the Lancia Martini of Patrese, Ghinzani and Heyer survives through the darkness, only to retire in the 17th hour with electrical problems. **Above:** the eighth Porsche victory came in 1983, for Al Holbert, Vern Schuppan and Hurley Haywood in the ultrasuccessful 956, one of 21 Porsches to start, and one of 15 to finish, underlining the marque's enormous strength. **Right:** Jaguar back at Le Mans, with Bob Tullius in one of the two Group 44 XJR-5s in 1984.

another convincing year for Stuttgart and, in spite of Porsche's dominance, a convincing year for the new Group C regime.

For Porsche, 1983 was even better. The works team was strong as ever and the 956 had already become a customer car, with top-notch private entries backing up the factory with huge strength in depth. 956s took the first eight places, 1-2 for the factory, the rest (plus tenth) for customers, in a race which on paper offered growing opposition but which in reality again offered little trouble.

Most intriguing weren't the Ford runners but the three-car Lancia team, moving up to Group C with its LC2 coupés. They used a 2.65 turbo V8 which was essentially a Ferrari unit, and with around 640bhp the closest anyone had yet come to ruffling Porsche's feathers. But although the Lancias were fast enough for Alboreto and Fabi to qualify on the front row, they were new and unreliable. Their problems started within the first hour and never went away, leading all three to retire. Ford's short-lived manufacturer effort had fizzled out, apparently along with their interest in producing a Porsche-chasing turbo engine, so Ford hopes reverted to the kit-cars, led again by Rondeau. Their three, all 3.9-powered, all had engine failures, and Rondeau only made the finish with older private cars in 19th and 20th places – a far cry from not so long ago.

They were also the only Ford-powered cars in the top twenty. The one interloper in the Porsche top ten was a 3.5 six-cylinder BMW-powered Sauber driven by Garcia, Naon and Montoya in ninth. There was a BMW-powered URD in 14th and the straightline-speed specialist 3.9 turbocharged Peugeot-engined WM (which made it a point of honour to be fastest on the Mulsanne) in 16th. The EMKA Aston Martin, a fairly compact Group C car, 5.3 Aston V8-powered, designed by the highly respected Len Bailey and privately entered by Michael Cane Racing, overcame suspension problems during the night to finish 17th on what was really a toe-in-the-water run.

With hindsight, perhaps the most interesting of all were the cars in 12th and 18th places, two screaming rotary-engined Mazda 717Cs, proving faster in 'Group C Junior' than many of the bigger cars, and showing again that Japan knew just where Le Mans was on the map.

However you looked at it, 1983 was Porsche's year. They lost the third Rothmans-liveried works car (having resisted entering a fourth) in the 22nd hour, after ignition problems and finally a blown engine stopped what could easily have been a winning run from Mass, Bellof and Barth. The winners were

Holbert, Haywood and Schuppan, chased all the way by Ickx and Bell. Their problems balanced out: the winner had lost a door, lost oil pressure, and finally lost its engine just yards after the finish; the second car (which Ickx started from pole) had hit one of the private 956's on the Mulsanne on the second lap, was delayed by electrical problems out on the circuit on Sunday morning, and with the fuel restrictions could never push quite hard enough to make up, by barely a minute. That was one of the few downsides of the new regulations – a pure win-or-bust charge was no longer likely to be on the cards. Behind them, the privateer 956s poured in: the Andrettis, father and son, Mario and Mike, with Phillipe Alliot for Kremer; Schickentanz, Merl and de Navarez fourth, Edwards, Keegan and Fitzpatrick fifth after struggling to make its fuel allowance last, then the cars sponsored by Marlboro cigarettes, Boss clothing, and Canon cameras. A far cry from 1923.

The past matters to true Le Mans enthusiasts, and one feature of the 1984 race was the return of one of the great names, Jaguar, to start another campaign that would take them right back to the top before the decade was over. For now, the naturally aspirated 6-litre V12 XJR-5 GTP cars entered by Bob Tullius's American team Group 44 were more significant for their publicity value (and ultimately for attracting thousands of new British fans to the circuit) than for their chance of a shock win, but they were further evidence that Le Mans was winning back real manufacturer names.

The top one was still Porsche, already with a 1980s hat-trick, now looking for four in a row – not with the works team, admittedly, but with all its finest privateers. They had a bit of a wake-up call. Pole didn't go to a Porsche: it went to one of the new Martini-sponsored Group C Lancia LC2-84s, and to Bob Wollek, sharing with Allesandro Nannini. There was another LC2 behind him (Mauro Baldi, Paolo Barilla and Hans Heyer), before the fastest Porsche, the 956 of Stefan Johansson, Jean-Louis Schlesser and Mauricio de Narvaez. The third Lancia, for Pierluigi Martini, Beppe Gabiani and Xavier Lapeyre might have been there too, except that it had a big practice accident and after a rebuild qualified only 12th.

If Porsche thought Lancia's practice performance was a fluke, they were wrong. From the unpleasantly hot start the Lancias led, and they apparently had the Porsches on the run. Rule changes, especially a higher minimum weight limit, suited Lancia better than Porsche, and the team were more than usually prepared. Raising a big French cheer, the WM Peugeot eclipsed both of them in the opening lap largely due to its now familiar Mulsanne speed, and came through in the lead. It swapped places a couple of times with Wollek's Lancia, but halfway round the third lap team boss Roger Dorchy outbraked himself into Mulsanne corner and wiped the nose off the car, putting it out of contention even before its gearbox broke on Sunday morning.

The script would now normally see Porsche taking the lead, juggling it between its fastest runners, and reeling off the hours to the finish, but not today. Wollek and the Lancia clung on, and through to the 16th hour they had never been below third on the hourly chart, and for nine of those hours they had led. The second Lancia had recovered from a slow start too, and climbed through eighth, sixth, fifth, fourth, third and eventually second to swap places with its team-mate for a couple of hours as overall leader before falling back with engine and gearbox woes.

'Group 44 Racing's first approach to Le Mans was clinical, in every sense. The personnel were clad in dazzling white and so were the cars, which were *perfectly* prepared … As to the conduct of the team, it was so cautious that even the drivers were bored.'

Autosport

Sadly, the gearbox did for Wollek and Nannini too, and what could so easily have been the win that Wollek never did achieve in 30 attempts turned to a frustrating eighth.

The status quo was soon restored. The Jaguars, driven by Redman, Bundy and Tullius and Watson, Ballot-Lena and Adamowicz had run well, both in the top six, one even leading briefly at the first round of pit-stops for the thirstier turbo cars. But both went out, one following accident damage, the other with gearbox failure. The second-string runners, still mainly looking for miracles from Cosworth, never had much of a look in. Both Nimrod Astons were involved in an accident on the Mulsanne which killed a marshal.

So the Porsches dropped into formation. But while it was obviously going to be another Porsche win, it would have been a brave punter who would have bet on which one, as the private teams, in the absence of the works, started one hell of a scrap. The last eight hours continued to be a race to remember. All the leading cars' minor problems had more or less balanced each other out. Pescarolo and Ludwig in the NewMan-sponsored Joest 956 had recovered from 30th position in the first hour to lead by the 17th, waging a huge battle with John Paul Jr, Jean Rondeau and Preston Henn in Henn's 956, and Jones, Schuppan and Jarier in the leading Kremer 956. The latter fell away to sixth with a late misfire and Pescarolo won his fourth Le Mans, with Ludwig. Henn was second; Hobbs, Streiff and van der Merwe came through for third. Lancia had some consolation in fastest lap, by Wollek, at 145.2mph. Porsche had four in a row, and just as important had equalled Ferrari's record tally of nine.

Below: 1984 was an emotional year on the podium as Henri Pescarolo scored his fourth win, exactly ten years after taking his third, and at his 18th attempt at the race. In the years between those two victories he had only finished the race twice, in 1976 and 1979, in eighth and tenth places.

Number five was tougher again, as tighter fuel limits narrowed the gap from Jaguar and Lancia in particular to the Porsches. There was another intriguing unknown too as, thirty years on from their darkest hour, the Mercedes name came back to Le Mans, on the twin-turbo 5-litre V8 of the new Sauber C8. This

year it was a 'private' partnership, but that wouldn't last long. For now, though, it was business as usual, with another Porsche 1-2-3-4-5.

It may have seemed strange to Le Mans drivers from earlier years, but qualifying at the very front was now an important part of the weekend. Not so much because of the tactical advantage, because even in a modern Le Mans 24 hours is a long time to make up a few yards, but because the early leaders could rely on so much television coverage. So, whether for tactics or for glory, the front-runners, Porsche and Lancia, treated qualifying almost as a race before the race – throwing ragged-edge engine tuning, minimal fuel loads and maximum attack driving at pole. Porsche, back with the works cars, won it, with an outstanding lap from the fast lap specialist, Hans Stuck. He finally beat Jacky Ickx's record. He did it as dusk fell, at an average of 155mph. And as he told *Autosport*, it was important to himself as well as to Porsche. 'Of course I am happy with myself. To beat Jacky's time around Le Mans is a difficult thing to do because he has been here so many times and he knows it all so well, every inch, every bump, every ripple. So I think this is an achievement and I am very satisfied even though I know I could have gone quicker.'

Porsche also put Ickx and Mass in the second car on the front of the grid, frustrating Lancia quite badly. They could manage only third for Wollek and Nannini, and sixth for Pescarolo, Baldi and Cesario, while Porsche had the rest of the top dozen. The Jaguars, struggling to get the most from their normally powerful and efficient V12s, allegedly because of poor 'official' fuel quality, only qualified 16th and 17th, for Tullius, Robinson and Ballot Lena, and Redman, Haywood and Adam. It was a disappointing start to a year when Tullius thought Group 44 Jaguar had a real chance to win.

The Lancias survived to finish sixth and seventh, and that was a fair reflection of their pace compared to the Porsches which overwhelmed them. The Tullius Jaguar finished 13th, a whopping 50 laps down on the winners, after electrical problems, engine problems, and worries about fuel consumption, having changed so much of the tuning to suit the questionable Le Mans fuel. The Redman XJR was out well before half distance with transmission failure.

Biggest surprise of the race, perhaps, was the Aston-powered Emka, which outqualified the Jaguars, led briefly thanks to some early pit-stop juggling, and survived with only minor problems to be first non-Porsche, non-Lancia home, in a creditable 11th overall, driven by Tiff Needell, Nick Faure and Steve O'Rourke.

'Klaus Ludwig and Paolo Barilla drove a perfect Le Mans last weekend, their NewMan Joest Racing Porsche 956B the class of the field.

The very same car that won this race last year ...'

Autosport

After the first couple of hours, only one car was going to win, and it was a Porsche, but not a factory one. It was the same car that won last year, Joest's NewMan 956B, and it had a near faultless run, in the lead from the third hour. It kept its pace partly because it was the most fuel-efficient of the 956s, even if no-one really knew why. It was driven by Klaus Ludwig, Paolo Barilla and for a few laps by 'John Winter' (a pseudonym). It was challenged early on by the Canon 956 of Jonathan Palmer and James Weaver, which fell back with electrical problems, then recovered its earlier second place and stayed there. Top factory car was Stuck and Bell in fourth, and Ickx and Mass just managed to make the top ten, but whether it was the factory's car or Joest's, the winner's log said Porsche again.

Oddly enough, this wasn't doing Le Mans any harm as a spectator attraction. Far from it. The game now was to beat the German cars fair and square. And one marque with major ambitions to be first to do that was Jaguar – now back with an even more serious effort. This time, backed by the works, run by Tom Walkinshaw's TWR, sponsored by Silk Cut cigarettes, and a winner at the often revealing Le Mans curtain-raiser race at Silverstone just a

Above: The Ickx and Mass 962C in 1985, as the works team returned after its spat with the organisers over fuel regulations. Ickx and Mass finished tenth while the best of the works cars was Stuck and Bell's 962 in third, behind the winning Joest NewMan 956 and the Canon 956 of Jonathan Palmer, James Weaver and Richard Lloyd.

couple of weeks before, it really did seem to have a chance. *Motor*'s preview stuck its neck out with the bold heading 'Jaguar's three-car team looks set to triumph at Le Mans on Sunday'. They didn't, of course, and to be fair the company hadn't been quite so upbeat about the possibility as the British press, but they gave it a very decent shot. And their presence swelled the crowd with a new influx of British fans.

Their new XJR-6s were state-of-the-art Group C cars, lighter and smaller than the already useful Group 44 cars, with carbon-fibre monocoques, low-drag aerodynamics, and happy to take advantage of an increase in this year's Le Mans fuel allowance. Not so happy, though, as to risk the team's thirstier four-valve engines as opposed to proven two-valve versions of their powerful V12s. They had been fastest at the Le Mans test day, albeit only facing one of Porsche's works cars, and well below Porsche's existing record – although that reflected a new road layout at Mulsanne corner, to bypass a new roundabout where the original escape road used to start!

It was cigarette wars between the works Porsches and Jaguars – Rothmans versus Silk Cut – and in qualifying two of the works 962Cs put the Jaguars back in their place, the Porsches hogging the front row, Mass was fastest (sharing with Wollek and Schuppan), then Stuck (with Bell and Al Holbert). There were two more private Porsches before the first Jaguars, the XJR-6s of Cheever, Warwick and Schlesser, with the Redman/Haywood/Heyer car just behind it. Quickest of the Saubers was back on the fifth row, and the first Nissan entry (for which many held unfeasibly high hopes) was disappointingly far adrift on the twelfth row.

Ludwig, in the Joest 962 looking for its third win, took the early initiative. But as the cars reached the reshaped Mulsanne corner for the first time, a blanket could have covered the first four Porsches and the two leading Jaguars. Group C was turning sports car racing into a spectacle again. But there would be a familiar ending. The Jaguars harried the Porsches for the first four hours, but had lost Heyer's car on the circuit with fuel problems. Another Jaguar went in the middle of the night with a driveshaft failure, but the Cheever car was holding a reasonably sound second on Sunday morning until an exploding tyre did enough damage to cause its retirement. Which once again left the Porsches.

Or some of them. Mass in one works car spun off on oil during the night, and Jo Gartner's 962 crashed on the Mulsanne, sadly killing the driver, and bringing the pace cars out for more than two hours. By the time the race started again Ludwig's engine had blown up and Joest's hopes of a hat-trick were gone. Once the last Jaguar had retired Bell, Stuck and Holbert reeled off the laps to win – Bell's fourth and his first without Jacky Ickx. As in 1981, Bell's celebration was muted by a fatal accident in the race, but the hordes of Brits, having seen the Jaguars shine but fail, at least had something to cheer.

In 1987 they were back in their thousands to see Jaguar piling on the pressure, but what they saw in the end was another victory for Porsche (their seventh in a row), and another (his fifth) for Bell.

Again, Jaguar arrived as favourites to stop the Porsche run, having beaten them in all four of the season's championship races to date. Last year Sir John Egan, chairman of Jaguar, had dropped the starting flag. This year he confirmed how important Le Mans was to Jaguar. 'The association of the Jaguar name with motor racing is deep-rooted. In fact, we think our racing heritage helped us considerably to survive through our difficult years. During that time we drew heavily on the bank of goodwill we had accumulated through our racing achievements of the '50s. A quarter of a century later, we felt the time has come to make a few more deposits at the bank.'

The popular enthusiasm for Jaguar at Le Mans was massive, and the next few years completely revitalised the whole event, first of all with the simple return of Jaguar, and even more so when the attraction became a head-to-head confrontation between Jaguar and old enemy Mercedes, all set against the might of Porsche and the continuing success of the Group C sports car generation.

There used to be an old adage that it takes three years to win Le Mans, and this was only Silk Cut Jaguar's second. But there was no doubt whatsoever that they were getting closer all the time. This year there was a feeling that they hadn't been beaten, but that they'd failed to win – yet certainly hadn't failed to show what was coming.

'Dusk: always one of the most spectacular aspects of this classic event, speeds virtually undiminished, the bright lights illuminating the road and the trees.'

Autosport

205

Frustratingly, Porsche had done much to support a Jaguar victory, losing two of their three works cars during the first hour. They also lost one Kremer and both Joest cars, and the Jonathan Palmer, Price Cobb, James Weaver car caught fire, but the fact that the works survivor was last year's winning combination of 962C plus Bell, Stuck and Holbert meant Jaguar still had a mountain to climb.

The 7-litre XJR-8LMs showed such promise. As the Porsches fell out (with engine problems, blamed on the same 'standard-issue' fuel that afflicted Group 44 Jaguar) they were first, third and fourth. Only one finished, Cheever/Boesel/Lammers, in fifth place. It was the best yet, but nothing like what it should have been. Win Percy (actually the reserve driver, just doing an odd stint) was lucky to escape unhurt when the XJR-8 shared by Lammers and Watson crashed in the biggest possible way on the Mulsanne after a rear tyre failure at 230mph. The car lost its entire rear bodywork, gearbox and wheels on the first impact, continued for several hundred yards airborne and upside down, then started rolling for several hundred more before it stopped. The second car, the Brundle/Nielsen one which had disputed the lead with the Porsche for so long, went out less dramatically but equally finally, with engine failure, and the survivor fell from second to fifth with a damaged gearbox, then damaged bodywork, then damaged suspension – which kept it there.

Left: in 1987 Hans Stuck, Derek Bell and Al Holbert repeated their 1986 win, and gave Porsche their seventh win in a row, overcoming the growing threat of Jaguar who had beaten them in four 1987 championship races prior to the big one. **Right:** the crowd thins out as darkness falls, but there will always be those who stay the night.

The Bell/Stuck/Haywood Porsche simply kept flying around – helped ironically by the time spent under the pace car, slowing the race after Percy's Jaguar accident, and taking away any lingering worries about eking out fuel for a fight to the finish. There was nobody much left to fight. The Sauber Mercedes were gone after showing early promise, one with broken transmission, the other with broken suspension after yet another high-speed tyre burst. None of the dark-horse Nissan entries made any impression at all, except perhaps for their unexpected lack of speed and reliability, and the Toyotas were quicker, but didn't see the finish. When Bell took the chequered flag, he was 20 laps ahead of the second-placed 962 of Jurgen Lassig, Pierre Yver and Bernard de Dryver. His fifth win had undoubtedly been easier than some of his others.

Jaguar's 31-year absence from the winner's circle ended just after 3 o'clock on Sunday 12 June 1988, to British cheers that would have done any previous British success more than proud. The last Jaguar win had been Flockhart and Bueb's famous victory with their Ecurie Ecosse D-type in 1957. The latest was for the Silk Cut XJR-9, driven by Jan Lammers, Andy Wallace and Johnny Dumfries. They had beaten the old enemy, Mercedes, here represented by Sauber, even before the race began. The German team was withdrawn shortly before the start after one of its cars burst a tyre on the Mulsanne at more than 220mph. Miraculously the driver survived, but the team's faith in its equipment apparently didn't. And Mercedes didn't want its first official entry since 1955 to have any echoes at all.

For Jaguar, Porsche still clouded the issue, looking for their eighth win in a row. But the Jaguar effort, the third in Silk Cut colours, was a serious one too, masterminded by Tom Walkinshaw Racing as the official works team. Like 1957 team boss David Murray, Walkinshaw is a Scot, originally from Prestonpans, not far from Ecurie Ecosse's Edinburgh base. TWR and Jaguar knew they could beat Porsche: they already had, repeatedly, in shorter world championship races. They threw everything at Le Mans in 1988. The logistics make an interesting comparison with the winning Ecosse effort described earlier, and say a lot about how Le Mans had changed, as well as about how the teams had grown.

TWR raced five cars, 7-litre 700bhp V12 XJR-9s: three from their headquarters at Kidlington near Oxford and two from the team's completely self-contained IMSA operation in Indiana. They also brought one complete spare car. The cars travelled in two huge articulated transporters and there were enough spares to rebuild all five cars: three additional truckloads, with a private plane constantly on call between Le Mans and Kidlington in case they were still missing anything. They brought 14 drivers, in a team of 110 people: 75 full-time staff, plus 21 additional volunteers. The European and American teams within the team each had its own director, and each car had its own technical crew and crew chief. There was a doctor, a physiotherapist, a dietician to keep the drivers on top of their game, and specialist signalling and fire crew for the pits. There was a separate catering operation – another 80 or so people to keep the team fed and its guests happy. They also had a ten-seat aeroplane for ferrying

team members, VIP guests and
provisions.

TWR had their own Dunlop
tyre engineer, with a stock of
2500 tyres to call on. Not all to
be used, but to cover all the
options. Two qualifying
compounds, six types of slick, one
full wet compound and
construction. All for five cars, for
qualifying and 24 hours racing.

Even a team like this has
dramas. Scrutineering
traditionally takes place in the
town during the week before the
race, immediately before practice
and qualifying. In 1988 the
Jaguars were the first to be
checked and they had to make
minor bodywork changes, to
shorten the tails slightly and
modify the underbody
aerodynamic 'tunnels'.

The race went off like a
sprint, and continued like one for
24 hours, to set record speeds
and distances for the Group C
generation. It was between the
Jaguars and the Porsches, with
half a dozen cars in contention
for most of the race. Porsche had
the first three places on the grid,
led by a 155mph lap from Hans

Stuck. His works 962C F6 topped 240mph on the Mulsanne, completely resurfaced for this year and
lined with triple-layer barriers, and showed that the new 'Dunlop S' (prompted by the needs of the
French motorcycle Grand Prix) had little effect on overall lap speeds. Stuck led from the start, chased by
Lammers' Jaguar. On the seventh lap Lammers took the lead. Jaguar and Porsche played different
early-race pit-stop strategies, and TWR's one-car-at-a-time approach proved better.

Through the race the lead changed 22 times, between the leading Jaguar and the three factory
Porsches – Bell, Stuck and Ludwig, the Andretti family, Mario, Michael and nephew John, and
Schuppan, Wollek and van der Merwe. Jaguar lost two cars, Porsche lost one. It rained, but the number
2 Jaguar led at 18 of the 24 hour marks, was second for five more and only fell to third once. The lead

was never more than a lap, often less than a minute, often less than half a minute. After 3313 miles there were two minutes 36 seconds in it. Lammers, Dumfries and Wallace had given Jaguar victory. The pace of the race had made it the second fastest Le Mans ever, after the 1971 records on the earlier circuit, and before further changes prompted by the worrying increase in high speed accidents. Bell, Stuck and Ludwig were second, Jelinski, Dickens and Winter third in the Joest 962. The second-place Porsche had had problems near the end but couldn't charge any harder to make up the deficit. At the end it apparently had 1.5 litres of fuel left. *Motor* noted, 'It wasn't until the French played "God Save The Queen" for the third time – and Derek Bell kissed Tom Walkinshaw on both cheeks – that it sank in that Jaguar had finally won Le Mans.'

Above: By the late 1980s, Japanese manufacturers were taking Le Mans seriously, with Mazda, Toyota and Nissan all represented by works-backed cars in 1988. All three got cars to the finish, and Mazda won the IMSA class with all three of their cars finishing. But the Japanese had their problems, too, including engine failures for two of the Nissan R88s.

Left: In 1985 Toyota powered the two 2.1-litre turbocharged Dome 85Cs, but promised more than they delivered, with major stability problems on the Mulsanne. This is the Elgh/Lees/Suzuki car which went out with clutch failure; Satoru, Sekiya and Hoshino finished twelfth.

By 1989, Mercedes had gone slightly longer than Jaguar had without winning – it had been 37 years since the 300SL won on its debut in 1952. Now it was their turn again, as Sauber Mercedes, in traditional Mercedes silver, with the three-pointed star large on their noses, scored one of the most unexpected wins in recent years.

The race was taking on a subtly different look again. There were no works Porsches, but the usual crowd of top-class private entries, again including Joest, Kremer, Richard Lloyd Racing and Repsol Brun, were the next best thing. There was an official Aston Martin team, with pukka carbon-fibre-tub, 6-litre V8 mid-engined AMR-1 Group C cars. And three of the big four Japanese manufacturers (Nissan, Toyota and Mazda) continued to get more and more serious about Le Mans. Nissan, after disappointing earlier showings, had carbon-fibre-chassised R89Cs (actually built by Lola) with twin-turbo 3.5 V8s and supposedly a massive amount of power. The Mazdas with their screaming four-rotor Wankel engines were chasing reliability. The Toyotas (entered on behalf of the factory by the British Team Tom's) were chasing qualifying speed, and first lap glory. They had evolved from the promising Domes and promised even more power – reputedly 1000bhp-plus from their 3.2 twin-turbo V8s in qualifying trim, with the boost turned up to a point where one big lap was your lot.

Above: When Jan Lammers, Johnny Dumfries and Andy Wallace won for Jaguar in 1988 they ended an unmatched run of seven Porsche victories. **Below:** Jaguar's efforts also brought British fans back in force.

To look at the records, it was Mercedes' weekend from practice on, but goodness, did they have to fight for it. They were fastest in first practice, the supposedly anti-Le Mans Jean-Louis Schlesser putting in a massively fast lap before the thunderstorms broke, pushing Neilsen's Jaguar to second, ahead of another Sauber and the first of the menacing, high-boost Toyotas. The Nissans had been fast in a straight line, but nasty to drive. Final qualifying promised to be a race in itself, and it was, between Sauber, Jaguar, Toyota and – no longer dominant – Porsche. Schlesser nailed it for Sauber, with one mighty lap setting an absolute record for this version of the circuit, before it changed again the following year. His average was almost exactly 250kph (155.3mph), with the second Sauber alongside him, the fastest Jaguars on the second row, and Toyota – denied the right to use special cars just for qualifying – well down behind the remaining Jaguars and the quickest Porsches.

The race was a stunning display by the new 'Silver Arrows' and the Jaguars. From the start it was a fascinating confrontation, the two teams desperately close on pace (and that now meant nudging 240mph on the Mulsanne), the Jaguars more driver-friendly, the Sauber Mercedes more brutally powerful – just. The Schlesser and Baldi Sauber took off ahead of the Davy Jones and Jan Lammers Jaguars, the Wollek and Stuck Porsche and the rest.

Jones in the Jaguar led at the end of the first lap, but Lammers was in the pits with a puncture. Few people could have stood the strain of that kind of knife-edge, waiting-for-the-bang race again ... The XJR of Jones, Derek Daly and Jeff Kline was clearly out to break the Mercedes, but Mercedes didn't rise to the bait, and that was where the race began to be won. They dropped back, as the Nielsen/Wallace/Cobb Jaguar, the fast-improving Bailey/Blundell/Donnelly Nissan, and the Wollek/Stuck Porsche powered by. And they waited. Bailey went first, after hitting Nielsen's Jaguar at Mulsanne corner. The Jaguar would get back (for a while), the Nissan wouldn't.

Two Jaguars now down the field, two near the front, including Jones leading, and pulling away from the Mercedes, but hounded by Wollek's Porsche. This was classic Le Mans tortoise and hare racing.

After the first pit stops, the Wollek Porsche led, until Jones stole it back and Mass, Jelinski and Stuck – Mercedes, Porsche, Porsche – slugged it out for second.

The next glitch was Jaguar's, and the leader's, as the Jones/Daly/Kline 'hare' XJR stopped and lost around half an hour limping back to the pits. Again, it wasn't Mercedes who charged into the gap, it

Above: Further spice was added to the end of the 1980s by the return of Mercedes, putting them head to head with Jaguar for the first time since the 1950s. After Jaguar's 1988 win, 1989 was Mercedes' year. The works-backed 5-litre turbocharged Sauber C9/88s finished first, second and fifth, sandwiching one Joest Porsche and one TWR Jaguar. This is the winning car, driven by Jochen Mass, Manuel Reuter and Stanley Dickens. **Overleaf:** Stuck, Holbert and Bell, winners in 1987.

was Porsche, in the guise of Stuck and Wollek, and they stayed there for more than four hours, until they were slowed by mechanical problems. That let a Jaguar, Lammers, Tambay and Gilbert-Scott, back to the front, with Sauber Mercedes apparently still happy to play the waiting game. And it was still working for them. Coming up to breakfast time on Sunday, the Jaguar was in trouble, and slipping back with gearbox problems. So finally, a Mercedes, driven by Acheson, Brancatelli and Baldi, inherited the lead, but even now this see-saw race was far from settled.

A mistake by Baldi and a spin through the Dunlop curves cost just long enough to let team-mates Jochen Mass, Stanley Dickens and Manuel Reuter into the lead, and this time they stayed there, to cruise home with just about five laps to spare over the Baldi car, which had recovered from its minor off but had spent the closing stages of the race stuck in fifth gear. Behind them came previous leaders the Wollek Porsche and the Lammers Jaguar (after a very rapid gearbox change), with the third Mercedes in fifth place – to crown a very convincing and courageously patient performance by an impressive team.

One of the two Aston Martin AMR1s survived to finish eleventh. The Astons carried black stripes on their bodywork, in honour of John Wyer, who had died a few weeks earlier. He would probably have appreciated Mercedes' brave tactical victory, but he might have been disappointed to see Le Mans end another decade without any particularly brave changes in the rules.

A GLOBAL CARNIVAL
THE 1990s AND BEYOND

In 1990, Le Mans changed forever. Late in 1989 the FIA finally turned its concerns over the dangers of the Mulsanne into an ultimatum: slow the cars or lose the circuit's licence. The Automobile Club de l'Ouest argued, but for once couldn't resist. Two chicanes were built into the famous straight, at a stroke changing the dominant feature of the circuit, for better or worse. Better undoubtedly meant lower maximum speeds and the likelihood of fewer major accidents. Worse meant an inevitable change of character, and two more places to have lower speed accidents. On balance, the changes were probably for the good, because the Mulsanne, for all its tradition, had long been a lethal problem.

Because the circuit was too new to be officially recognised, Le Mans lost its world championship status for a second year, and Mercedes cited that as their reason for not returning. Inevitably, too, the changes were met with mixed feelings. The biggest criticism was that the first chicane was very bumpy, giving both drivers and cars a hard time. No-one liked the brake marker boards either, which were originally at 50-metre intervals from 350 metres before the corners. As *Autosport* said, 'at 215mph they flashed past as one giant blur'. They were quickly thinned out to 100-metre intervals after several teams complained.

So the chicanes were another technical challenge, but few denied the potential safety benefits – especially Jonathan Palmer. During first practice his Porsche 962 suffered a rear suspension failure between the two chicanes, and the result was a classic Mulsanne accident. The car struck the barriers on the left, spun and hit again with the rear, then flew across the track to the other barrier, airborne for 100 metres before landing, thankfully right way up, and eventually coming to a stop just before the second chicane. Palmer was badly shaken but essentially uninjured. He had been doing around 200mph when the accident began. A year earlier, pre-chicanes, similar cars had been nudging 240mph. How that would have affected the outcome of the accident is open to conjecture, but not difficult to imagine. Round one to the chicanes?

Of course, they slowed the lap speeds. The 1989 pole time was 3m 15.04s; in 1990 it was 3m 27.02s. And that was a mighty lap by the fastest of seven Nissans entered for this year, with Mark

Previous Spread: one of the greatest ever Le Mans names made its comeback in 2001, and covered itself in glory. The Bentley team's two coupés didn't win, but the surviving car of the pair finished a strong third, driven by Wallace, van der Poele and Leitzinger. **Above:** Jaguar's 1990 win provided the perfect leaving present for outgoing Jaguar boss Sir John Egan, the man who had supported the team's efforts right from the start of the 1980s comeback. **Right:** American Price Cobb shared the win with Dane John Neilsen and Briton Martin Brundle. It was Cobb's fifth Le Mans and, for him, it was third time lucky with the Silk-Cut Jaguars.

Blundell six seconds quicker than the first Porsche. With the boost wound up for this one Banzai lap, the carbon-braked V8 turbo Nissan was reckoned to offer as much as 1100bhp, but not for long ...

Any thoughts that the circuit changes would destroy the race were soon forgotten. *Autosport* wrote, 'Chicanes or not, Le Mans is still a classic event, and this was one of the best'. It was especially good for Jaguar. Before the race, Tom Walkinshaw was upbeat about the four TWR Silk Cut XJR-12s. 'Last year our cars were significantly quicker than anything else out there, but we were unable to keep them running for 24 hours without having problems. We know what those problems were, we know what was causing them and we have addressed those problems. I am fairly confident that we have the strongest combination of cars and drivers in the race; we've got everything we need to win Le Mans this time.'

They did win, and this was a special Le Mans for Jaguar, not only to wipe out the frustration of 1989 but because chairman Sir John Egan, the driving force behind Jaguar's Le Mans efforts, was about to leave the company. First and second places were a perfect leaving present, and Egan was at the circuit again to enjoy it.

It was as tough a race as Jaguar had ever contested here. The Japanese challenge, including three Toyotas and three Mazdas as well as the Nissans, was more serious than ever. The Porsche entry included nineteen 962s plus two Porsche-engined Cougars, split between ten of the finest private teams in the sport – although Joest had lost one pre-race favourite in the Palmer accident.

Nissan had the embarrassment of losing one car on the warm-up lap when Kenny Acheson ran out of brakes and broke the gearbox while trying to stop. On the other hand, they had the satisfaction of seeing Julian Bailey in the pole-sitting R90CK head the field from the start, chased hard by Oscar Larrauri in the Repsol Brun Porsche.

It went virtually to the flag – a race of speed versus attrition. The naturally aspirated Jaguar of Martin Brundle, Alain Ferté and David Leslie stalked the Nissan and Porsche turbo cars. The 962C of Larrauri, Jesus Pareja and team chief Walter Brun regularly traded the lead with the Bailey, Blundell and Gianfranco Brancatelli Nissan. Nissan's hopes took a major blow, though, around 8.30 on Saturday evening when Brancatelli collided with Aguri Suzuki's Toyota, falling way back, before further mechanical problems sidelined it completely. Now the American-entered Nissan driven by Geoff Brabham, Chip Robinson and Derek Daly (and managed by Jacky Ickx) took up the fight, and led on and off during the night.

But around dawn the American Nissan's challenge faded with a leaking fuel tank, as the race began to show its teeth. Over the next few hours Jaguar lost two cars, but its two survivors rolled on, fast and generally untroubled – except by the Brun Porsche. For many hours the 962 split the Jaguars, and looked certain of at least second place, until Pareja stopped on the Mulsanne fifteen minutes short of the finish, with a dead engine, and tears in his eyes. The two Jaguars finished first and second, driven by John Nielsen and Price Cobb, plus a car-hopping Brundle, and by Jan Lammers, Andy Wallace and Franz Konrad. Tiff Needell, David Sears and Anthony Reid climbed steadily to third in their British-entered Alpha Racing Porsche, ahead of Joest's Stuck/Bell/Frank Jelinski 962C.

There were more changes in 1991, as the old pits, built in 1956 after the Levegh disaster, were demolished and a vast new complex erected. Its modern glass frontage hid hospitality units and press offices above 46 impressive new garages. A few decades before, few teams had had factories as clean,

spacious and well equipped as the big new garages. At the same time, the pit lane was widened, the paddock extended, and a five-storey race control built alongside the start line. The old carnival spirit of Le Mans survived though.

After the race *Autosport* reported, 'The complex was inaugurated on Friday night with a spectacular firework display and *son et lumière*. Cars, bikes and karts made their way through the smoke and flares down the pit straight, highlighted by a skid school car, fitted with roman candles, spinning merrily up the track'.

There was more big news. In 1990 Le Mans had opened its first MacDonalds; in 1991 the famous old Hunaudières café was revamped as a Chinese restaurant. In 1990 the all-Japanese Nissan of Hasemi, Hoshino and Suzuki had been fifth, the Toyota of Lees, Sekiya and Ogawa sixth. It was the best Japanese result so far, but was about to be eclipsed, in one of Le Mans' biggest shocks. 1991 was the year of the Mazda, and the year of the rotary engine.

The regulations changed again, in line with the world series, to which Le Mans returned. That meant 3.5-litre cars with no more than twelve cylinders and a minimum weight of 750kg. Those were thin on the ground, so the organisers allowed another category, for 1000kg cars of unlimited capacity, running to a fuel-consumption limit. The catch was the engine had to be from a manufacturer already involved in the world championship, which let in cars from Mercedes, Jaguar, Porsche and Ford but sidelined Nissan and Toyota.

It resulted in the smallest grid in almost sixty years, just 38 cars. But it was an interesting mixture – including three Mazdas (again managed by Ickx), four Jaguars, three Sauber Mercedes, thirteen Porsches, three Cougars and a pair of works Peugeots, the first since the 1920s. After mostly wet qualifying, the Peugeot 905 coupés started from the front, but hadn't been fastest. The rules said the championship cars had the first five rows to themselves, whatever their practice times. The fastest car, Schlesser's Sauber Mercedes C11, started from the sixth row. The Peugeots

Above: Nissan Motor Sports' competitions director Sam Machida oversaw NISMO's big budget Le Mans challenge in the early 1990s, but the team never achieved as much as it promised with its super-powerful cars.

Below: when Japan finally won Le Mans, in 1991, it was an unlikely marque which took the first victory. Not a Nissan or a Toyota but the screaming rotary-engined Mazda of Weidler, Gachot and Herbert – here leading the sports car class winner, the Ford-engined Spice SE 90c of all-Japanese squad Misaki, Yokoshima and Nagasaka.
Overleaf: Peugeots dominated the poorly supported 1992 race. Dalmas, Warwick and Blundell in number 1 won, Baldi, Alliot and Jabouille were third.

were bumped forward too by the withdrawal of the fastest car in their own category, the Jaguar XJR-14 as qualified by Andy Wallace.

The Peugeots had their moment, leading the opening laps before being overwhelmed by the three Mercedes. Clearly the quickest cars in the race, they cruised into the first three places and for a long time looked like staying there. But this was a race with a twist.

The V10 Peugeots were both out before one-third distance. The Jaguars were proving too thirsty to run at full pace and challenge the Mercedes. And the quickest Mazda was harrying them all – helped mainly by running to a considerably lighter weight limit than the Mercedes or Jaguars, to the benefit of outright performance, brake and tyre wear, and fuel economy. But it wasn't just speed that won, it was reliability. The Mazda had it, Mercedes didn't.

Overnight the race was led by Mercedes' 'junior' squad – Fritz Kreutzpointer, Karl Wendlinger and one Michael Schumacher, who set fastest lap. But the German cars hit problems. By daybreak one had gone with engine failure following minor accident damage, and the 'junior' car had fallen well back with accident damage and gearbox problems. Then, with only three hours to go, the Schlesser, Mass and Ferté Mercedes was in the pits and clearly in trouble, with an overcooked engine. The screaming four-rotor Mazda powered into the lead. Its drivers were Volker Weidler, Bertrand Gachot, and Johnny Herbert, who was so tired after doing the last, crucial driving stint that he collapsed with heat exhaustion. The Jaguars were second, third and fourth, the Schumacher Mercedes fifth, but this year only one car counted, and it was Le Mans' first Japanese winner.

RAY 2
11 12 1
10 DUTRAY 2
3
10 3
4
5 2 3 8 LE MANS 4
DUTRAY 2
10 3
9 3
8 LE MANS 4

In 1992 the world sports car championship was on its last legs, but championship round or not, Le Mans was one race everyone still wanted to see. They came even with the smallest field since the early 1930s. But it was slightly ironic that the ACO had erected miles of debris fencing to protect spectators, and hundreds of yards of fencing to discourage the traditional end-of-race track invasion, in a year which saw just 28 starters and a miserable 14 finishers. That said, though, it wasn't a bad race ...

This sixtieth Le Mans was headlined as a showdown between Peugeot and Toyota, and to be honest the rest of the field looked decidedly make-weight, even given the raft of dispensations the FIA had given to allow non-championship cars to compete. There were three 3.5-litre V10 Peugeots, three V10 and two V8 Toyotas, and a couple of Mazdas, now with V10 Judd engines rather than the unique rotaries. There were five Porsches, the most promising a pair of 3-litre turbo 962s from Kremer, but finally showing their age. There was even a BRM, a 3.5 V12 P351 from the now defunct Grand Prix manufacturer whose first involvement with Le Mans had been with the Rover turbine cars in the early 1960s.

There were serious worries, too, that this breed of car might be good for a sprint race but would find 24 hours hard going. Which

goes to show that at Le Mans you should take nothing at all for granted.

It was a sparse field but a fascinating race. The Peugeots had the practice advantage, as Phillipe Alliot took pole in the car he shared with Mauro Baldi and Jean-Pierre Jabouille. It was the other Peugeot though, of Derek Warwick, Mark Blundell and Yannick Dalmas, which won. After it overhauled the fast-starting Herbert, Weidler and Gachot Mazda, a car taking maximum advantage of miserable weather at the start, it never actually lost the lead. But behind it there was always something to ponder. The

Above: the Peugeots were back in 1993, and in the last year of the old rules the 905s scored a dominant 1-2-3. This is Brabham, Bouchut and Helary, who headed the three Peugeots home, a lap clear of Boutsen, Dalmas and Fabi, and eight laps ahead of Alliot, Baldi and Jabouille. It was the team's swansong, as Toyota failed in the race and Jaguar returned to test the water for the new GT category which would move the emphasis away from Group C by 1994.

Peugeots regained the advantage as the Mazdas switched to a self-preservation strategy, and the Toyota challenge came off the rails. Or in the case of the fastest Toyota, off the track, when Geoff Lees, blinded by spray and slowing, was hit from behind by Peugeot driver Alain Ferté at the beginning of the Mulsanne. Both were patched up and resumed, but well out of contention. Both finally retired, while their team mates raced on.

As rain came and went, the remaining Peugeots sandwiched the rapid Mazda, the second 905 eventually finding a way past, until it had steering problems and an accident early in the morning. That let the Mazda back into second, and the Sekiya, Raphanel and Acheson Toyota into third. The lead Peugeot had a morning scare with a misfire, but had enough in hand to hang on. Its sister car had enough problems to give the Toyota a sniff of second place, and it took it, just, in spite of late pit stops and a hard charge from the Peugeot, which took third, nine laps ahead of the Mazda. The consensus was that Le Mans would suffer not at all from being beyond the pale of the sports car chamionship next time round.

There were some interesting young names at Le Mans in 1993, showing that not so long ago future Grand Prix drivers still knew what a sports car was. There was David Coulthard in one of the GT Jaguars, Eddie Irvine in a Toyota, and many other well-known Formula One names. Again this was billed as Peugeot versus Toyota, again it was Peugeot's race, again it was a pointer to another Le Mans future, as the 3.5-litre Group C sports prototypes were bolstered by a new GT category, opening up some fascinating possibilities.

Peugeot not only won, they dominated in a way no-one had since Porsche more than ten years before, with a comprehensive 1-2-3. Toyota pushed them, on pace at least, between their numerous problems. Eddie Irvine had led for the Japanese team in the early stages, and looked fairly well in control, until Irvine handed over to his team mates, Toshio Suzuki and Masanori Sekiya, neither of whom could get anything near as much out of the car as Irvine had. The second Toyota developed a misfire on Saturday evening and although Pierre-Henri Raphanel, Kenny Acheson and Andy Wallace fought hard to get back in the running, gearbox problems cost them a lot of time later on, and eventually stopped the car out on the circuit. The Irvine Toyota lost time that even he couldn't make up, with electrical problems. And the third Toyota, driven by Geoff Lees, Jan Lammers and Juan Manuel Fangio II, was unluckiest of all, as young Fangio was hit from behind while braking for the second Mulsanne chicane, repair time dropping the car way down the field.

Peugeot had their problems too, but by Toyota's standards they were trivial, and the team had time to sort them out without their lead being threatened. A broken oil pipe cost the Alliot, Baldi, Jabouille car nine laps and the lead; the Boutsen, Dalmas, Fabi car then inherited first place – and lost it during the night after a catalogue of problems, from an electrical fault to body damage and finally a broken exhaust. By the time that let the third car (driven by Geoff Brabham, Eric Helary and Christophe Bouchut) into the lead, and Toyota's problems had let the Alliot car back to third, Peugeot team manager Jean Todt was in defensive mode. He issued instructions that this was how it should stay – his cars wouldn't race with each other, even though they clearly could have.

So Peugeot took 1-2-3, and Toyota 4-5-6, with fifth and sixth for the older, Category II 'Group C 1990' cars of Ratzenberger, Martini and Nagasaka, and Fouche, Elgh and Andskar. Considerably further back, John Nielsen, David Brabham and David Coulthard were first home in the new GT category in their Jaguar XJ220C, but with clouds gathering over a protest that the cars – supposedly IMSA versions of the 'production' models – should have used catalytic converters, just as the type-approved road cars did. Some weeks later they were disqualified, and the GT win went to Porsche.

It wasn't an auspicious start for the new GT category, but soon there was a chance, at least, that a genuinely production-based car might just win Le Mans. And to achieve that the Automobile Club de l'Ouest came up with a clever 'equivalency' formula, which would let the GT cars compete head-to-head with the Group C prototypes and production-based IMSA GTS cars, and head-to-head with each other, regardless of capacity or complexity.

They proposed to do it by fitting each car with an air restrictor to control maximum output. The bigger and more exotic the engine the smaller the restrictor – the object being to have one GT class allowing up to 600bhp (100bhp more than the current Group Cs) and another up to 450bhp. The less powerful cars could also be lighter, and there were other differences to try to level the playing field – such as 50 per cent bigger fuel tanks for the GTs compared to the lighter Group C cars. It was a sort of supercar charter, so suddenly Le Mans had real road car clones again: Ferrari F40, Honda NSX, Mazda RX7, Bugatti EB110S, Ferrari 348, Dodge Viper, De Tomaso Pantera, Venturi 400 GTR and 600LM, Lotus Esprit and, of course, various versions of Porsche 911. But where there's a rule, there's a loophole, and this year it was the Dauer Porsche which found it.

The Dauer Porsches were ostensibly (and by the rules officially) LM GT1 cars, and thus allowed 600bhp. They were also, behind the thin disguise, Porsche 962s, based on a roadgoing version of the race car, built by Jochen Dauer and shown at a number of motor shows.

Above: the 1994 rules were meant to promote a return to 'production' GTs, as interest in sports car racing waned. As ever some teams outfoxed the rule makers. The winning Dauer Porsche of Dalmas, Baldi and Haywood was road legal, but you didn't have to look too hard to see that it was really a 962.

The main prototype challenge was from the Gulf-sponsored Kremer Porsche spyders, the Courage Porsches, and a brace of Toyotas. Derek Bell, in what he promised was his last Le Mans, led briefly from the start in the Gulf car, but the Toyota was really the one to beat. The winning Dauer Porsche beat all the other GT cars and the Toyotas. Most of those suffered more for lack of Le Mans experience than anything, and virtually all of them had some kind of trouble, while the vastly experienced Porsche operation just plugged on. The fast but troublesome Bugatti had turbo problems (and it did have four turbos), all bar one Venturi retired and the last one finished on just five cylinders out of six, while the F40 went out on Saturday evening with electronic problems. Aside from the Dauer 962, best of the 'real' GT1s was the Viper of René Arnoux, Bertrand Balas and Justin Bell – son of five times winner Derek. In GT2 the demise of the Lotuses, Hondas and Ferraris left the Dupuy, Gouhier and Palau Porsche Carrera RSR with a comfortable win, while Millen, Morton and O'Connell won the IMSA class in their Nissan 300ZX.

Still, the overall win should have gone to Toyota, which had led from Saturday evening as the Dauer Porsches lost time with driveshaft problems. With less than two hours to go, Toyota's Irvine, Jeff Krosnoff and Mauro Martini could taste the champagne, but then the car's gear linkage broke. The Dauer crew tried to rob themselves of victory by losing time with both cars in the pits together, but it took so long to sort out the Toyota's gearshift problems that it was academic. The Baldi, Dalmas and Haywood Porsche won, with the Toyota second and the other Dauer car, of Boutsen, Stuck and Sullivan, third. The crowd probably went home happy, the rule makers went away to think again.

In 1995, the theory worked out better – the winning McLaren F1 GTR might have been a racing

car for all to see, but at least the F1 genuinely was a production car of sorts, if you had around £650,000 to spend and didn't mind waiting for it to be built. It was also the fastest road car of all time, so it clearly had the measure of the GT opposition. And overall, if not for outright speed, thanks to the clever rules it probably had the measure of the protoypes, too. Its problem so far as Le Mans was concerned was that it had never done anything resembling an endurance race. It had never raced in the wet, and Le Mans 1995 was mostly wet. The last time that McLaren designer Gordon Murray had even been to Le Mans was in the early 1970s, when he designed his last Le Mans car, for de Cadenet. But the GTR's debut was a triumph. Seven were entered, five made it to the finish, to take first, third, fourth, fifth and thirteenth places.

There was little about the grid to point to this remarkable outcome. The fastest McLaren, the Dalmas, Lehto and Sekiya car, languished back in ninth place, behind two WR-Peugeot prototypes, two Courage prototypes, a Kremer Porsche, and three Ferrari F40s – so the McLaren wasn't even the fastest GT on the grid. But the GTRs dominated the race in remarkable fashion, one or other leading all but eleven of the 298 laps which won the race.

Fortunately they worked well in the wet, and there were around 16 hours of rain during the 24. From the start the McLarens really only had to contend with each other. One who took a turn in the lead, early on Sunday, was Derek Bell, out of 'retirement' to drive the Harrods-sponsored GTR, and for a while surely scenting a sixth victory, with son Justin and another former winner, Andy Wallace. They were still ahead with three hours to go, but being caught by the McLaren of Dalmas, Lehto and Helary. With Lehto less than a minute behind, Bell was suffering gearchange problems, as the clutch was failing. It cost him a couple of off-course moments, and eventually a pit stop which was just long enough to hand Lehto the lead.

Below: in 1995, five-times winner Derek Bell shared the Harrods-sponsored Mach 1 Racing McLaren with son Justin and Andy Wallace – and came tantalisingly close to adding a sixth win to equal his great friend Ickx's record.

When Gordon Murray conceived the McLaren F1 coupé, he planned it as the world's fastest road car – and it was. But the revamping of the Le Mans regulations to encourage 'production' GT cars made the F1 a natural Le Mans contender.

Much of Murray's road car design philosophy for the F1 was already exactly what defines a racing car: minimum weight, minimum size, maximum power-to-weight ratio with the broadest power spread. Which was why the carbon-fibre-tubbed F1 weighed almost exactly 1000kg and used a large-capacity, naturally aspirated engine rather than a smaller capacity turbo engine. But the 6.1-litre BMW V12 was developed by BMW's Motorsport division and a light, compact, 600bhp-plus road car with a maximum of around 240mph and 0-100mph in 6.3 seconds was tailor-made for the Le Mans GT regulations. Even its innovative centre seat was probably an advantage. So the GTR was created as a racing version of the car, stripped of what few unnecessary bits the road cars had – and the appropriate Le Mans intake restrictors meant power was certainly no more than the road cars', possibly a touch less. The main downside, so far as Le Mans was concerned, however, was that the GTR had simply never been designed as an endurance racer, and even after it had proved successful in shorter GT championship races, no-one knew whether it would last for 24 hours. In fact most people (Murray included) suspected that its transmission, rather than anything else, probably wouldn't. On its Le Mans debut in 1995, it proved them largely wrong, with a fine win. But as other makes from Porsche to Mercedes to Toyota to Nissan pushed the GT1 envelope, even the F1 was soon outgunned.

> 'McLaren Cars of Woking won the 1995 edition of Le Mans outright, claimed the top four positions in the Grand Touring category and, for good measure, placed four cars in the top five positions.'
>
> *Motor Sport*

Left: McLaren's 1995 debut win, for Sekiya, Lehto and Dalmas, with other F1s taking third, fourth and fifth.
Overleaf: night time pit stop for the Stuck, Wollek and Boutsen Porsche GT1 in 1997.

'Win or not, if I
feel like I do right
now, I'm going
back again next
year. It's not that
I'll go and, if I win
it, say "Goodbye".
No I won't,
because I enjoy it
so much ...'

Mario Andretti, 1996

They hung on, but only just. The Kremer prototype had started from the back after it wouldn't start on the grid, and proved almost undrivable in the wet, probably as a result of rushed repairs after a heavy accident in practice. The Courage, however, came within an ace of spoiling the McLarens' party. Early in the race Mario Andretti hit the barriers and lost some six laps in the pits. With Bob Wollek and Eric Hélary he hauled it back into contention as the track dried on Sunday, but at the end they were still second, less than a lap adrift. It was Wollek's 25th Le Mans, and yet again he had come oh, so close to the win he never did achieve.

Wallace and the Bells tiptoed home for third, and Ray Bellm, Maurizio Sala and Mark Blundell took fourth in their Gulf-backed McLaren, after damaging the car in a minor accident early on. This time there was a feeling that it really was a GT car that had won.

The fact that around 20 cars failed to make it through pre-qualifying was an indicator of how competitive 1996 was going to be, and how much quicker than just a year before. McLaren were now a known quantity, and Porsche had joined the 'production' GT ranks with what was either the ultimate derivative of the 911, or the cleverest interpretation yet of the GT rules, with the 911 GT1. It was a racing car, of course, but Porsche showed a road legal version, and opened up the order book for private customers – for next year. McLaren topped the GT1 qualifiers, Porsche second, McLaren third and fourth, Porsche fifth, McLaren six to eight. A fine prospect, but quickest of all in pre-qualifying was a Ferrari 333SP prototype, and the chances of a Ferrari win added further spice.

Come the race, though, the script went out of the window, and Le Mans produced another of its frequent twists. The Ferrari wasn't on pole, a Porsche was. Not one of the GT1s but a hybrid – a chassis built by TWR (originally for Jaguar), powered by Porsche and run by Joest, one of the most successful privateers in the business.

In the race it ran away from virtually every other car in the field, including the Ferraris, the Oldsmobile-powered Riley & Scott prototypes, the Courage-Porsches and the rest. It ran virtually without a problem, and the only other car that got near it (even led for a short time) was the quicker of the two works 911 GT1s. The McLarens, after all the high expectations, weren't quick enough and weren't reliable enough. The best of them, driven by Ray Bellm, James Weaver and JJ Lehto, battled into the top three but lost a lot of time to a gearbox change just before Sunday midday, so a 911 GT1 took third, too, with the first McLaren home being that of John Neilsen, Thomas Bscher and Peter Kox. The other McLarens, including a pair officially backed by the car's engine supplier, BMW, struggled.

In the prototypes, one Ferrari was out within three hours, out of fuel after already surviving a spin on only the second lap. The other, having been in the top five, crashed early on Sunday morning. Mario Andretti damaged one Courage and Alliot crashed another. The Riley & Scott broke its transmission, both Kremer Porsche K8 spyders crashed, even the second Joest WSC95 broke a driveshaft.

But its sister car, driven by Davy Jones, Manuel Reuter and Alexander Wurz only had to hold off the quickest 911 GT1 to win, and in spite of minor brake problems, and looking decidedly smoky towards the end, it did, by just a lap, from Stuck, Boutsen, and perpetual bridesmaid Wollek. There was just one nagging thought. In the seventh hour, both the works Porsches had off-road moments, while driven by Stuck and Dalmas respectively. They fell back to fourth and tenth, and even then the Dalmas, Wendlinger and Goodyear car clawed back to third at the end. Without their offs, it might have been a very different story.

The records show 1997 as Porsche's fifteenth win, but so far as the factory was concerned, for the

second year running it was a win for the right name on the wrong car. As last year, the script said the works 911 GT1s should have won. Reality saw the same Porsche-powered, TWR-built Joest Porsche WSC95 victorious again. It was even wearing the same number, 7.

Last year the new Porsche 911 GT1s had been immediately on the pace of the dominant McLaren F1 GTRs. This year Porsche knew they were more than capable of handling the GTRs, and with Mercedes failing to show, with their not-quite-ready CLKs, the further developed works GT1s should have had the 1997 race all sewn up.

But luck wasn't with them. Last year, in spite of its newness, the GT1 should have won. Although it was slower outright than the Joest prototype, it had the legs of all the rest, prototypes included. The advantages the rules gave it in fuel stops, and tyre and brake wear, should have been enough to tip the scales. But the GT1s had their minor problems and the Joest car was more fuel efficient than anyone had thought, leaving Porsche with just second and third – before they won every other race in the 1996 championship. Controversially, though, McLaren among others suggested that some production-based GTs were more production-based than others ...

This depends on definition. By 1997 the mid-engined, water-cooled, 3.2 twin-turbo 911 GT1 was listed as a 544bhp, 194mph 'production' model – and at £457,075, rather less than the latest quoted price for the McLaren, at £634,500. Porsche planned a run of thirty cars, and quickly took orders for most of them.

The latest factory cars had brake and engine modifications to meet revised regulations, and new front bodywork previewing the upcoming second generation mainstream 911. In classic Porsche style, the Mobil-liveried works cars were backed now by seven customer versions, still with last year's bodywork – making nine Porsche GT1s versus five McLaren F1 GTRs. That meant more Porsches in GT1

Above: in 1997, for the second time in recent memory, the Joest team scored a second successive win with the same car. First time around it had been back-to-back wins for the NewMan Porsche in the mid 1980s. This time it was win number two for the TWR-built, Porsche-powered WSC95 – updated and in different livery but still wearing the same race number, 7. This year the drivers were Alboreto, Johansson and Kristensen.

than in GT2, where just seven 911 clones faced the Viper GTS-Rs, Callaway Corvettes, Saleen Mustangs and a single Marcos 600LM. But also facing the Porsche and McLaren GT1s were the dark horse Nissan R390 GT1s (another TWR creation), the fine handling and very aerodynamic front-engined Panoz GTRs, and outsiders like the British Listers and Lotuses.

In qualifying, only Michele Alboreto and the Joest Porsche were quicker than Boutsen in the fastest GT1, shared with Stuck and Wollek. In the race, there were dogfights down the field between the McLarens, Nissans and private GT1s, between the Courage and Ferrari prototypes and the Viper and 911 GT2s. But at the front the battle was solely between Joest and the works cars.

Alboreto and Wollek (briefly) both led in the first hour, before a spin for Wollek at Indianapolis let the Dalmas, Kelleners and Collard GT1 into second by the second hour and into the lead by the third hour. As night fell, Boutsen, Stuck and Wollek were ahead again, and they stayed there through the night, rarely more than a couple of seconds ahead of their team-mates, with the Joest Porsche shadowing at a distance.

Then just as the hardiest spectators were contemplating breakfast, Wollek parked the leading GT1 in the Porsche Curves, after spinning over the kerbs. Dalmas retook the lead, and although the Joest Porsche was breaking lap records, the protoype versus GT1 balance of pit calls and fuel efficiency was still favouring the GT1.

It wasn't over. By 2pm, six hours after Wollek hit the kerbs, only four other cars had retired, and the Dalmas Porsche continued to lead. But on lap 328 it lost drive on the Mulsanne and burst into flames, as Kelleners scrambled clear. The Joest car, exactly the same car as last year in all but detail and livery, shared by Alboreto, Stefan Johansson and Tom Kristensen, led, and it won. Kristensen's impressive debut included a new lap record, and they won by a lap from the Gulf McLaren of Raphanel, Gounon and Olofson, with the 'works' BMW Motorsport McLaren of Kox, Ravaglia and Helary third. So with the Schubel Engineering 911 GT1 of Armin Hahne, Pedro Lamy and Patrick Goueslard in fifth, Porsche had lost the race overall to Joest and the GT1 class to McLaren. They had the consolation of winning GT2 with the Elf Haberthur Racing 911, so on paper they had won two of the three classes, overall victory and fastest lap, but not with the big budget 911 GT1 programme. And the following year, it seemed its task could only get harder ...

In 1998 Porsche didn't only face Nissan, Toyota, Panoz, McLaren and the Porsche-powered Joest, Kremer and Courage prototypes, they faced a new prototype effort from BMW, and the return of a works team from Mercedes.

Like Porsche, McLaren, Toyota and Nissan, Mercedes had interpreted the GT1 rules with a spectacular 'production' car. Seven years after conceding the race to Mazda on their last appearance in 1991, and nine years after their last win in 1989, they were back with all their formidable organisation and experience, and their presence made the 1998 race one of the most exciting prospects in years. Depending on who you listened to, there were anything between five and a dozen teams with a realistic chance.

For Mercedes, the high-profile return started well. Two of the 5-litre, 600bhp, V8-engined Le Mans spec CLK-LM cars were entered, for FIA GT champion Bernd Schneider, Klaus Ludwig and Mark Webber, and for Jean-Marc Gounon, Christophe Bouchut and Brazilian Ricardo Zonta. A year ago the CLKs had been considered unready for Le Mans, but since then they had won the world sports car championship, and two weeks ago they had won the Silverstone sprint, which many people see as a traditional curtain raiser and pointer to Le Mans prospects. They were here to win – but then so were all the other top teams, and especially the other GT1s.

The entry was big enough to need a pre-qualifying session a month before race week, and that

Below: the 911 GT1 was Porsche's interpretation of the 'production' GT rules which had allowed McLaren onto the winner's podium in 1995. It could and probably should have won the race in either or both its first appearances, in 1996 and 1997, but it didn't take the big prize until 1998. Then McNish, Ortelli and Aiello led Müller, Alzen and Wollek home to a 911 GT1 1-2 – helped by hard-charging Toyota's last-gasp bad luck.

only heightened expectations. The Porsche GT1-98 of McNish, Ortelli and Dalmas was quickest, and the single AMG Mercedes (the only car they needed to prequalify) a close third, driven by Schneider. They were split by the spectacular new Toyota GT One of Brundle and Collard. Its interpretation of the 'road-car related' rules had already raised a few more eyebrows than either its Porsche or Mercedes rivals, and to many people an impending race win for the Toyotas was seen as little more than a formality.

The big shock in qualifying was that Toyota didn't win pole. After a mighty battle between the big three, Toyota, Porsche and Mercedes, Mercedes came out on top. They took pole with a car set up for minimum drag, including blanking off some of the cooling ducts, for one maximum-effort lap from Schneider. He was a

Right: BMW had made many appearances at Le Mans over the years, from before World War II to the 1970s, both with complete cars and with BMW engines for other marques. A BMW V12 powered McLaren to victory in 1996, but it wasn't until 1999 that a BMW car powered by a BMW engine took outright victory – the LMR driven by Dalmas, Winkelhock and Martini.

fraction of a second faster than the fastest Toyota, the second Mercedes, the two works Porsche GT1-98s, and the first of the promising new open BMWs, which headed the prototype category.

The pace car peeled off from the parade lap at 2pm on Saturday 6 June, a week ahead of the traditional date in deference to the football World Cup, and a further two hours ahead for the French Open tennis finals in Paris. The Schneider Mercedes led briefly, with a brake-smoking moment up through the Dunlop Curves and under the Dunlop Bridge before being swallowed up on the Mulsanne by the sheer speed of Brundle's Toyota.

That was not a surprise, and to most of the others not an immediate problem, as they pursued their own strategies. For the first hour and the first round of pit stops the Mercedes, and to a slightly lesser extent the quickest of the Porsches, BMWs and Nissans, weren't giving too much ground, and waiting for the Toyota to have problems. But Mercedes hit trouble first. With not much more than an hour gone, the Schneider car was stranded at the pit exit, its driver negotiating what was permissible with the marshals, his team a hundred yards too far back to help. A steering pump drive had broken, taken the

'I felt the front come up and saw sky and thought "I'm in trouble". The first thing I thought about was the trees – I didn't want to hit them ...'

Peter Dumbreck, 1999

Above and Below: Mark Webber's Mercedes flew both in practice and during the warm-up for the 1999 race, but the team didn't withdraw its other two cars. Peter Dumbreck was fortunate to escape from another take-off in the race, after which Mercedes finally pulled out its remaining car.

shared drive for the engine oil pump along with it, and led to a major engine failure.

Bad as that was for Mercedes, worse was to come. Less than an hour later, the second CLK suffered an identical failure out on the circuit and with 21 hours still to go, Mercedes' race was run. And for the new front runners there was now a new problem, with the threat of rain which had already delayed the start of the tennis in Paris.

With both Mercedes gone, the Brundle, Collard and Hélary Toyota had another hour of glory before it too started to feel the pace, with wheel bearing problems which first caused Helary to spin in the Ford chicane and then to lose eight laps in the pits. That let the Boutsen, Kelleners and Lees Toyota into the lead, and they stayed there for around four hours, during which both the prototype-leading BMWs also went out – the first with wheel bearing failure, the second withdrawn by the team as a safety precaution. And all the time the factory Porsches continued to breathe down the Toyota's neck.

Meanwhile, with three-quarters of the race still to go, Brundle, clawing his way back into the top ten, set fastest lap – but the Toyotas were starting to struggle. All three had gearbox problems, which might have accounted for their catalogue of spins and excursions. In the end, Toyota could change a gearbox in around ten minutes, but by then they'd had plenty of practice ... This let a familiar scenario unfold at the front, as the factory GT1-98 Porsches took the lead through most of the night and towards the dawn, with the race two hours older than it would usually be. But still the twists weren't over. While it rained during the night, Porsche GT1 driver Alan McNish had stayed on slicks to avoid an additional pit stop, but had still been heroically fast – and that may have been the deciding factor in a fascinating finale.

He put a full lap on the other factory Porsche, driven by Müller, Alzen and Wollek, until 6am when the Porsches faltered. McNish's car was overheating, Müller's was in the pits after a minor off-road moment. The Boutsen Toyota was waiting to pounce. When the McNish GT1 emerged from twenty minutes in the garage it began a battle which see-sawed between Porsche and Toyota for most of the rest of the race. They were never more than a lap apart, often much closer, changing places during pit-stops, but still looking good for Toyota. Until, that is, Boutsen stopped out on the circuit, at Arnage, with less than two hours to go.

So in the company's fiftieth year, Porsche won Le Mans for the sixteenth time, with McNish, Ortelli and Aiello leading home Müller, Alzen and Wollek – and the Nissan of Hoshino, Suzuki and Kageyama.

In 1999 the race went to the wire again, and it made worldwide headlines – but it made the front pages for reasons Le Mans would have preferred not to face. It had also attracted more manufacturers than it had in many years, including Toyota, Audi, Mercedes, Nissan, dark-horse Panoz – and BMW.

For their second appearance, the works BMW team had all-new V12 LMR cars run by Schnitzer, supported by two of last year's cars, updated by David Price Racing for Price+Bscher and the Japanese Team Goh. All had looked good in pre-qualifying, and the works car had also won the American Le Mans Series race at Sebring in March.

Between pre-qualifying and the race, BMW pared its squad down from three to two cars, but this was still an all-out effort. Number 15 was for Pierluigi Martini, Yannick Dalmas and Jo Winkelhock; 17 was for JJ Lehto, Tom Kristensen and Jorg Müller. Between them they had 22 Le Mans starts and five wins – including those for Lehto and Dalmas with the BMW-powered McLaren in 1995, which was Dalmas's third win.

The cars were fast and reliable, with a huge amount of mainly trouble-free testing. And they had the advantage of the open-car rule differences, so they might not be as fast over a single lap as the quickest coupés but they should have a tyre wear advantage and less time in the pits. But in qualifying they weren't as fast as the Toyota GT Ones, which continued to be Le Mans' 'cars most likely'.

Their three cars were driven by 1990 winner Brundle with Emmanuel Collard and Vicenzo Sospiri, Boutsen, Kelleners and last year's winner McNish, and Ukyo Katayama, Toshio Suzuki and 1995 GT2 winner Keiichi Tsuchiya. Brundle put pole beyond reach with a mighty lap of 3m 29.93s, a 145.8mph average and six seconds quicker than last year's Mercedes pole. Boutsen was second, Lehto third in the fastest BMW, then Mercedes and the first of the thunderous front-engined Panoz Roadsters. Five places, four makes.

Newcomers Audi, with two German-run open cars and two British-run coupés, were playing themselves in with ninth and eleventh. Nissan in twelfth were down to one car but relieved that Eric van der Poele had survived a huge accident with the other one.

Mercedes were about to suffer even bigger problems. During Thursday evening practice Mark Webber's CLR took off on the 200mph run from Mulsanne to Indianapolis, performing a back somersault and landing on its wheels before hitting the barriers. The front had lifted slightly over bumps and air had rushed under the controversial flat bottom required by the regulations, after which Webber was a passenger. Amazingly he was virtually unhurt, but in raceday warm-up he did it again, on the Mulsanne. Again he walked away, and Mercedes withdrew his car, but opted to race the other two, with minor changes to the front bodywork. That raised a few eyebrows ...

The race started like a sprint, and continued that way. Brundle and Boutsen's Toyotas led, hounded by Schneider's Mercedes and Dalmas's BMW, with the second BMW also ahead of the third Toyota. At the first pit-stops the leading Toyotas and Mercedes stopped almost together and Kristensen's BMW led, its team mate second – already giving the others cause for concern with their fuel efficiency.

Above: Australian Mark Webber had plenty to think about in the run up to the 1999 race, but was spared the ordeal of actually starting. The other drivers did start, officially with no qualms after long discussions with the team. But Dumbreck's high-flying accident in the race brought the team perilously close to a major disaster. Webber obviously didn't follow the arrow behind ...

The picture changed all the time. At ninety minutes there was half a second between the leading pair, and five seconds covered the top four – Mercedes, Toyota, Toyota, BMW. The Audi coupés and the lone Ferrari 333SP already had problems, but it was the fourth hour before there was an official retirement. The Toyotas were fast, the BMWs frugal, usually going at least one more lap between stops, and hugely quick when their fuel load was low. The Toyotas often lost time leaving the pits as they didn't start easily, and Mercedes shadowed both the leading teams.

Left: the Panoz Roadster of Brabham, Bernard and Leitzinger in 1999. The front-engined Panoz spyders were a breath of fresh air at Le Mans, and American team owner Don Panoz spread the Le Mans gospel with his American Le Mans Series.

After four hours there were still four cars on the lead lap, BMW duelling with Toyota, and the occasional sprinkle of rain. Then everything changed. At 8.45 Peter Dumbreck's fourth-placed Mercedes was hounding Boutsen's Toyota towards Indianapolis when, just like Webber's, the nose came up and he went into a horrifying series of twisting back somersaults, over the barriers, into the trees. Even before news filtered through of his miraculous survival, Mercedes had withdrawn their other car – and prepared to face the question of whether they should have raced at all. Dumbreck said, 'I felt the front come up and saw sky and thought "I'm in trouble". The first thing I thought about was the trees – I didn't want to hit them ...'

It was now a straight fight between BMW and Toyota, swapping lap records, swapping the lead, the Toyotas with minor problems, the BMWs with their pit-stop advantage. Then just before midnight Brundle punctured on the Mulsanne and thumped the first chicane. Three hours later Boutsen, still hounding the leading number 17 BMW, had an even bigger accident in the Dunlop Curves and was trapped in the car for almost half an hour. This left the BMW with three laps over its sister car, chased by the Audi spyder of Pirro, Biela and Theys, then by the surviving Japanese-crewed Toyota.

Just before midday Lehto crashed heavily approaching the Porsche Curves after his throttle stuck open, and the second BMW led, chased by the hugely fast Toyota. For three hours the advantage see-sawed, dictated by speed and pit-stop strategy. With less than an hour to go Katayama miraculously held on after a tyre exploded on the Mulsanne, a few seconds after he had tangled with Bscher in the private BMW and probably collected some debris. The chase was over, and the works BMW of Martini, Dalmas and Winkelhock could finally reel off the laps to victory, while Katayama rejoined, but resigned to second. Dalmas, now a four-time winner, simply said, 'Le Mans is the greatest race one can win'. For the moment, BMW agreed.

Yet the works BMWs didn't return in 2000, and the sole BMW entry, the V12 LM98 of Bscher, Lees and Gounon was out after 180 laps with accident damage, but where BMW left off, Audi took over.

They dominated the race, and just after four o'clock cruised across the line in formation. Emmanuele Pirro in the winning car which he shared with Tom Kristensen and Frank Biela held both arms aloft, waving an Audi flag and, for once, the crowd was held back as the cars actually crossed the finish line. The three-car Audi team had been managed by Reinhold Joest, who was getting good at this.

The only car to head the Audis at all was a Panoz, as the team took advantage of a safety-car period after one of the DAMS Cadillacs had caught fire on the circuit. They brought David Brabham in for an early, and quick, pit-stop, and when the race resumed he was ahead of the three Audis. But only for four laps, until they started, one by one, to overwhelm him again. Brabham was sharing that car with Jan Magnussen – and Mario Andretti, in his sixtieth year and back to have one more go at adding Le Mans to his Grand Prix world title and Indy wins. But it wasn't to be. Once the threat of the very fast Panoz Roadsters had faded, around mid-distance, the Audis only had to worry about each other, and such problems as they had through the race were considered minor. Minor, in this context, included an early spin for Ortelli, a puncture for Kristensen, a puncture for Biela, underbody aerodynamic repairs for the McNish car, minor electrical problems for Ortelli, another puncture for Abt while in the lead, and routine changes of brake discs for two of the three cars.

That says a lot about the Joest Audi team's approach, because two of the cars also needed gearbox changes during the night. But they'd come prepared for that eventuality, with a design whose entire rear end, gearbox and suspension combined, could be changed in minutes. The winner probably won because it was the only one of the three which didn't need the high-speed gearbox change. But the fact that even the second and third-placed Audi R8s (driven by Laurent Aiello, Allan McNish and Stephane Ortelli, and by Michele Alboreto, Christian Abt and Rinaldo Capello) were twenty-odd laps in front of the next finisher handsomely underlined their superiority. As it was, fourth place for the Bourdais, Grouillard and Clerico Courage-Peugeot, and fifth for the Katoh, O'Connell and Raphanel Panoz, were the best anyone else could have hoped for. And unlike BMW, Audi would be back ...

Above: victory formation for the totally dominant Audi team in 2000, a remarkable performance on only the second appearance for the German marque at Le Mans. In 1999 they were beaten to third and fourth places by BMW and Toyota. By 2000 both those challengers had turned their backs on the race, and the Audis were easily the class of the field, led home by Pirro, Biela and Kristensen, waving the flag in number 8.

At the end of the 2001 race, the Oliver Reed Appreciation Society, in white shirts and black bow ties, set up table, chairs and battered candelabra in front of the podium, in front of thousands of other pushing, cheering enthusiasts. They opened their champagne and raised a glass to the new Bentley Boys, class of 2001, who had briefly donned baggy white 1920s overalls and flying helmets.

The Bentleys hadn't won, but they had achieved more than anyone dared hope – a strong third, leaving the thousands of flag-waving Brits crammed into the terraces to celebrate as only they know how. Seventy-one years after their last official appearance, Bentley were back with a works team, and on the podium. Only two Audis stood between them and the British marque's sixth Le Mans win.

The bare facts were simple. Works Audis first and second, the winner driven by Tom Kristensen, Frank Biela and Emanuele Pirro, the second car by Rinaldo Capello, Laurent Aiello and Christian Pescatori. Behind them the glorious survivor of the two-car Bentley team, driven by Andy Wallace, Eric van de Poele and Butch Leitzinger.

One thing above all shaped the race – the weather. Sometimes it rained, then the sun shone. Sometimes it rained on one part of the circuit, sometimes on others. Much of the time it was wet everywhere – and when it was wet it was very, very wet.

Ten minutes after the start the first deluge put half a dozen cars into the scenery. It brought the pace car out for the first of many appearances, and brought some

Right: Martin Brundle in the number 7 Bentley in 2001. The wet race gave both the cars and the drivers a hard time, with drowning gearbox electronics and badly compromised visibility. Until its retirement this was the quicker of the two Bentleys, but it was its team-mate which soldiered on for a remarkable third place on Bentley's popular return.

LA PASSION DU FUTUR

fantastic moments for the huge British contingent, steadfastly waving their sodden Bentley and MG banners. Seven laps in and the clock was wound back to the 1920s. A Bentley led Le Mans, as Martin Brundle power-boated past Aiello's number 2 Audi. For two hours, the rain and pace cars came and went, and Bentley slogged it out with Audi. For many hours, both Bentleys in their turn snapped at the leading Audis' heels as other challenges faded.

The rain caught many cars. Some drowned in it, some spun off, often triggering long-term mechanical problems. The leading Bentley, originally the quicker of the two, driven by Brundle, Stephane Ortelli and Guy Smith, went out in the fifth hour, stuck in top gear, its overheated turbochargers briefly setting the bodywork alight. Both Bentleys suffered with the rain – in the electrics, in the cockpit, in the pit-to-car radio. For most of the race their drivers were blinded by the heavily-misted screen and out of radio contact. The number 4 Audi in the pale blue and orange colours of Gulf Oil, another famous winner returning this year, had already gone – its electronics drowned. So had the quicker of the two MGs, and one of the promising Cadillacs. So had half a dozen other front runners.

It became a battle to survive – but stick around and anything looked possible. Works MGs were also back for the first time in decades, in the smaller prototype class, and like the Bentleys they covered themselves in glory. After endless practice problems few expected them to last the first hour, but after twenty minutes they were sixth and seventh, the two crews of Anthony Reid, Jonny Kane and Warren Hughes, and Mark Blundell, Kevin McGarrity and Julian Bailey giving most of the bigger cars a serious fright. At eighty minutes Blundell was up to fifth, then past the second Bentley into fourth, and briefly, as the first round of routine pit stops began, into third. It was a mighty effort, but the first MG had gone with engine problems by the sixth hour, while the second hung on until after midnight but eventually drowned and couldn't be resuscitated.

One by one any threats followed it into retirement, and by Sunday morning Le Mans was unusually quiet. Around half the 48-car field was already on the sidelines. By breakfast time the second private Audi – the Champion car of Ralf Kelleners, Johnny

'This was the most difficult race of my career. Jacky Ickx told Frank Biela and myself before we went onto the podium that he had never experienced such a hard race at Le Mans himself. When that comes from him it really means something.'

Tom Kristensen, June 2001

Right: in 2001, for the second year in a row, Audi had the measure of the field, but in a race punctuated by appallingly wet weather and several pace-car periods, winners Kristensen, Biela and Pirro were continuously pushed by their team-mates, and to a lesser degree by the hugely impressive Bentleys.

Herbert and Didier Theys had gone too, its clutch cooked. Both the promising Japanese Domes and both Panozes, all of which had scrapped for the lead early on, were out. So was one Chrysler, one Cadillac, one Courage, and at least one car from virtually every team.

Only the Audis and the surviving Bentley looked comfortable, and the Bentley team eventually had their car dry enough so the gears would select pretty well, the radio worked and the drivers could occasionally see the road. But they never saw the two works Audis. When the clock ticked past four o'clock on Sunday they were more than a dozen laps clear, and a after a brief flurry of fighting between themselves as the last pace car session ended, the German cars cruised home in formation, with the Bentley and the rest tagging along behind, the overall positions so well set that the last throes of the race had been reduced to a finish-at-all-costs tip-toe – a nightmare of its own in the appalling conditions.

It was a strange Le Mans, and as someone remarked, if it hadn't been for the Audis, for a long time it would have been a very close run one, but one thing's for certain, it cheered up the Brits. Le Mans has been described as the biggest British motor race in France. Many things make it special. The atmosphere, the subtleties, the uncertainty, and those British fans. The Bentley performances of the 1920s and 1930s brought them here in the first place, and put Le Mans on the international sporting map. This year's Bentley effort (and the MGs too) brought them back in the sort of numbers that haven't been seen since the glory days of Jaguar. The result was a bonus, almost guaranteeing that both teams would be back for 2002 and Le Mans' seventieth anniversary. The magic is still there.

1923

	Drivers	Car	
1	André Lagache/René Leonard	Chenard et Walcker 'Sport'	2,209 kilometres at 92.064kph
			Winner, 2,001-3,000 cc class
2	Raoul Bachmann/Christian Dauvergne	Chenard et Walcker 'Sport'	
3	Raymond de Tornaco/Paul Gros	Bignan 'Desmo'	Winner, 1,501-2,000 cc class
4	John Duff/Frank Clement	Bentley 'Sport'	Fastest lap: 9m 39s (107.328kph)
5	Philippe de Marne/Jean Martin	Bignan 'Commercial'	
6	André Dils/Nicolas Caerels	Excelsior 'Albert 1er'	Winner, 5,001-8,000 cc class
8	Gérard de Courcelles/André Rossignol	Lorraine Dietrich B3-6	Winner, 3,001-5,000 cc class
10	Max de Pourtales/Sosthène de la Rochefoucauld	Bugatti Brescia 16S	Winner, 1,101-1,500 cc class
12	Lucien Desvaux/Georges Casse	Salmson AL	Winner, 751-1,100 cc class

1924

1	John Duff/Frank Clement	Bentley 'Sport'	2,077 kilometres at 86.555kph
			Winner, 2,001-3,000 cc class
2	Henry Stoffel/Edouard Brisson	Lorraine-Dietrich	Winner, 3,001-5,000 cc class
3	Gérard de Courcelles/André Rossignol	Lorraine-Dietrich	
4	André Pisard/'Chavee'	Chenard et Walcker	Winner, 1,501-2,000 cc class
5	Christian Dauvergne/Manso de Zuniga	Chenard et Walcker	
11	Fernand Gabriel/Henri Lapierre	Aries 8-10 CV	Winner, 751-1,100 cc class
			Fastest lap: André Lagache,
			Chenard et Walcker, 9m 19s (111.168kph)

1925

1	Gérard de Courcelles/André Rossignol	Lorraine-Dietrich B3-6	2,233.98 kilometres at 93.082kph
			Winner, 3,001-5,000 cc class
2	Jean Chassagne/Sammy Davis	Sunbeam 'Sport'	Winner, 2,001-3,000 cc class
3	Edouard Brisson/'Stalter'	Lorraine-Dietrich B3-6	
=4	Tino Danieli/Mario Danieli	OM 665S 'Superba'	=Winner,1,501-2,000 cc class
=4	Julio Foresti/Aimé Vassiaux	OM 665S 'Superba'	=Winner,1,501-2,000 cc class
8	Louis Balart/Robert Doutrebente	Corre La Licorne W15	Winner, 1,101-1,500 cc class
10	Raymond Glazmann/Manso de Zuniga	Chenard et Walcker	Winner, 751-1,100 cc class
			Winner, Coupe Biennial 1924-
13	Robert Senechal/Albéric Locqueneux	Chenard et Walcker	Winner, Coupe Triennial, 1923-1924-1925
			Fastest lap: André Lagache,
			Chenard et Walcker, 9m 10s (112.987kph)

1926

1	Robert Bloch/André Rossignol	Lorraine-Dietrich B3-6	2,552.414 kilometres at 106.350kph
			Winner, 3,001-5,000 cc class
2	Gérard de Courcelles/Marcel Mongin	Lorraine-Dietrich B3-6	Fastest lap: de Courcelles,
			9m 03s (114.444kph)
3	Edouard Brisson/'Stalter'	Lorraine-Dietrich B3-6	
4	Nando Minoia/Giulio Foresti	OM 665 SS 'Superba'	Winner, 1,501-2,000 cc class
			Winner, Coupe Biennale 1925-1926
			Winner, Index of Performance
5	Tino Danieli/Mario Danieli	OM 665 SS 'Superba'	
8	Henri de Costier/Pierre Bussienne	EHP DS	Winner, 1,101-1,500 cc class
9	Georges Casse/André Rousseau	Salmson GS	Winner, 751-1,100 cc class

1927

1	Sammy Davis/Dr John Benjafield	Bentley Sport	2,369.807 kilometres at 98.740kph
			Winner, 2,001-3,000 cc class
2	André de Victor/J. Hasley	Salmson GS	Winner, 751-1,100 cc class
3	Georges Casse/André Rousseau	Salmson GS	Winner, Coupe Biennale 1926-1927
			Winner, Index of Performance
4	Lucien Desvaux/Fernand Vallon	SCAP	Winner, 1,101-1,500 cc class
5	Guy Bouriat/Pierre Bussienne	EHP DS	
			Fastest lap: Frank Clement,
			Bentley Super Sport, 8m 46s (118.142kph)

1928

1	Woolf Barnato/Bernard Rubin	Bentley 4.4	2,669.272 kilometres at 111.219kph
			Winner, 3,001-5,000 cc class
2	Edouard Brisson/Robert Block	Stutz Black Hawk	
3	Henry Stoffel/André Rossignol	Chrysler 72	
4	C. Ghica/G. Ghica	Chrysler 72	
5	Tim Birkin/Jean Chassagne	Bentley 4.4	Fastest lap: Birkin, 8m 07s (127.604kph)
6	Maurice Harvey/Harold Purdy	Alvis TA	Winner, 1,101-1,500 cc class
7	Michel Dore/Jean Treunet	BNC	Winner, 751-1,100 cc class
10	Georges Casse/André Rousseau	Salmson GS	Winner, Coupe Biennale 1927-1928
			Winner, Index of Performance

1929

1	Woolf Barnato/Henry Birkin	Bentley Speed Six	2,843.83 kilometres at 118.492kph
			Winner, 5,001-8,000 cc class
			Winner, Coupe Biennale 1928-1929
			Winner, Index of Performance
			Fastest lap: Birkin, 7m 21s (133.551kph)
			Winner, 3,001-5,000 cc class
2	Jack Dunfee/Glen Kidston	Bentley 4.4	
3	Dr John Benjafield/André d'Erlanger	Bentley 4.4	
4	Frank Clement/Jean Chassagne	Bentley 4.4	
5	Guy Bouriat/'Georges Philippe'	Stutz DV	
8	Kenneth Peacock/Sammy Newsome	Lea Francis Hyper Sport	Winner, 1,101-1,500 cc class
9	Louis Balart/Louis Debeugny	Tracta	Winner, 751-1,100 cc class

1930

1	Woolf Barnato/Glen Kidston	Bentley Speed Six	2,930.663 kilometres at 122.111kph
			Winner, 5,001-8,000 cc class
			Winner, Coupe Biennale 1929-1930
2	Frank Clement/Richard Watney	Bentley Speed Six	
3	Brian Lewis/Hugh Eaton	Talbot 90	Winner, 2,001-3,000 cc class
			Winner, Index of Performance
4	John Hindmarsh/Tim Rose-Richards	Talbot 90	
5	Lord Howe/Leslie Callingham	Alfa Romeo 6C	
7	Kenneth Peacock/Sammy Newsome	Lea Francis	Winner, 1,501-2,000 cc class
8	Jean-Albert Gregoire/Fernand Vallon	Tracta A29	Winner, 751-1,100 cc class
			Fastest lap: Henry Birkin, Bentley 4.4,
			6m 48s (144.362kph)

1931

1	Lord Howe/Henry Birkin	Alfa Romeo 8C	3,017.654 kilometres at 125.735kph
			Winner, 2,001-3,000 cc class
			Winner, Coupe Biennale 1930-1931
			Winner, Index of Performance
2	Boris Ivanowski/Henry Stoffel	Mercedes-Benz SSK	Winner, 5,001-8,000 cc class
			Fastest lap: Ivanowski,
			7m 03s (139.234kph
3	Tim Rose-Richards/A. Saunders-Davies	Talbot 105	
4	Henri Trebor/Louis Balart	Lorraine-Dietrich B3-6	Winner, 3,001-5,000 cc class
5	Auguste Cesar Bertelli/Maurice Harvey	Aston Martin LM5	Winner, 1,101-1,500 cc class
6	Just Emile Vernet/Fernand Vallon	Caban Speciale	Winner, 751-1,100 cc class

1932

1	Raymond Sommer/Luigi Chinetti	Alfa Romeo 8C	2,954.038 kilometres at 123.084kph
			Winner, 2,001-3,000 cc class
			Winner, Index of Performance
2	Franco Cortese/Gian Battista Guidotti	Alfa Romeo 8C	
3	Brian Lewis/Tim Rose-Davies	Talbot 105	
4	Mme Odette Siko/'Sabipa'	Alfa Romeo 6C	Winner, 1,501-2,000 cc class
5	Sammy Newsome/Hugh Widengren	Aston Martin	Winner, 1,101-1,500 cc class
7	Auguste Cesar Bertelli/Patrick Driscoll	Aston Martin	Winner, Coupe Biennale 1931-1932
8	Charles Auguste Martin/Auguste Bodoignet	Amilcar	Winner, 751-1,100 cc class
			Fastest lap: Nando Minoia,
			Alfa Romeo 8C, 5m 41s (142.437kph)

1933

1	Raymond Sommer/Tazio Nuvolari	Alfa Romeo 8C	3,144 kilometres at 131.001kph
			Winner, 2,001-3,000 cc class
			Winner, Coupe Biennale 1932-1933
			Fastest lap: Sommer, 5m 31.4s (146.386kph)
2	Luigi Chinetti/Philippe Varent	Alfa Romeo 8C	
3	Brian Lewis/Tim Rose-Richards	Alfa Romeo 8C	
4	Kenneth Peacock/Alex v.d. Becke	Riley 9 Brooklands	Winner, 751-1,100 cc class
			Winner, Index of Performance
5	Patrick Driscoll/S.C. Penn Hughes	Aston Martin Ulster	Winner, 1,101-1,500 cc class
6	John Ludovic Ford/Maurice Baumer	MG Midget	Winner, up to 750 cc class
8	André Rousseau/François Paco	Alfa Romeo 6C	Winner, 1,501-2,000 cc class

1934

1	Philippe Etancelin/Luigi Chinetti	Alfa Romeo 8C	2,886.938 kilometres at 120.289kph
			Winner, 2,001-3,000 cc class
			Fastest lap: Etancelin, 5m 41s (142.437kph)
2	Jean Sebilleau/Georges Delaroche	Riley 9	Winner, 1,101-1,500 cc class
3	Freddie Dixon/Cyril Paul	Riley 9 Brooklands	
4	Roy Eccles/Charlie Martin	MG Magnette K3	Winner, 751-1,100 cc class
5	Kenneth Peacock/Alex v.d. Becke	Riley 9 Brooklands	Winner, Coupe Biennale 1933-1934
			Winner, Index of Performance

1935

1	John Hindmarsh/Luis Fontes	Lagonda Rapide	3,006.797 kilometres at 125.283kph
			Winner, Over 4,000 cc class
2	'Helde'/Henry Stoffel	Alfa Romeo 8C	Winner, 3,001-4,000 cc class
3	Charles Martin/Charles Brackenbury	Aston Martin Ulster	Winner, 1,101 to 1,500 cc class
			Winner, Coupe Biennale 1934-1934
			Winner, Index of Performance
4	Alex v.d. Becke/Cliff Richardson	Riley MPH	
5	'Michel Paris'/Marcel Mongin	Delahaye 135	
9	Philippe Maillard Brune/Charles Druck	MG Magnette K3	Winner, 1,501-2,000 cc class
16	Stanley Barnes/Archie Langley	Singer Le Mans Replica	Winner, up to 1,000 cc class
			Fastest lap: Earl Howe, Alfa Romeo 8C,
			in 5m 47.9s (139.612kph)

1936

No event

1937

1	Jean-Pierre Wimille/Robert Benoist	Bugatti type 57G	3,287.938 kilometres at 136.997kph Winner, 3,001-5,000 cc class Winner, Index of Performance Fastest lap: Wimille, 5m 13s (155.179kph)
2	Joseph Paul/Marcel Mongin	Delahaye 135S	
3	René Dreyfus/Henry Stoffel	Delahaye 135S	
4	Louis Gerard/Jacques de Valence	Delage D6	Winner, 2,001-3,000 cc class
5	J.M. Skeffington/Murton Neale	Aston Martin Ulster	Winner, 1,101 to 1,500 cc class
12	Just Emile Vernet/Mme Suzanne Largeot	SIMCA	Winner, 751-1,100 cc class
17	Jean Viale/Albert Alin	SIMCA Cinq	Winner, up to 750 cc class

1938

1	Eugène Chaboud/Jean Tremoulet	Delahaye 135S	3,180.940 kilometres at 132.539kph Winner, 3,001-5,000 cc class
2	Gaston Serraud/Yves Giraud Cabantous	Delahaye 135S	
3	Jean Prenant/André Morel	Talbot Lago SS	
4	Louis Villeneuve/René Biolay	Delahaye 135S	
5	Charles de Cortanze/Marcel Contet	Peugeot DS402	Winner, 1,501-2000 cc class
6	Peter Orssich/Rudolph Sauerwein	Adler Super Trumpf	Winner, Coupe Biennale 1937-1938
7	Hans Otto Lhoer/Paul von Guilleaume	Adler Trumpf	Winner, 1,101-1,500 cc class
8	Jacques Savoye/Pierre Savoye	Singer Savoye Special	
			Winner, 751-1,000 cc class
14	Maurice Aime/Charles Plantivaux	SIMCA Cinq	Winner, up to 750 cc class Fastest lap: Raymond Sommer, Alfa Romeo 8C, 5m 13.8s (154.783kph)

1939

1	Jean-Pierre Wimille/Pierre Veyron	Bugatti 57C	3,354.760 kilometres at 139.781kph Winner, 3,001-5,000 cc class
2	Louis Gerard/Georges Monneret	Delage	Winner, 2,001-3,000 cc class
3	Arthur Dobson/Charles Brackenbury	Lagonda V12	
4	Lord Selsdon/Lord Waleran	Lagonda V12	
5	Prince von Schambourg Lippe/Fritz Hans Wencher	BMW 328 Touring	Winner, 1,501-2,000 cc class
10	Amédée Gordini/Roger Scaron	SIMCA Huit	Winner, 751-1,000 cc class Winner, Coupe Biennale 1938-1939 Winner, Index of Performance
14	Peter Clark/Marcus Chambers	HRG	Winner, 1,101-1,500 cc class Fastest lap: Robert Mazaud, Delahaye 135S, 5m 12.1s (155.627kph)

1940 to 1948

No event

1949

1	Luigi Chinetti/Lord Selsdon	Ferrari 166 MM	3,178.279 kilometres at 132.420kph Winner, 1,501-2,000 cc class Winner, Coupe Biennale 1939-1949 Winner, Index of Performance
2	Henri Louveau/Juan Jover	Delage D6S	Winner, 2,001-3,000 cc class
3	Norman Culpan/H.J. Aldington	Frazer Nash	
4	Louis Gerard/Francesco Godia Fales	Delage D6S	
5	Georges Grignard/Robert Brunet	Delahaye 135S	Winner, 3,001-5,000 cc class
8	Eric Thompson/Jack Fairman	HRG Lightweight LM	Winner, 1,101-1,500 cc class
12	Jean de Montremy/Eugène Dussous	Monopole Sport	Winner, 751-1,100 cc class
15	Otto Krattner/Frank Sutner	Aero Minor	Winner, 501-750 cc class Fastest lap: André Simon, Delahaye 175S, 5m 12.5s (155.427kph)

1950

1	Louis Rosier/Jean-Louis Rosier	Talbot Lago T26 GS	3,465.120 kilometres at 144.380kph Winner, 3,001-5,000 cc class Fastest lap: Louis Rosier, 4m 53.5s (165.490kph)
2	Pierre Meyrat/Guy Mairesse	Talbot Lago	
3	Sydney Allard/Tom Cole	Allard J2	Winner, 5,001-8,000 cc class
4	Duncan Hamilton/Tony Rolt	Healey 6	
5	George Abecassis/Lance Macklin	Aston Martin DB2	Winner, 2,001-3,000 cc class =Winner, Index of Performance
9	T.A.S.O. Mathieson/Dickie Stoop	Frazer Nash MM	Winner, 1,501-2,000 cc class
16	Tommy Wisdom/Tom Wise	Jowett Jupiter Javelin	Winner, 1,101-1,500 cc class
22	Jean de Montremy/Jean Hemard	Monopole 'Tank' X84	Winner, Coupe Biennale 1949-1950 =Winner, Index of Performance

1951

1	Peter Walker/Peter Whitehead	Jaguar XK120C	3,611.193 kilometres at 150.466kph Winner, 3,001-5,000 cc class
2	Pierre Meyrat/Guy Mairesse	Talbot Lago T26GS	
3	Lance Macklin/Eric Thompson	Aston Martin DB2	Winner, 2,001-3,000 cc class
4	Pierre 'Levegh'/René Marchand	Talbot Lago	
5	George Abecassis/Brian Shawe Taylor	Aston Martin DB2	
12	Giovanni Lurani/Giovanni Bracco	Lancia Aurelia B20	Winner, 1,501-2,000 cc class
18	John Fitch/Phil Walters	Cunningham C-2R	Winner, 5,001-8,000 cc class
20	Auguste Veuillet/Edmond Mouche	Porsche 356	Winner, 751-1,100 cc class
22	Marcel Becquart/Gordon Wilkins	Jowett Jupiter	Winner, 1,101-1,500 cc class
23	François Landon/André Briat	Renault 4CV	Winner, 501-750 cc class
24	Jean de Montremy/Jean Hemard	Monopole X84 Sport	Winner, Coupe Biennale 1950-1951 Winner, Index of Performance Fastest lap: Stirling Moss, Jaguar XK120C, 4m 46.8s (169.356kph)

1952

1	Hermann Lang/Fritz Riess	Mercedes-Benz 300 SL	3,773.800 kilometres at 155.575kph Winner, 2,001-3,000 cc class
2	Theo Helfrich/Norbert Niedermayer	Mercedes-Benz 300 SL	
3	Leslie Johnson/Tommy Wisdom	Nash-Healey	Winner, 3,001-5,000 cc class
4	Briggs Cunningham/Walter Spear	Cunningham C-4R	Winner, 5,001-8,000 cc class
5	André Simon/Lucien Vincent	Ferrari 340 America	
11	Auguste Veuillet/Edmonde Mouche	Porsche 356	Winner, 751-1,100 cc class
13	Marcel Becquart/Gordon Wilkins	Jowett R1 Jupiter	Winner, 1,101-1,500 cc class
14	Jean Hemard/Eugène Dussous	Monopole X84 Sport	Winner, Coupe Biennale 1951-1952 Winner, Index of Performance Winner, 501-750 cc class Fastest lap: Alberto Ascari, Ferrari 250S, 4m 40.5s (173.159kph)

1953

1	Tony Rolt/Duncan Hamilton	Jaguar XK120C	4,088.064 kilometres at 170.336kph Winner, 3,001-5,000 cc class
2	Peter Walker/Stirling Moss	Jaguar XK120C	
3	Phil Walters/John Fitch	Cunningham C5-R	Winner, 5,001-8,000 cc class
4	Peter Whitehead/Ian Stewart	Jaguar XK120C	
5	Paolo Marzotto/Giannino Marzotto	Ferrari 340 MM	
6	Maurice Trintignant/Harry Schell	Gordini T24S	Winner, 2,001-3000 cc class
13	Ken Wharton/Bob Mitchell	Frazer Nash LMR	Winner, 1,501-2,000 cc class
15	Richard von Frankenburg/Paul Frère	Porsche 550	Winner, 1,101-1,500 cc class
17	René Bonnet/André Moynet	DB HBR	Winner, 501-750 cc class
18	Mario Damonte/'Helde'	OSCA MT4	Winner, 751-1,100 cc class
21	Pierre Chancel/Robert Chancel	Panhard X88	Winner, Coupe Biennale 1952-1953 Winner, Index of Performance Fastest lap: Alberto Ascari, Ferrari 367 MM, 4m 27.4s (181.642kph)

1954

1	Froilan Gonzales/Maurice Trintignant	Ferrari 375 Plus	4,061.150 kilometres at 169.215kph Winner, 3,001-5,000 cc class Fastest lap: Gonzales, 4m 16.8s (189.139kph)
2	Tony Rolt/Duncan Hamilton	Jaguar XK D-type	
3	William Spear/Sherwood Johnson	Cunningham C-4R	Winner, 5,000-8,000 cc class
4	Roger Laurent/Jacques Swaters	Jaguar XK120C	
5	Briggs Cunningham/John Bennett	Cunningham C-4R	
6	André Guelfi/Jacques Pollet	Gordini T30S	Winner, 2,001-3,000 cc class
7	Peter Wilson/Jim Mayers	Bristol 450	Winner, 1,501-2,000 cc class
10	René Bonnet/Elie Bayol	DB HBR	Winner, Coupe Biennale 1953-1954 Winner, Index of Performance Winner, 501-750 cc class
12	Johnny Claes/Pierre Stasse	Porsche 550	Winner, 1,101-1,500 cc class

1955

1	Mike Hawthorn/Ivor Bueb	Jaguar XK D-type	4,135.380 kilometres at 172.308kph Winner, 3,001-5,000 cc class Fastest lap: Hawthorn, 4m 06.6s (196.963kph)
2	Peter Collins/Paul Frère	Aston Martin DB3S	Winner, 2,001-3,000 cc class
3	Johnny Claes/Jacques Swaters	Jaguar XK D-type	
4	Helmuth Polensky/Richard von Frankenberg	Porsche 550	Winner, Coupe Biennale 1954-1955 Winner, Index of Performance Winner, 1,101-1,500 cc class
5	Wolfgang Seidel/Olivier Gendebien	Porsche 550	
7	Peter Wilson/Jim Mayers	Bristol 450C	Winner, 1,501-2,000 cc class
13	Zora Arkus Duntov/Auguste Veuillet	Porsche 550	Winner, 751,1-100 cc class
16	Louis Cornet/Robert Mougin	DB HBR	Winner, 501-750 cc class

1956

1	Ron Flockhart/Ninian Sanderson	Jaguar XK D-type	4,034.929 kilometres at 168.122kph
			Winner, 3,001-5,000 cc class
2	Stirling Moss/Peter Collins	Aston Martin DB3S	Winner, 2,001-3,000 cc class
3	Maurice Trintignant/Olivier Gendebien	Ferrari 625 LM	
4	Jacques Swaters/Freddy Rousselle	Jaguar XK D-type	
5	Wolfgang von Trips/Richard von Frankenberg	Porsche RS 550A	Winner, 1,001-1,500 cc class
6	Mike Hawthorn/Ivor Bueb	Jaguar XK D-type	Fastest lap: Hawthorn,
			4m 20s (186.383kph)
7	Reg Bicknell/Peter Jopp	Lotus XI	Winner, 751-1,000 cc class
10	Gerard Laureau/Paul Armagnac	DB HBR5	Winner, Coupe Biennale 1955-1956
			Winner, Index of Performance
			Winner, 501-750 cc class

1957

1	Ron Flockhart/Ivor Bueb	Jaguar XK D-type	4,397.108 kilometres at 183.217kph
			Winner, 3,001-5,000 cc class
2	Ninian Sanderson/John Lawrence	Jaguar XK D-type	
3	Jean Lucas/'Mary'	Jaguar XK D-type	
4	Paul Frère/Freddy Rousselle	Jaguar XK D-type	
5	Stuart Lewis-Evans/Martino Severi	Ferrari 315S	
6	Duncan Hamilton/Masten Gregory	Jaguar XK D-type	
7	Lucien Bianchi/Georges Harris	Ferrari 500 TR	Winner, 1,501-2,000 cc class
8	Ed Hugus/Godin de Beaufort	Porsche RS 550A	Winner, 1,101-1,500 cc class
9	Herbert McKay Frazer/Jay Chamberlain	Lotus XI	Winner, 751-1,000 cc class
11	Jean-Paul Colas/Jean Kerguen	Aston Martin DB3S	Winner, 2,001-3,000 cc class
14	Cliff Allison/Keith Hall	Lotus XI	Winner, Index of Performance
			Winner, 501-750 cc class
			Fastest lap: Mike Hawthorn,
			Ferrari 335 MM, 3m 58.7s (203.015kph)

1958

1	Olivier Gendebien/Phil Hill	Ferrari 250 TR	4,101.926 kilometres at 170.914kph
			Winner, 2,001-3,000 cc class
2	Peter Whitehead/Graham Whitehead	Aston Martin DB3S	
3	Jean Behra/Hans Herrmann	Porsche RSK	Winner, 1,501-2,000 cc class
4	Edgar Barth/Paul Frère	Porsche RSK	Winner, 1,101-1,500 cc class
5	Godin de Beaufort/Herbert Linge	Porsche RS	
11	Alessandro de Tomaso/Colin Davis	OSCA Sport 750 TN	Winner, Index of Energy
			Winner, 501-750 cc class
			Fastest lap: Mike Hawthorn,
			Ferrari 250 TR, 4m 08.0s (195.402kph)

1959

1	Roy Salvadori/Carroll Shelby	Aston Martin DBR1	4,347.000 kilometres at 181.163kph
			Winner, 2,001-3,000 cc class
2	Maurice Trintignant/Paul Frère	Aston Martin DBR1	
3	'Beurlys'/'Elde'	Ferrari 250 GT	Winner, Grand Touring class
4	André Pilette/George Arents	Ferrari 250 GT	
5	Bob Grossman/Fernand Tavano	Ferrari 250 GT California	
7	Ted Whiteaway/John Turner	AC Ace	Winner, 1,501-2,000 cc class
8	Peter Lumsden/Peter Riley	Lotus Elite	Winner, 1,101-1,500 cc class
9	Louis Cornet/René Cotton	DB HBR4	Winner, Coupe Biennale 1958-1959
			Winner, Index of Performance
			Winner, 501-750 cc class
11	Bernard Consten/Paul Armagnac	DB HBR4	Winner, Index of Energy
			Fastest lap: Jean Behra,
			4m 00.9s (201.161kph)

1960

1	Olivier Gendebien/Paul Frère	Ferrari TR 60	4,217.527 kilometres at 175.730kph
			Winner, 2501-3,000 cc class
2	Ricardo Rodriguez/André Pilette	Ferrari TR60	
3	Roy Salvadori/Jim Clark	Aston Martin DBR1	
4	Fernand Tavano/'Loustel'	Ferrari 250 GT	Winner, Grand Touring class
5	George Arents/Alan Connell	Ferrari 250 GT	
8	John Fitch/Bob Grossman	Chevrolet Corvette	Winner, 4,001-5,000 cc class
10	Herbert Linge/Hans Walter	Porsche 1600 GS	Winner, 1,301-1,600 cc class
12	Ted Lund/Colin Escott	MGA Twin-Cam	Winner, 1,601-2,000 cc class
13	Roger Masson/Claude Laurent	Lotus Elite	Winner, 1,151-1,300 cc class
14	John Wagstaff/Tony Marsh	Lotus Elite	Winner, Index of Energy
15	Gérard Laureau/Paul Armagnac	DB HBR4	Winner, Coupe Biennale 1959-1960
			Winner, Index of Performance
			Winner, 701-850 cc class
16,	Jack Dalton/John Colgate	Austin Healey Sprite	Winner, 851-1,000 cc class
			Fastest lap: Masten Gregory,
			Maserati Tipo 61, 4m 04.0s (198.605kph)

1961

1	Olivier Gendebien/Phil Hill	Ferrari TR 61	4,476.580 kilometres at 186.527kph
			Winner, 2,501-3,000 cc class
2	Willy Mairesse/Mike Parkes	Ferrari TR 61	
3	Pierre Noblet/Jean Guichet	Ferrari 250 GT	Winner, Grand Touring class
4	Augie Pabst/Dick Thompson	Maserati Tipo 63	
5	Masten Gregory/Bob Holbert	Porsche RS 61	Winner, 1,601-2,000 cc class
10	Herbert Linge/Ben Pon	Porsche 695 GS	Winner, 1,301-1,600 cc class
12	Bill Allen/Trevor Taylor	Lotus Elite	Winner, 1,151-1,300 cc class
14	Denny Hulme/Angus Hyslop	Abarth 850S	Winner, 701-850 cc class
16	Peter Harper/Peter Procter	Sunbeam Alpine	Winner, Index of Energy
18	Gérard Laureau/Robert Bouharde	DB HBR4	Winner, Index of Performance
			Fastest lap: Ricardo Rodriguez,
			Ferrari TR 61, 3m 59.09s (201.202kph)

1962

1	Olivier Gendebien/Phil Hill	Ferrari 330 LM	4,451.255 kilometres at 185.469kph
			Winner, 3,001-4,000 cc class
			Winner, Experimental Group
			Fastest lap: Hill, 3m 57.3s (204.202kph)
2	Jean Guichet/Pierre Noblet	Ferrari 250 GTO	Winner, Grand Touring class
			Winner, 2,501-3,000 cc class
3	'Elde'/'Beurlys'	Ferrari 250 GTO	
4	Briggs Cunningham/Roy Salvadori	Jaguar E-type	
5	Peter Lumsden/Peter Sargent	Jaguar E-type	
7	Edgar Barth/Hans Herrmann	Porsche 695 GS	Winner, 1,301-1,600 cc class
8	David Hobbs/Frank Gardner	Lotus Elite	Winner, Index of Energy
			Winner, 1,151-1,300 cc class
13	Chris Lawrence/Richard Shepherd Barron	Morgan Plus 4 SS	Winner, 1,601-2,000 cc class
16	André Guillaudin/Alain Bertaut	CD	Winner, Index of Performance
			Winner, 701-850 cc class
17	Bernard Consten/José Rosinski	Rene Bonnet Djet	Winner, 851-1,000 cc class

1963

1	Lodovico Scarfiotti/Lorenzo Bandini	Ferrari 250P	4,561.710 kilometres at 190.071kph
			Winner, 2,501-3,000 cc class
			Winner, Index of Performance
			Winner, Prototype Group
2	'Beurlys'/Gerald von Ophem	Ferrari 250 GTO	Winner, Grand Touring class
3	Mike Parkes/Umberto Maglioli	Ferrari 250P	
4	'Elde'/Pierre Dumay	Ferrari 250 GTO	
5	Jack Sears/Peter Salmon	Ferrari 330 LMB	Winner, 3,001-4,000 cc class
7	Peter Bolton/Ninian Sanderson	AC Cobra	Winner, 4,001-5,000 cc class
8	Edgar Barth/Herbert Linge	Porsche 718/8	Winner, 1,601-2,000 cc class
9	Briggs Cunningham/Bob Grossman	Jaguar E-type	Winner, 3,001-4,000 cc class
10	John Wagstaff/Patrick Ferguson	Lotus Elite	Winner, 1,151-1,300 cc class
11	Jean-Pierre Beltoise/Claude Bobrowski	René Bonnet Aerodjet LM6	Winner, 1,101-1,300 cc class
			Winner, Index of Energy
			Fastest lap: John Surtees,
			Ferrari 250P, 3m 53.3s (207.714kph)

1964

1	Jean Guichet/Nino Vaccarella	Ferrari 275P	4,695.310 kilometres at 195.638kph
			Winner, 3,001-4,000 cc class
			Winner, Prototype Group
			Winner, Index of Performance
2	Graham Hill/Jo Bonnier	Ferrari 330P	
3	John Surtees/Lorenzo Bandini	Ferrari 330P	
4	Dan Gurney/Bob Bondurant	AC Cobra Daytona	Winner, 4,001-5,000 cc class
			Winner, Grand Touring class
5	Lucien Bianchi/'Beurlys'	Ferrari 250 GTO	Winner, 2,501-3,000 cc class
6	Innes Ireland/Tony Maggs	Ferrari 250 GTO	
7	Robert Buchet/Guy Ligier	Porsche 904	Winner, 1,601-2,000 cc class
13	Roberto Businello/Bruno Deserti	Alfa Romeo Giulia Tubolare	Winner, 1,301-1,600 cc class
14	Edgar Berney/Pierre Noblet	Iso Rivolta	Winner, over 5,000 cc class
17	Henry Morrogh/Roger de Lageneste	Alpine Renault M64	Winner, 1,001-1,150 cc class
			Winner, Index of Energy
22	Clive Hunt/John Wagstaff	Lotus Elite	Winner, 1,151-1,300 cc class
			Fastest lap: Phil Hill, Ford GT40,
			3m 49.2s (211.429kph)

1965

1	Jochen Rindt/Masten Gregory	Ferrari 275 LM	4,677.110 kilometres at 194.880kph
			Winner, 3,001-4,000 cc class
			Winner, Prototype Group
2	Pierre Dumay/Gustave Gosselin	Ferrari 275 LM	
3	Willy Mairesse/'Beurlys'	Ferrari 275 GTB	Winner, Grand Touring class
4	Herbert Linge/Peter Nocker	Porsche 904/6	Winner, 1,601-2,000 cc class
			Winner, Index of Performance
5	Gerhard Koch/Anton Fischaber	Porsche 904/4	Winner, Index of Energy
7	Pedro Rodriguez/Nino Vaccarella	Ferrari 365 P2	
9	Regis Fraissinet/Jean de Mortimart	Iso Grifo	Winner, 4,001-5,000 cc class
			Winner, over 5,000 cc class
12	Paul Hawkins/John Rhodes	Austin Healey Sprite	Winner, 1,151-1,300 cc class
13	Jean-Jacques Thuner/Simo Lampinen	Triumph Spitfire	Winner, 1,101-1,500 cc class
			Fastest lap: Phil Hill, Ford Mk2,
			3m 37.5s (222.803kph)

1966

1	Bruce McLaren/Chris Amon	Ford Mk2	4,843.090 kilometres at 210.795kph
			Winner, over 5,000 cc class
			Winner, Prototype Group
2	Ken Miles/Denny Hulme	Ford Mk2	
3	Ronnie Bucknum/Dick Hutcheson	Ford Mk2	
4	Jo Siffert/Colin Davis	Porsche 906/6	Winner, 1,601-2,000 cc class
			Winner, Index of Performance
5	Hans Herrmann/Herbert Linge	Porsche 906/6	
6	Udo Schutz/Peter de Klerk	Porsche 906/6	
7	Gunther Klass/Rolf Stommelen	Porsche 906/6	Winner, Sport class
8	Piers Courage/Roy Pike	Ferrari 275 GTB	Winner, 3,001-5,000 cc class
			Winner, Grand Touring class
9	Henry Grandsire/Leo Cella	Alpine Renault A210	
11	Jacques Cheinisse/Roger de Lageneste	Alpine Renault A210	Winner, Index of Energy
14	'Franc'/Jean Kerguen	Porsche 911S	Winner, Grand Touring up to 2,000 cc
			Fastest lap: Dan Gurney, Ford Mk2,
			3m 30.6s (230.103kph)

1967

1	Dan Gurney/A.J. Foyt	Ford Mk4	5,232.900 kilometres at 218.038kph
			Winner, over 5,000 cc class
			Winner, Prototype Group
			Winner, Index of Efficiency
2	Lodovico Scarfiotti/Mike Parkes	Ferrari 330 P4	
3	Willy Mairess/'Beurlys'	Ferrari 330 P4	
4	Bruce McLaren/Mark Donohue	Ford Mk4	
5	Jo Siffert/Hans Herrmann	Porsche 907/6	Winner, 1,601-2,000 cc class
			Winner, Index of Efficiency
6	Rolf Stommelen/Jochen Neerpasch	Porsche 910/6	
7	Vic Elford/Ben Pon	Porsche 906/6	Winner, Sport class
9	Henry Grandsire/José Rosinski	Alpine Renault A210	Winner, 1,151-1,300 cc class
11	Rico Steinemann/Dieter Spoerry	Ferrari 275 GTB	Winner, Grand Touring class
13	Jean Vinatier/Mauro Bianchi	Alpine Renault A210	Winner, 1,301-1,600 cc class
16	Marcel Martin/Jean Mesange	Abarth 1300 OT	Winner, Sport class up to 1,300 cc
			Fastest lap: Mario Andretti, Ford Mk4,
			3m 23.6s (238.014kph)

1968

1	Pedro Rodriguez/Lucien Bianchi	Ford GT40	4,452.880 kilometres at 185.536kph
			Winner, 3,001-5,000 cc class
			Winner, Sport Group
2	Rico Steinemann/Dieter Spoerry	Porsche 907/8	Winner, 2,001-2,500 cc class
			Winner, Sports-Prototype Group
3	Rolf Stommelen/Jochen Neerpasch	Porsche 908/8	Winner, 2,501-3,000 cc class
			Fastest lap: Stommelen,
			3m 38.1s (222.321kph)
4	Ignazio Giunti/Nanni Galli	Alfa Romeo 33/2	Winner, 1,601-2,000 cc class
5	Carlo Facetti/Spartaco Dini	Alfa Romeo 33/2	
9	Alain Le Guellec/Alain Serpaggi	Alpine Renault A210	Winner, 1,151-1,600 cc class
10	Jean-Luc Therier/Bernard Tramont	Alpine Renault A210	Winner, Index of Energy
12	Jean-Pierre Gaban/Roger Vanderschrick	Porsche 911T	Winner, Grand Touring Group
14	Jean-Claude Andruet/Jean-Pierre Nicolas	Alpine Renault A210	Winner, 1,001-1,150 cc class
			Winner, Index of Performance

1969

1	Jacky Ickx/Jackie Oliver	Ford GT40	4,998.00 kilometres at 208.250kph
			Winner, 3,001-5,000 cc class
2	Hans Herrmann/Gérard Larrousse	Porsche 908	Winner, 2,501-3,000 cc class
			Winner, Sports-Prototype category
3	David Hobbs/Mike Hailwood	Ford GT40	
4	Jean-Pierre Beltoise/Piers Courage	Matra-Simca MS 650	
5	Jean Guichet/Nino Vaccarella	Matra-Simca MS 630	
9	Christian Poirot/Pierre Maublanc	Porsche 910	Winner, 1,601-2,000 cc class
10	Jean-Pierre Gaban/Yves Deprez	Porsche 911S	Winner, Grand Touring category
12	Alain Serpaggi/Christian Ethuin	Alpine Renault A210	Winner, 1,001-1,150 cc class
			Winner, Index of Performance
			Fastest lap: Vic Elford,
			Porsche 917, 3m 27.2s (234.017kph)

1970

1	Hans Herrmann/Richard Attwood	Porsche 917L	4,607.810 kilometres at 191.992kph
			Winner, 3,001-5,000 cc class
2	Gérard Larrousse/Willi Kauhsen	Porsche 917LH	Winner, Index of Energy
3	Rudi Lins/Helmut Marko	Porsche 90	Winner, 2,501-3,000 cc class
			Winner, Sports-Prototype category
			Winner, Index of Performance
4	Sam Posey/Ronnie Bucknum	Ferrari 512S	
5	Hughes de Fierlandt/Alistair Walker	Ferrari 512S	
6	Guy Chasseuil/Claude Ballot-Lena	Porsche 914/6	Winner, 1,601-2,000 cc class
			Winner, Grand Touring Special group
7	Nicolas Koob/Erwin Kremer	Porsche 911S	Winner, 2001-2,500 cc class
			Fastest lap: Vic Elford, Porsche 917LH,
			3m 21.0s (241.235kph)

1971

1	Helmut Marko/Gijs van Lennep	Porsche 917K	5,335.313 kilometres at 222.304kph
			Winner, 3,001-5,000 cc class
			Winner, Sport category
			Winner, Index of Performance
2	Herbert Mueller/Richard Attwood	Porsche 917K	
3	Sam Posey/Tony Adamowicz	Ferrari 512M	
4	Chris Craft/David Weir	Ferrari 512M	
5	Bob Grossmann/Luigi Chinetti Jr	Ferrari 365 GTB4	Winner, Index of Energy
6	Raymond Touroul/'Anselme'	Porsche 911S	Winner, 2,001-2,500 cc class
			Winner, Grand Touring Special group
7	Walter Brun/Peter Mattli	Porsche 907	Winner, 1,601-2,000 cc class
			Winner, Sports-Prototype group
			Fastest lap: Jackie Oliver, Porsche 917LH,
			3m 18.4s (244.387kph)

1972

1	Henri Pescarolo/Graham Hill	Matra-Simca MS670	4,691.343 kilometres at 195.472kph
			Winner, 2,501-3,000 cc class
2	François Cevert/Howden Ganley	Matra-Simca MS670	
3	Reinhold Joest/Mario Casoni/Michael Weber	Porsche 908LH	
4	Andréa de Adamich/Nino Vaccarella	Alfa Romeo 33 TT 3	
5	Claude Andruet/Claude Ballot-Lena	Ferrari 365 GTB4	Winner, 3,001-5,000 cc class
			Winner, Grand Touring Special group
10	Gerry Birrell/Claude Bourgoignie	Ford Capri 2600 RS	Winner, Special Touring group
13	Michael Keyser/Jurgen Barth/Sylvain Garant	Porsche 911S	Winner, 2,001-3,000 cc class
14	René Ligonnet/Barrie Smith	Lola Ford T290	Winner, 1,601-2,000 cc class
15	Dave Heinz/Bob Johnson	Chevrolet Corvette	Winner, over 5,000 cc class
			Fastest lap: Gijs van Lennep, Lola Ford T280,
			3m 46.9s (216.423kph)

1973

1	Henri Pescarolo/Gérard Larrousse	Matra-Simca MS670B	4,853.945 kilometres at 202.247kph
			Winner, 2,501-3,000 cc class
2	Carlos Pace/Arturo Merzario	Ferrari 312PB	
3	Jean-Pierre Jabouille/Jean-Pierre Jaussaud	Matra-Simca MS670B	
4	Gijs van Lennep/Herbert Mueller	Porsche 911 Carrera	
5,	Bernard Cheneviere/Juan Fernandez/		
	Francisco Torredemer	Porsche 908/03	
6	Vic Elford/Claude Ballot-Lena	Ferrari 365 GTB4	Winner, 3,001-5,000 cc class
			Winner, Grand Touring Special group
8	Erwin Kremer/Clemens Schickentanz/Paul Keller	Porsche 911 Carrera	Winner, Index of Energy
11	Toine Hezemans/Dieter Quester	BMW 3.0 CSL	Winner, Special Touring group
12	Henri Greder/Marie-Claude Beaumont	Chevrolet Corvette	Winner, over 5,000 cc class
			Fastest lap: François Cevert,
			Matra-Simca MS670B, 3m 39.6s (223.607kph)

1974

1	Henri Pescarolo/Gérard Larrousse	Matra-Simca MS670B	4,606.571 kilometres at 191.940kph
			Winner, 2,501-3,000 cc class
2	Gijs van Lennep/Herbert Mueller	Porsche 911 Turbo RSR	
3	Jean-Pierre Jabouille/François Migault	Matra-Simca MS670B	
4	Derek Bell/Mike Hailwood	Gulf Mirage Ford GR7	
5	Cyril Grandet/Dominique 'Bardini'	Ferrari 365 GTB4	Winner, 3,001-5,000 cc class
			Winner, Grand Touring Special group
			Winner, Index of Energy
15	Jean-Claude Aubriet/'Depnic'	BMW 3.0 CSL	Winner, Special Touring group
17	'Christine'/Yvette Fontaine/Marie Laurent	Chevron Ford B23	Winner, 1,601-2,000 cc class
18	Henri Greder/Marie-Claude Beaumont	Chevrolet Corvette	Winner, over 5,000 cc class
			Fastest lap: Jean-Pierre Jarier,
			Matra-Simca MS680, 3m 42.7s (220.494kph)

1975

1	Jacky Ickx/Derek Bell	Gulf Mirage Ford GR8	4,595.577 kilometres at 191.482kph
			Winner, 2,501-3,000 cc class
2	Jean-Louis Lafosse/Guy Chasseuil	Ligier Ford JS2	
3	Vern Schuppan/Jean-Pierre Jaussaud	Gulf Mirage Ford GR8	
4	Reinhold Joest/Jurgen Barth/Mario Casoni	Porsche 908 3L	
5	John Fitzpatrick/Gijs van Lennep/Manfred Schurti	Porsche 911 Carrera RSR	
10	Gerhard Maurer/Christian Beez/Eugen Straehl	Porsche 911 Carrera RS	Winner, Grand Touring category
12	Teddy Pilette/Hugues de Fierlandt/		
	Jean-Claude Andruet	Ferrari 365 GTB4	Winner, 3,001-5,000 cc class
15	Bernard Beguin/Peter Zbinden/Claude Haldi	Porsche 911 Turbo	Winner, GTX category
16	Pierre Rubens/Paolo Bozetto	De Tomaso Panter	Winner, over 5,000 cc class
20	Rene Boubet/Philippe Dermagne	Porsche 911 Carrera RS	Winner, combined class
21	Michele Mouton/Marianne Hoepfner/		
	Christine Dacremont	Moynet LM75	Winner, 1,601-2,000 cc class
26	André Haller/Hans Schuller/Benoit Maechler	Datsun 240Z	Winner, 2,001-2,500 cc class
27	Daniel Brillat/Giancarlo Gagliardi/		
	Michel Degoumois	BMW 2002	Winner, GTS category
			Fastest lap: Chris Craft, De Cadenet-Lola Ford,
			3m 53.8s (210.025kph)

1976

1	Jacky Ickx/Gijs van Lennep	Porsche 936	4,769.923 kilometres at 198.746kph
			Winner, 2,501-3,000 cc class
			Winner, Group 6 category
2	Jean-Louis Lafosse/François Migault	Mirage Ford GR8	
3	Alain de Cadenet/Chris Craft	De Cadenet-Lola Ford	
4	Rolf Stommelen/Manfred Schurti	Porsche 935	Winner, 3,001-4,000 cc class
			Winner, Group 5
5	Derek Bell/Vern Schuppan	Mirage Ford GR8	
8	Henri Pescarolo/Jean-Pierre Beltoise	Inaltera Ford GT	Winner, GTP category
11	Hubert Striebig/Annie-Charlotte Verney/		
	Hughes Kirschhoffer	Porsche 934	Winner, 4,001-5,000 cc class
12	'Segolen'/Marçel Ouviere/'Ladagi'	Porsche 911 Carrera RS	Winner, Group 4 category
14	John Rulon Miller/Tom Waugh/		
	Jean-Pierre Laffeach	Porsche 911 Carrera RSR	Winner, IMSA category
15	Francois Trisconi/Georges Morand/		
	André Chevalley	Lola Ford T292	Winner, 1,601-2,000 cc class
			Winner, Group 6 up to 2-litres
20	Lella Lombardi/Christine Dacremont	Lancia Stratos	Winner, Coupe des Dames
24	Jean-Louis Ravenel/Jacky Ravenel/		
	Jean-Marie Detrin	BMW 3.0 CSL	Winner, Group 2 category
			Fastest lap: Jean-Pierre Jabouille,
			Alpine Renault A442, 3m 43.0s (220.197kph)

1977

1	Jacky Ickx/Jurgen Barth/Hurley Haywood	Porsche 936	4,671.630 kilometres at 194.651kph
			Winner, 2,501-3,000 cc class
			Winner, Group 6 category
			Fastest lap: Ickx, 3m 36.5s (226.808kph)
2	Vern Schuppan/Jean-Pierre Jarier	Mirage Ford GR8	
3	Claude Ballot-Lena/Peter Gregg	Porsche 935	Winner, 3,001-4,000 cc class
			Winner, Group 5 category
			Winner, GTP category
4	Jean Ragnotti/Jean Rondeau	Inaltera Ford GT	
5	Alain de Cadenet/Chris Craft	De Cadenet-Lola Ford	
6	Michel Pignard/Albert Dufrene/Jacques Henry	Chevron Ford B36	Winner, 1,601-2,000 cc class
			Winner, Group 6 up to 2-litres
			Winner, Index of Energy
7	Bob Wollek/Philippe Gurdjian/'Steve'	Porsche 934	Winner, Group 4 category
8	Pierre Dieudonné/Spartaco Dini/Jean Xhenceval	BMW 3.0 CSL	Winner, IMSA category
11	Lella Lombardi/'Christine'	Inaltera Ford GR8	Winner, Coupe des Dames
16	François Migault/Lucien Guitteny	Ferrari 365 GTB4	Winner, 4,001-5,000 cc class
17	Robin Hamilton/Mike Salmon/David Preece	Aston Martin AM V8	Winner, over 5,000 cc class

1978

1	Didier Pironi/Jean-Pierre Jaussaud	Renault Alpine A442B	5,044.530 kilometres at 210.188kph
			Winner, 2,501-3,000 cc class
			Winner, Group 6 category
			Winner, Index of Efficiency
2	Bob Wollek/Jurgen Barth/Jacky Ickx	Porsche 936/77	Winner, Index of Efficiency
3	Hurley Haywood/Peter Gregg/Reinhold Joest	Porche 936/78	
4	Jean Ragnotti/Guy Frequelin/José Dolhem	Renault Alpine A442	
5	Dick Barbour/Brian Redman/John Paul	Porsche 935	Winner, IMSA category
6	Jim Busby/Rick Knoop/Chris Cord	Porsche 935	Winner, Group 5
9	Jean Rondeau/Jacky Haran/Bernard Darniche	Rondeau Ford M378	Winner, GTP category
11	Michel Pignard/Laurent Ferrier/Lucien Rossiaud		Winner, Group 6 up to 2-litres
12	Annie-Charlotte Verney/Xavier Lapiere/		
	François Servanin	Porsche 911 Carrera	Winner, Group 4 category
			Fastest lap: Jean-Pierre Jabouille,
			Renault Alpine A443, 3m 34.2s (229.244kph)

1979

1	Klaus Ludwig/Bill Whittington/Don Whittington	Porsche 935 K3	4,173.930 kilometres at 173.913kph
			Winner, over 2,000 cc class
			Winner, Group 5 category
			Winner, IMSA category
2	Dick Barbour/Paul Newman/Rolf Stommelen	Porsche 935	
3	Laurent Ferrier/François Servanin/François Trisconi	Porsche 935	
4	Herbert Mueller/Angelo Pallaviccini/Marco Vanoli	Porsche 934	Winner, Group 4 category
5	Bernard Darniche/Jean Ragnotti	Rondeau Ford M379	Winner, Group 6 category
14	Max Mamers/Jean-Daniel Raulet	WM Peugeot P79	Winner, GTP category
17	Tony Charnell/Richard Jones/Robin Smith	Chevron Ford B36	Winner, Group 6 up to 2-litres
			Fastest lap: Jacky Ickx, Porsche 936,
			3m 36.01s (227.003kph)

1980

1	Jean Rondeau/Jean-Pierre Jaussaud	Rondeau Ford M379B	4,608.020 kilometres at 192.000kph
			Winner, over 2,000 cc class
			Winner, Group 6 category
			Winner, Index of Energy
2	Jacky Ickx/Reinhold Joest	Porsche 908/80	Fastest lap: Ickx, 3m 40.6s (222.373kph)
3	Gordon Spice/Jean-Michel Martin/Philippe Martin	Rondeau Ford M379B	Winner, GTP category
4	Guy Frequelin/Roger Dorchy	WM Peugeot P79/80	
5	John Fitzpatrick/Brian Redman/Dick Barbour	Porsche 935 K3	Winner, IMSA category
8	Dieter Schornstein/Harald Grohs/		
	Goetz von TschirnhauS	Porsche 935	Winner, Group 5 category
16	Thierry Perrier/Roger Carmillet	Porsche 911 SC	Winner, Group 4
17	Bruno Sotty/Philippe Hesnault/		
	Daniel LaurentChevron	Ford B36	Winner, Group 6 up to 2-litres
19	Carlo Facetti/Martino Finotto	Lancia Beta	Winner, Group 5 up to 2-litres

1981

1	Jacky Ickx/Derek Bell	Porsche 936/81	4,825.348 kilometres at 201.056kph
			Winner, Group 6 category
2	Philippe Streiff/Jean-Louis Schlesser/Jacky Haran	Rondeau Ford M379C	
3	François Migault/Gordon Spice	Rondeau Ford M379C	
4	Claude Bourgoignie/Dudley Wood/John Cooper	Porsche 935 K3	Winner, Group 5 category
5	Claude Ballot-Lena/Jean-Claude Andruet	Ferrari 512 BB LM	Winner, IMSA GTX category
8	Eddie Cheever/Michele Alboreto/Carlo Facetti	Lancia Beta Monte Carlo	Winner, Group 5 up to 2-litres
11	Manfred Schurti/Andy Rouse	Porsche 924 GTR	Winner, IMSA GTO category
12	Jochen Mass/Hurley Haywood/Vern Schuppan	Porsche 936/81	Fastest lap: Haywood,
			3m 34.0s (229.231kph)
17	Thierry Perrier/Valentin Bertapalle/Bernard Salam	Porsche 934	Winner, Group 4 category
18	Jean-Philippe Grand/Yves Courage	Lola Ford T298	Winner, Group 6 up to 2-litres

1982

1	Jacky Ickx/Derek Bell	Porsche 956	4,899.086 kilometres at 204.128kph
			Winner, Group C category
			Winner, Index of Energy
2	Jochen Mass/Vern Schuppan	Porsche 956	
3	Hurley Haywood/Al Holbert/Juergen Barth	Porsche 956	
4	John Fitzpatrick/David Hobbs	Porsche 935	Winner, IMSA GTX category
5	Dany Snobeck/François Servanin/René Metge	Porsche 935 K3	
8	Claude Bourgoignie/Paul Smith/John Cooper	Porsche 935 K3	Winner, Group 5 category
12	Jean-Marie Lemerle/Max Cohen Olivar/		
	Joe Castellano	Lancia Beta Monte Carlo	Winner, Group 5 up to 2-litres
13	Richard Cleare/Tony Dron/Richard Jones	Porsche 934	Winner, Group 4 category
16	Jim Busby/Doc Bundy	Porsche 924 GTR	Winner, IMSA GT category
			Fastest lap: Jean Ragnotti,
			Rondeau Ford M382,
			3m 36.9s (226.166kph)

1983

1	Al Holbert/Hurley Haywood/Vern Schuppan	Porsche 956	5,047.934 kilometres at 210.330kph
			Winner, Group C category
			Winner, Index of Energy
2	Jacky Ickx/Derek Bell	Porsche 956	Fastest lap: Ickx, 3m 29.7s (233.922kph)
3	Mario Andrétti/Michael Andrétti/Philippe Alliot	Porsche 956	
4	Clemens Schickentanz/Volkert Merl/		
	Mauriçio de Narvaez	Porsche 956	
5	Guy Edwards/John Fitzpatrick/Rupert Keegan	Porsche 956	
11	John Cooper/Paul Smith/David Ovey	Porsche 911 Turbo	Winner, Group B category
12	Yoshimi Katayama/Yojiro Terada/Tahashi Yorino	Mazda 717C	Winner, Group C Junior category

1984

1	Klaus Ludwig/Henri Pescarolo	Porsche 956	4,900.276 kilometres at 204.178kph
			Winner, Group C category
2	Jean Rondeau/Preston Henn/John Paul Jr	Porsche 956	
3	David Hobbs/Philippe Streiff/Sarel van der Merwe	Porsche 956	
4	Walter Brun/Leopold von Bayern/Bob Akin	Porsche 956	
5	Volkert Merl/'John Winter'/Dieter Schornstein	Porsche 956	
6	Alan Jones/Vern Schuppan/Jean-Pierre Jarier	Porsche 956	Winner, Index of Energy
10	John O'Steen/John Morton/Yoshimi Katayama	Lola Mazda T616	Winner, Group C2 category
14	Pierre de Thoisy/Philippe Dagoreau/		
	Jean-François Yvon	BMW M1	Winner, Group B category
17	Raymond Touroul/Valentin Bertapelle/		
	Thierry Perrier	Porsche 911 Turbo	Winner, IMSA GTO category
			Fastest lap: Alessandro Nannini, Lancia LC2,
			3m 28.9s (234.818kph)

1985

1	Klaus Ludwig/Paolo Barilla/'John Winter'	Porsche 956	5,088.507 kilometres at 212.021kph
			Winner, Group C category
			Winner, Index of Energy
2	Jonathan Palmer/James Weaver/Richard Lloyd	Porsche 956	
3	Derek Bell/Hans Stuck	Porsche 962C	
4	Jo Gartner/David Hobbs/Guy Edwards	Porsche 956	
5	George Fouché/Sarel van der Merwe/		
	Mario Hytten	Porsche 956	
10	Jacky Ickx/Jochen Mass	Porsche 962C	Fastest lap: Ickx, 3m 25.1s (239.169kph)
13	Bob Tullius/Chip Robinson/Claude Ballot-Lena	Jaguar XJR-5	Winner, IMSA GTP category
14	Gordon Spice/Ray Bellm/Mark Galvin	Tiga Ford GC84	Winner, Group C2 category
15	Edgar Doeren/Martin Birrane/Jean-Paul Libert	BMW M1	Winner, Group B category

1986

1	Derek Bell/Hans Stuck/Al Holbert	Porsche 962C	4,972.731 kilometres at 207.197kph
			Winner, Group C category
2	Oscar Larrauri/Jesus Pareja/Joël Gouhier	Porsche 962C	
3	George Follmer/John Morton/Kemper Miller	Porsche 956	
4	Emilio de Villota/Fermin Velez/George Fouché	Porsche 956	
5	Juergen Laessig/Fulvio Ballabio/Dudley Wood	Porsche 956	
7	René Metge/Claude Ballot-Lena	Porsche 961	Winner, IMSA GTX category
8	Ian Harrower/Evan Clements/Tom Dodd-Noble	Gebhardt Ford JC843	Winner, Group C2 category
14	Richard Cleare/Lionel Robert/Jack Newsum	March Porsche 85G	Winner, IMSA GTX category
			Fastest lap: Klaus Ludwig, Porsche 956,
			3m 23.3s (239.551kph)

1987

1	Derek Bell/Hans Stuck/Al Holbert	Porsche 962C	4,791.777 kilometres at 199.657kph
			Winner, Group C category
2	Pierre Yver/Bernard de Dryver/Juergen Laessig	Porsche 962C	
3	Yves Courage/Pierre-Henri Raphanel/		
	Hervé Regout	Cougar Porsche C20	
4	George Fouché/Franz Konrad/Wayne Taylor	Porsche 962C	
5	Eddie Cheever/Raul Boesel/Jan Lammers	Jaguar XJR-8LM	
6	Gordon Spice/Fermin Velez/Philippe de Henning	Spice (Ford) Pontiac	Winner, Group C2 category
7	David Kennedy/Pierre Dieudonné/Mark Galvin	Mazda 757	Winner, IMSA category
			Fastest lap: Johnny Dumfries, Sauber Mercedes C9,
			3m 25.04s (237.224kph)

1988

1	Jan Lammers/Andy Wallace/Johnny Dumfries	Jaguar XJR-9LM	5,332.790 kilometres at 221.665kph
			Winner, Group C category
2	Derek Bell/Hans Stuck/Klaus Ludwig	Porsche 962C	Fastest lap: Stuck, 3m 22.5s (240.622kph)
3	Frank Jelinski/Stanley Dickens/'John Winter'	Porsche 962C	
4	Derek Daly/Kevin Kogan/Larry Perkins	Jaguar XJR-9LM	
5	David Hobbs/Didier Theys/Franz Konrad	Porsche 962C	
13	Gordon Spice/Ray Bellm/Pierre de Thoisy	Spice Ford SE88C	Winner, Group C2 category
15	Yojiro Terada/David Kennedy/Pierre Dieudonné		Winner, IMSA category

1989

1	Jochen Mass/Stanley Dickens/Manuel Reuter	Sauber Mercedes C9	5,265.115 kilometres at 219.990kph
			Winner, Group C category
2	Mauro Baldi/Kenny Acheson/ Gianfranco Brancatelli	Sauber Mercedes C9	
3	Hans Stuck/Bob Wollek	Porsche 962C	
4	Jan Lammers/Patrick Tambay/ Andrew Gilbert-Scott	Jaguar XJR-9LM	
5	Jean-Louis Schlesser/Jean-Pierre Jabouille/ Alain Cudini	Sauber Mercedes C9	
7	David Kennedy/Pierre Dieudonné/Chris Hodgetts	Mazda 767B	Winner, IMSA category
14	Jean-Claude Andruet/Philippe Farjon/ Shenji Kasuya	Cougar Porsche C20	Winner, Group C2 category
			Fastest lap: Alain Ferté, Jaguar XJR-9LM,
			3m 21.27s (243.093kph)

1990

1	John Nielsen/Price Cobb/Martin Brundle	Jaguar XJR-12	4,882.400 kilometres at 204.036kph
			Winner, Group C category
2	Jan Lammers/Andy Wallace/Franz Konrad	Jaguar XJR-12	
3	Tiff Needell/David Sears/Anthony Reid	Porsche 962C	
4	Derek Bell/Hans Stuck/Frank Jelinski	Porsche 962C	
5	Masahiro Hasemi/Toshio Suzuki	Nissan R90 CP	
20	Yoshimi Katayama/Yojiro Terada/Tahashi Yorino	Mazda 767B	Winner, IMSA GTP category
21	Richard Piper/Olindo Iacobelli/Mike Youles	Spice Ford SE89C	Winner, Group C2 category
			Fastest lap: Bob Earl, Nissan R90 CK,
			3m 40.03s (222.515kph)

1991

1	Volkert Weidler/Johnny Herbert/Bertrand Gachot	Mazda 787B	4,922.810 kilometres at 205.333kph
			Winner, Sport category
2	Davy Jones/Raul Boesel/Michel Ferté	Jaguar XJR-12	
3	Bob Wollek/Teo Fabi/Kenny Acheson	Jaguar XJR-12	
4	Derek Warwick/John Nielsen/Andy Wallace	Jaguar XJR-12	
5	Michael Schumacher/Karl Wendlinger/ Fritz Kreuzpointner	Sauber C11-Mercedes	Fastest lap: Schumacher,
			3m 35.564s (227.125kph)
12	Kiyoshi Misaki/Hisashi Yokoshima/ Naoki Nagasaka	Spice Ford SE90C	Winner, Sport Category 1

1992

1	Derek Warwick/Yannick Dalmas/Mark Blundell	Peugeot 905	4,787.200 kilometres at 199.340kph
2	Masanori Sekiya/Pierre-Henri Raphanel/ Kenny Acheson	Toyota TS-010	
3	Mauro Baldi/Philippe Alliot/Jean-Pierre Jabouille	Peugeot 905	
4	Johnny Herbert/Volkert Weidler/Bertrand Gachot	Mazda MX-R01	
5	George Fouché/Steven Andskar/Stefan Johansson	Toyota 92C-V	
8	Jan Lammers/Teo Fabi/Andy Wallace	Toyota TS-010	Fastest lap: Lammers, 3m 32.295s (230.622kph)

1993

1	Eric Hélary/Geoff Brabham/Christophe Bouchut	Peugeot 905B	5,100.00 kilometres at 213.358kph
			Winner, 3.5 litre Protoype category
2	Thierry Boutsen/Yannick Dalmas/Teo Fabi	Peugeot 905B	
3	Jean-Pierre Jabouille/Philippe Alliot/Mauro Baldi	Peugeot 905B	
4	Eddie Irvine/Masanori Sekiya/Toshio Suzuki	Toyota TS010	Fastest lap: Irvine, 3m 30.48s (232.611kph)
5	Roland Ratzenberger/Mauro Martini/ Naoki Nagasaka	Toyota 92CV	Winner, Group C 1990 category
15	John Nielsen/David Coulthard/David Brabham	Jaguar XJ220C	Winner, Grand Touring category
25	Patrick Gonin/Bernard Santal/Alain Lamouille	WR Peugeot LM	Winner, Le Mans Prototype category

1994

1	Yannick Dalmas/Hurley Haywood/Mauro Baldi	Dauer 962LM GT Porsche	4,678.4 kilometres at 195.265kph
			Winner, Le Mans GT1 category
2	Eddie Irvine/Mauro Martini/Jeff Krosnoff	Toyota 94CV	Winner, Prototype 1 category
3	Hans Stuck/Thierry Boutsen/Danny Sullivan	Dauer 962LM GT Porsche	Fastest lap: Boutsen, 3m 52.54s
			(210.544kph)
4	Bob Wollek/Steven Andskar/George Fouché	Toyota 94CV	
5	Steve Millen/Johnny O'Connell/John Morton	Nissan 300ZX	Winner, IMSA GTS category
8	Dominique Dupuy/Jesus Pareja/Carlos Palau	Porsche 911 RSR	Winner, Le Mans GT2 category

1995

1	JJ Lehto/Yannick Dalmas/Masanori Sekiya	McLaren BMW F1 GTR	4,055.80 kilometres at 168.992kph
			Winner, Le Mans GT1 category
2	Bob Wollek/Mario Andretti/Eric Hélary	Courage Porsche C34	Winner, WSC Prototype 1 category
3	Derek Bell/Andy Wallace/Justin Bell		McLaren BMW F1 GTR
4	Ray Bellm/Maurizio Sala/Mark Blundell	McLaren BMW F1 GTR	
5	Fabien Giroix/Jean-Denis Deletraz/ Olivier Grouillard	McLaren BMW F1 GTR	
8	Kunimitsu Takahashi/Keiichi Tsuchiya/Akira Iida	Honda NSX	Winner, Le Mans GT2 category
20	Patrice Roussel/Edouard Sezionale/Bernard Santal	Debora LMP295	Winner, Le Mans Prototype 2 category
			Fastest lap: Patrick Gonin, WR-Peugeot LM95,
			3m 51.41s (211.573kph)

1996

1	Manuel Reuter/Davy Jones/Alexander Wurz	Joest TWR Porsche WSC	4,814.40 kilometres at 200.60kph
			Winner, Le Mans Prototype category
2	Hans Stuck/Thierry Boutsen/Bob Wollek	Porsche 911 GT1	Winner, Le Mans GT1 category
3	Yannick Dalmas/Karl Wendlinger/Scott Goodyear	Porsche 911 GT1	
4	John Nielsen/Thomas Bscher/Peter Kox	McLaren BMW F1 GTR	
5	Lindsay Owen-Jones/Pierre-Henri Raphanel/ David Brabham	McLaren BMW F1 GTR	
12	Guy Martinolle/Ralf Kelleners/Bruno Eichmann	Porsche 911 GT2	Winner, Le Mans GT2 category
			Fastest lap: Eric van de Poele, Ferrari 333 SP,
			3m 46.958s (215.723kph)

1997

1	Michele Alboreto/Stefan Johansson/ Tom Kristensen	Joest TWR Porsche WSC	4,909.6 kilometres at 204.186kph
			Winner, Le Mans Prototype category
			Fastest lap: Kristensen, 3m 45.068s (217.534kph)
2	Jean-Marc Gounon/Pierre-Henri Raphanel/ Anders Olofsson	McLaren BMW F1 GTR	
3	Peter Kox/Roberto Ravaglia/Eric Hélary	McLaren BMW F1 GTR	Winner, Le Mans GT1 category
4	Didier Cottaz/Jerome Policand/Marc Goossens	Courage Porsche C41	
5	Pedro Lamy/Patrice Goueslard/Armin Hahne	Porsche 911 GT1	
9	Michel Neugarten/Guy Martinolle/ Jean-Claude Lagniez	Porsche 911 GT2	Winner, Le Mans GT2 category

1998

1	Allan McNish/Laurent Aiello/Stephane Ortelli	Porsche 911 GT1-98	4,783.78 kilometres at 199.324kph
			Winner, Le Mans GT1 category
2	Joerg Müller/Uwe Alzen/Bob Wollek	Porsche 911 GT1-98	
3	Kazuyoshi Hoshino/Aguri Suzuki/ Masahiko Kageyama	Nissan R390 GT1	
4	Tim Sugden/Steve O'Rourke/Bill Auberlen	McLaren BMW F1 GTR	
5	John Nielsen/Franck Lagorce/Michael Krumm	Nissan R390 GT1	
8	Wayne Taylor/Eric van de Poele/Fermin Velez	Ferrari 333 SP	Winner, Le Mans Prototype category
11	Justin Bell/David Donohue/Luca Drudi	Chrysler Viper GTS/R	Winner, Le Mans GT2 category
			Fastest lap: Martin Brundle, Toyota GT-One,
			3m 41.809s (220.812kph)

1999

1	Yannick Dalmas/Pierluigi Martini/ Joachim Winkelhock	BMW V12 LMR	4,967.991 kilometres at 207.00kph
			Winner, Le Mans Prototype category
2	Ukyo Katayama/Toshio Suzuki/Keiichi Tsuchiya	Toyota GT-One	Winner, Le Mans GT1 category
			Fastest lap: Katayama, 3m 35.032s (227.771kph)
3	Emanuele Pirro/Frank Biela/Didier Theys	Audi R8R	
4	Michele Alboreto/Rinaldo Capello/Laurent Aiello	Audi R8R	
5	Thomas Bscher/Bill Auberlen/Steve Soper	BMW V12 LM-98	
10	Olivier Beretta/Karl Wendlinger/ Dominique Dupuy	Chrysler Viper GTS-R	Winner, Le Mans GTS category
13	Uwe Alzen/Patrick Huisman/Luca Riccitelli	Porsche 911 GT3	Winner, Le Mans GT3 category

2000

1	Tom Kristensen/Frank Biela/Emanuele Pirro	Audi R8	5,007.988 kilometres at 208.666kph
			Winner, Le Mans Prototype category
2	Allan McNish/Laurent Aiello/Stephane Ortelli	Audi R8	Fastest lap: McNish, 3m 37.359s (225.332kph)
3	Michele Alboreto/Christian Abt/Rinaldo Capello	Audi R8	
4	Sebastien Bourdais/Olivier Grouillard/ Emanuele Clerico	Courage Peugeot C52	
5	Hiroki Katoh/Johnny O'Connell/ Pierre-Henri Raphanel	Panoz LMP-1	
7	Olivier Beretta/Karl Wendlinger/ Dominique Dupuy	Chrysler Viper GTS-R/T	Winner, Le Mans GTS category
16	Hideo Fukuyama/Bruno Lambert/Atsushi Yogo	Porsche 911 GT3R	Winner, Le Mans GT3 category
25	Scott Maxwell/John Graham/Greg Wilkins	Lola Nissan B2K/40	Winner, LMP675 category

2001

1	Emanuele Pirro/Frank Biela/Tom Kristensen	Audi R8	4,342.776 kilometres at180.949kph
			Winner, Le Mans Prototype category
2	Rinaldo Capello/Laurent Aiello/Christian Pescatori	Audi R8	Fastest lap: Aiello, 3m 39.046s (223.597kph)
3	Andy Wallace/Butch Leitzinger/Eric van de Poele	Bentley EXP Speed 8	Winner, Le Mans GT Prototype category
4	Olivier Beretta/Karl Wendlinger/Pedro Lamy	Chrysler LMP	
5	Pascal Fabre/Jordi Gene/Jean-Denis Deletraz	Reynard-VW	Winner, Le Mans Prototype 675 category
6	Gabrio Rosa/Fabio Babini/Luca Drudi	Porsche 911 GT3RS	Winner, Le Mans GT category
7	Gunnar Jeannette/Romain Dumas/ Philippe Haezebrouck	Porsche 911 GT3RS	
8	Ron Fellows/Johnny O'Connell/Scott Pruett	Chevrolet Corvette C5-R	Winner, Le Mans GTS category

PICTURE ACKNOWLEDGMENTS

Allsport: 1, 4–5, 6, 7 bottom, 14, 16–17, 41, 87, 166, 192, 196–197, 202, 204, 205, 207, 208–209, 210–211, 212–213, 214, 216–217, 218–219, 221, 222 right, 226, 228 bottom, 229, 230–231, 232–233, 234, 235 bottom, 237, 238–239, 242–243, 246–247, 253

Corbis: 179 top

Ian Dawson: 9

DPPI: 48–49, 49, 160–161, 187, 240–241 bottom insets

GP Library: 12, 13, 30 bottom right, 51, 70, 78–79, 81, 94, 98–99, 108, 125 top right, 140–141, 179 bottom, 180, 184

Hulton Getty: 19, 68–69, 95, 110 bottom right, 115, 118–119, 158 bottom left

Keystone (Paris): 167 top right, 169 bottom right

Kobal: 163, 164, 164–165

LAT Archive: 10–11, 15, 17, 20–21, 22–23, 24 top left, 25, 26, 27, 28–29, 30 top left, 34–35, 36, 37, 38, 38–39, 40, 42–43, 45, 46, 47, 50, 52–53, 54, 55, 56, 56–57, 58, 59, 60–61, 62–63, 64, 65, 66, 67, 71, 72–73, 74, 75, 76, 77, 82, 83, 84, 84–85, 86 both pictures, 88–89, 90–91, 100, 101, 102–103, 105, 106, 109, 110 top right, 112–113, 114, 117, 120 top left, 123, 124, 125 bottom, 126, 127 top right, 128–129, 130–131, 132, 133, 134, 136–137, 139, 142, 143, 144–145, 156 bottom left, 158 top, 162, 167 bottom, 170–171, 172, 174, 178, 181, 182–183, 185, 190, 228 top, 248, 249

Mark Leech/L'Equipe: 31, 32–33, 92–93, 96, 99, 104, 107, 120–121, 127 bottom left, 194–195, 195 top right, 244

National Motor Museum: 18, 20 bottom left, 24 bottom left, 80, 97, 111, 157

S. Weiss/Rapho: 2–3, 135, 138, 147, 150–151,

Sutton Motorsport: 8, 32, 44, 69, 144, 146, 148, 149, 152, 153, 154–155, 156 top right, 159, 168, 169 top right, 173, 175, 176–177, 188–189, 191, 193, 198, 199, 200, 201, 203, 206, 215, 220, 222 left, 223, 224–225, 227, 235 top, 236, 240, 241, 245, 251

Front cover image: L.A.T. Archive

Special thanks to Chris Dixon at L.A.T. Archives, Paul Sutton, Mark Leech, Kerr Robertson and Phil Burnham-Richards